KT-524-486

The Golden & the

Brazen World

PUBLISHED UNDER THE AUSPICES OF THE

WILLIAM ANDREWS CLARK MEMORIAL LIBRARY

UNIVERSITY OF CALIFORNIA, LOS ANGELES

Publications from the
CLARK LIBRARY PROFESSORSHIP, UCLA

THE GOLDEN &
THE BRAZEN WORLD

*Papers in Literature and
History, 1650-1800*

Edited by

JOHN M. WALLACE

Clark Library Professor, 1982-1983

UNIVERSITY OF CALIFORNIA PRESS
BERKELEY • LOS ANGELES • LONDON

BATH COLLEGE

PBH
809.WAL
1105750

University of California Press
Berkeley and Los Angeles, California

University of California Press, Ltd.
London, England

Copyright © 1985 by The Regents of the University of California

Library of Congress Cataloging in Publication Data
Main entry under title:

The Golden & the brazen world.

Contents: Need Clio quarrel with her sister muses? /
Cleanth Brooks — "That sober liberty" : Marvell's
Cromwell in 1654 / Derek Hirst — Dryden in 1678-1681 /
Phillip Harth — [etc.]
    1. Literature and history—Addresses, essays, lectures.
I. Wallace, John M., 1928-
PN50.G6   1985   809   84-16233
ISBN 0-520-05401-6

Printed in the United States of America

1 2 3 4 5 6 7 8 9

CONTENTS

PREFACE

"Nature," declared Sir Philip Sidney in his *Defence of Poetry,* "never set forth the earth in so rich tapestry as divers poets have done; neither with pleasant rivers, fruitful trees, sweet-smelling flowers, nor whatsoever else may make the too much loved earth more lovely. Her world is brazen, the poets only deliver a golden." Sidney had already admitted that "there is no art delivered to mankind that hath not the works of Nature for his principal object," and the arts he had in mind included history ("what men have done") which he characterized as a mixture of hearsay and "old mouse-eaten records." The historians come off very badly in the *Defence* as denizens of the brazen world, tied not to what should be but to what is, and floundering in a wealth of minutiae which "draweth no necessary consequence, and therefore a less fruitful doctrine."

Yet the contention in the Renaissance between poets and historians for the superiority of their art also had the effect of bringing the opponents closer together, because the two activities had much in common and were more obviously related than they are today. The crucial connection in Sidney's argument is that both history and poetry are allegedly examples of moral philosophy, intended to illustrate ethical truths. Had a historian been allowed to interrupt, he would have claimed that the great advantage of historical examples was their truth, which thus made them more morally persuasive. Sidney was well aware of the strength of this position and countered it with the assertion that the clutter of historical details was so confusing that even when a clear lesson could be deduced from them, it was likely to be a wrong one. In recognizing that history as well as poetry had great power to move men's minds and their passions, he insisted that feigned examples were more easily harnessed to moral precepts and therefore would move the hearer more directly and consistently toward the good.

Examples, as Cicero said, were stepping-stones toward a truth, which would declare itself with a certain surprise when the right moment came. Examples, too, could offer the brilliant enhancement of a thought, bringing to life the theme to which they were attached. Whether feigned or true, they had an emotional force that made them potentially dangerous but preferable to the "wordish descriptions" that made moral philosophy pedagogically unattractive. Sidney knew that philosophy was the "chief of all knowledges," but though he followed Plutarch in finding a moral use for poetry, it was only the rhetoric of a "defence" that led him to deny an equal value for the study of history.

Sidney was describing a fruitful tension or benign disagreement between literature and history which was to continue at least into the eighteenth century and covers the period traversed by the essays in this book. In spite of new forms of historical investigation and constant innovation in literature, both arts maintained close ties with moral philosophy, and the preceptual reading of them was still common. A great history, such as Clarendon's, was very much an exercise in moral judgment, and the poets and playwrights who turned increasingly to history for their subject matter cemented an alliance that, at least theoretically, could claim to enjoy the best of both worlds by bringing the force of historical examples into literature without compromising the prerogatives of the poet. Only the faint echoes of former combat are to be heard in the comments of Richard Braithwait on his slight preference for the study of history: "to be short, my opinion positively is this: That Historian which can joyne profit with a modest delight together in one body or frame of one united discourse grounding his story upon an essentiall truth, deserves the first and principall place: and he who (upon a feigned discourse) can proportion it to a likenesse of truth, merits ye next" (*A Survey of History*, 1638).

Poetry and history had their proper domains, but by the end of the seventeenth century in England, the old quarrel, which had always been academic, had become more of a conversation. The two arts were more secure in their social standing than they had been in Sidney's time, and men of letters could move freely between the realms of poetry and history without feeling the need to choose between them. Both had indispensable parts to play in the intellectual life of cultivated men and women, and it is the competition between the arts of poetry and painting, not poetry and history, that we tend to associate with the eighteenth century.

The idea that poetry and history continue to challenge each other was implicit, however, in the invitation from the Clark Library committee to arrange a series of seminars on the subject of "literature and history," although my guess would be that the reason for picking the topic was a general sense that nowadays historians and literary critics often pay little attention to each other's work, and that bringing a few of them together would lead to interesting discussion of an interdisciplinary kind; and all interdisciplinary matters have enjoyed a great vogue in recent years on the assumption that if two subjects are brought together they will enrich themselves rather than water each other down.

The poets in this meeting of minds are now represented by critics, whereas the historians still speak for themselves, but the wish to bring them together arises from the complicated history of Anglo-American literary criticism over the last twenty or thirty years. In a recent and helpful guide to its many phases, *After the New Criticism* (University of Chicago Press, 1980), Frank Lentricchia notes in his preface that "the traces of the New Criticism are found . . . in the repeated and often subtle denial of history by a variety of contemporary theorists" (p. xiii). It is an intricate story as Lentricchia tells it, but some of us have vivid memories of the critical climate in the fifties, in which our senior professors, trained in the older school of literary history and research, had been challenged by the New Criticism to become critics themselves — more learned critics, they believed, than their rivals who dominated the scene. In effect, they accepted formalist principles, and the close reading of poems as a high form of criticism, but they encouraged their students to study the history of ideas, the classical topoi, the political backgrounds, and any other contexts of learning that might be relevant to the interpretation of particular works of literature. Theirs was certainly an attempt to bring traditional historical scholarship into the popular practice of explication, and at the time it seemed a promising direction that would combine the best of the old with the excitement of the new.

It was not to happen as they planned it. Within a very few years, the influence of Northrop Frye's *Anatomy of Criticism* (1957), followed by the unprecedented growth of literary theory, made such a program seem obsolete, although a number of scholars remain faithful to it. One can attribute the theoretical turmoil of the last twenty years in part to a widespread and deep dissatisfaction (and perhaps boredom) with literary criticism as it had recently been practiced. The period has seen the proliferation of books and courses with titles beginning, "Literature and . . . ," as if criticism were searching for a partner with which to share its future. History is now merely one of many subjects linked to literature, not as rivals but as adjuncts. It is in this spirit of cooperation rather than polemic that the present collection of essays has been assembled. It reflects my personal conviction that some of the best and most lasting criticism combines acute literary perception and informed historical knowledge. I thought this conviction should be demonstrated in practice rather than argued at an abstruse theoretical level.

Cleanth Brooks kindly agreed to open the series. His own important contributions to the history of modern criticism have included a celebrated dispute with the late Douglas Bush about the role of historical knowledge in literary criticism. His conciliatory attitude of thirty years ago remains consistent with his present reading of Bishop Henry King's "The Exequy." Following his essay, the order is roughly chronological. The second essay is Derek Hirst's analysis of Marvell's "The First Anniversary of the Government under O. C." He is the first professional historian to have examined the poem closely since Caroline Robbins did so in her dissertation over fifty years ago. He advances a new and highly plausible reading, which will be the starting point for further controversy. At the Clark Library—home of the California edition of Dryden's works—Phillip Harth's lecture on Dryden in 1678-1681 provoked a long and ardent debate. If he is right, and I find his evidence convincing, Dryden's biography for those crucial years will have to be rewritten, and a new perspective is obtained on *Absalom and Achitophel.* Nowhere are politics and literature more intimately connected than in the drama, and few would question that Robert Hume is our most active historian of the Restoration and eighteenth-century stage. His lecture "Henry Fielding and Politics at the Little Haymarket, 1728-1737," expanded here, greatly clarifies Fielding's early career and exonerates him from changing political sides. Susan Staves, whose lecture "Where is History but in Texts?" was actually second in the program, on Guy Fawkes Day, brings her wide knowledge of law and legal procedures to bear upon some of the methodological problems involved in writing a history of marriage in the eighteenth century. It transpires they are no less tricky than the law courts themselves. James Chandler's essay, "Wordsworth's Reflections on the Revolution in France," offers surprising evidence for a much deeper and earlier influence of Burke upon Wordsworth than anyone has suspected. He has also pointed to the psychological difficulty Wordsworth experienced in acknowledging this influence even to himself. Edmund Morgan has written extensively about the Puritans in early New England, so no one can speak more authoritatively about Arthur Miller's treatment of the Salem witch trials in *The Crucible*. His courteous criticism of some aspects of the play ends with a striking declaration of one lesson to be drawn from history — a lesson of the widest application. Lastly, we were highly fortunate to have another historian of international repute, Arnaldo Momigliano, whose extraordinary erudition elucidates "The Introduction of History as an Academic Subject and Its Implications." Professor Momigliano first characterizes the classical and postclassical attitudes toward the reading and writing of history, then offers an explanation for the very late start, in the seventeenth and eighteenth centuries, of the professional teaching of history in European universities. As the great historian of historiography, Professor Momigliano brought the series to a fitting conclusion.

Because of the reputations of the speakers, the lectures proved to be popular, and on behalf of the large audiences I wish to thank the lecturers for the intellectually exciting afternoons they provided. Discussion often continued until dusk during the winter months, in the library garden tended so well by Frank Orden. I should like to acknowledge the honor of being appointed to the Clark professorship and to thank those who brought the appointment about. I am also most grateful to the director of the library, Professor Norman Thrower, for his unfailing helpfulness and hospitality. The Clark has become justly famous as a place to work, and all readers are deeply obliged to the librarian, Dr. Thomas Wright, and his efficient staff. I owe special thanks to those members of it who not only arranged the receptions that followed the lectures but afforded all readers the daily amenities of library life: John Bidwell, Carol Briggs, Susan Green, Pat McCloskey, Beverly Onley, Raymond Reece, Nancy Shea, Carol Sommer, Neady Taylor and Leonard White. Finally, as editor of this volume, I should like to dedicate my small share in it to Robert and Lorraine Vosper, who have played such a significant part in the Clark Library's history and who continue so staunchly to support its activities.

J. M. W.

CONTRIBUTORS

Cleanth Brooks, Gray Professor of Rhetoric emeritus, Yale University.

James K. Chandler, Associate Professor of English, The University of Chicago.

Phillip Harth, Merritt Y. Hughes Professor of English and Fellow of the Institute for Research in the Humanities, The University of Wisconsin, Madison.

Derek Hirst, Professor of History, Washington University.

Robert D. Hume, Professor of English, The Pennsylvania State University.

Arnaldo Momigliano, Professor, Scuola Normale Superiore, Pisa, and Alexander White, Visiting Professor, The University of Chicago.

Edmund S. Morgan, Sterling Professor of History, Yale University.

Susan Staves, Professor of English, Brandeis University.

John M. Wallace, Professor of English, The University of Chicago.

I

NEED CLIO QUARREL WITH HER SISTER MUSES? THE CLAIMS OF LITERATURE AND HISTORY

Cleanth Brooks

Is there any justification for a quarrel between the Muse of History and her sister Muses? Neither Hesiod nor any other of the ancient Greek authorities refer to even a tiff within this sisterhood. According to Homer, the Olympian gods wrangled frequently, but never the Muses. Yet some of their devotees have kept up a long-standing bickering down to this day. I think there are no just grounds for their contention. I appear before you on this occasion in the guise of peacemaker, all but waving a large olive branch.

Since I have little confidence in abstract presentations of literary issues, I mean to let the examination of a particular poem make most of my points for me. I have chosen an English poem, "The Exequy," by Bishop Henry King, composed circa 1624. Because the English language has changed so much in 360 years, we shall need all the help from the historian we can get in order to come to grips with this remarkable poem. Among other things, we shall rely heavily on the *Oxford English Dictionary,* a dictionary which proclaims itself to be founded "On Historical Principles."

My discussion will also involve some account of seventeenth-century theological beliefs and burial customs, the meager deposit of biographical facts about the author, especially his literary career, and the chronological order of his poems. As I hope this essay will make evident, the historian and notably the historian of language holds one of the most important of the several keys necessary to unlock the poem's full meaning. Yet I will show that a full knowledge of history, though absolutely necessary, does not in itself suffice. For history can explore the historical matrix of a mediocre poem or a worthless poem as readily as that of an excellent poem. Dates are dates, facts are facts, whether they have to do with the American popular ballad "Casey Jones," Longfellow's vapid "Psalm of Life," or Keats's magnificent "Ode to a Nightingale." History cannot in and of itself determine literary value.

"The Exequy" is a poem on the death of Bishop King's wife in 1624. The poem has elicited high praise from poets as radically different as T. S. Eliot and Edgar Allan Poe. Eliot regarded lines 111-112, in which the mourning husband says to the dead wife,

> But hark! My Pulse, like a soft Drum
> Beates my Approach, Tells Thee I come,

as constituting one of the finest examples of the "conceit," the involved intellectual figure beloved by the seventeenth-century metaphysical poets. Poe could be expected to like "The Exequy," if for no other reason, for its subject matter, the death of a beautiful and beloved woman. His own showpiece is "The Raven," in which a lover mourns the death of his lost Lenore.

King also apparently had a liking for poems of this sort. He wrote many laments and elegies, but they have received little praise. "The Exequy" employs much the same literary conventions, rhetorical devices, and "conceited" imagery that characterize all King's funereal verse. Why, then, does his masterpiece so far surpass his other poems in this genre? The obvious answer is that he was deeply and sincerely grieved at the loss of his wife, Anne, whereas he merely followed the polite conventions, expressing a formal sorrow, in "An Elegy Upon the immature losse of the most vertuous Lady Anne Riche," or "An Elegy Upon Mrs. Kirk, unfortunately drowned in Thames." "The Exequy," so this argument runs, is the outcome of genuine emotion. What was Lady Anne Riche to him or he to Mistress Kirk?

Though this way of accounting for the superior merit of "The Exequy" makes a certain sense, biographers and literary historians can tell us absolutely nothing about the relation of our poet to any of these three esteemed ladies. We possess no real evidence. We simply "know" from reading "The Exequy" that the grief is real and from reading the other two poems that it is not. The argument is clearly circular: our only basis for judging the sincerity of the poem is the character of the poems themselves. What we should be asking is this: What is there in the makeup of "The Exequy" which convinces us that the sentiments expressed are authentic? Even when demonstrable by biographical evidence, the sincerity of the author doesn't guarantee poetic virtue. The skeptic may be referred to the agony column of the average city newspaper. The sorrowing mother who begins, " 'Tis one year and a day / Since our little Willie passed away" is expressing a heartfelt sorrow. Even the professional poet wracked by genuine grief is capable of shameless sentimentalism. James Russell Lowell's "After the Burial," though it contains some beautiful lines, is an example of this. Thus, if most readers of "The Exequy" feel that it expresses genuine sorrow, that belief must be an inference from the poem itself.

I think we shall have to seek the poetic merit of "The Exequy" in what it is able to convey to the reader, both explicitly and by implication. The structure of the poem lives up to its title. The word *exequy* means funeral rites and ultimately derives from the Latin *exequi,* "to follow out," or, as the *OED* expands it, "follow to the grave." This is the framework of the poem. As the poem opens, the funeral procession has evidently reached the already opened grave. The bereaved husband now lays on his wife's bier "a strew of weeping verse" rather than the usual cluster of "sweet flowres." The first sixty lines of the poem are addressed to her, whereas lines 61-78 are addressed to the earth, which is to receive her body.

In "The Exequy" King makes use of the literary conventions, witty imagery, and verbal play of the time. He begins the poem with what seems a flourish of rhetorical extravagance. He addresses his dead wife as a "Saint" and lays the poem as an offering upon her "Shrine." A more careful reading makes it plain that, in fact, the husband has not claimed canonization for his wife nor established for her, even in metaphor, an ornate shrine like that befitting a medieval saint. Nor does he liken himself to a pilgrim come to pay his devotion and veneration to the holy relics enclosed in the shrine. He is much more modest in his claims. The bereft husband addresses the *body* of his dead wife. The shrine in question is the body itself. He calls it a shrine because it once contained her spirit, as a medieval shrine contains the bones or other relics of a saint.

King draws on the familiar Christian concept of the body as the temple of the Holy Ghost, the earthly case containing the immortal soul. Shakespeare makes use of the same concept in Sonnet 146 when he writes, "Poor soul the center of my sinful earth." King uses the term *saint* to signify the devout and committed Christian. Such usage was general at the time. A few years later, Milton was to use *saint* in just this sense in the sonnet in which he refers to his dead wife as "my late espoused Saint." That the shrine referred to in the first line of King's poem is indeed the dead body is confirmed by line 11, in which he addresses her body as "Lov'd Clay."

Though he addresses the inanimate remains as if the dead woman were still able to hear him, this notion hardly transcends accepted poetic license. Traditional verse and prose have for centuries been full of anguished lovers speaking to the loved one's corpse as if it still contained the breath of life. Even so, King does not press the issue. In writing "Thou might'st see [me] / Quite melted into Teares for Thee" (lines 5-6), he uses the conditional, not the indicative "Thou may'st see," for he well knows that the dead eyes cannot see anything.

The word "glasses" in line 15 (where he refers to his eyes as "wett glasses") perhaps requires a gloss. Though in the seventeenth century *glasses* could refer as now to telescopes and spectacles, the word could also signify the unaided eyes themselves, and such has to be the meaning here.

The mourner goes on to say that through his tear-blinded eyes (because of their blurred vision or in spite of it?) he finds out

How lazily Time creepes about
To one that mournes.
(lines 16-17)

And time is not merely slowed; it actually runs

> Backward and most praeposterous.
>
> (line 22)

Preposterous is used in its precise, etymological sense, "hindside-before," though by the seventeenth century the present meaning ("absurd, ridiculous") had already developed.

The mourning husband reflects that it is no wonder his sense of time is confused, for in losing his wife he has lost the "cleere Sunne" of his life (line 29). Therefore he finds himself, even in broad daylight, benighted, encompassed in an "Eve of blacknes" (line 24). In fact, the course of his sun has run contrary to normal expectations. It has now set beneath earth's rim before ever reaching full "Noon-tide" (line 26).

The husband presses this circumstance of early and untimely death further, implying again that his wife had scarcely completed her full day. He remarks in lines 28-29,

> Thou scarce hadst seene so many Yeeres
> As Day tells [that is, numbers] Howres.

The historian can confirm the implication. The scant records we possess indicate that Anne King was not quite twenty-four when she died. The allusion seems neat and precise. This kind of figurative detail is, of course, the hallmark of the great metaphysicals.

King develops the sun figure still further. His sun has set, but unlike that other sun that by reappearing every morning brings light and warmth to mankind, his cannot be expected to return to him. He finds a more accurate and mournful analogy for her departure than the great daystar: a shooting star, which after a brief transit across the sky, falls to earth and loses its light forever.

With line 35 the poet shifts to yet another metaphorical description of what has befallen his sun. It has suffered eclipse—an unexpected and shocking eclipse since no "Almanake" predicted it. The figurative language reflects the very mechanism of an eclipse:

> And 'twixt mee and my Soule's deare wish
> The Earth now interposed is.
>
> (lines 35-36)

This sounds like an eclipse of the moon, in which the earth's shadow blots out the moon's light. If the eclipse is of the sun, it is the moon that interposes itself between the sun and the observer. (Several of the manuscripts actually read, "An Earth." The moon as a planetary body of the order of the earth might indeed be called an Earth.) Yet, whether the eclipse is of the sun or the moon, the point of the figure is the same: the grieving lover will be left in lasting darkness, for he has no hope of recovery of the wished for light.

Indeed, the poet says that if he only knew that in ten years his light would return, he might be able to endure his present state. But it may be eons before his light will put "off [her] ashy Shrowd" (line 45). For the modern reader, lines 47-48,

> But woe is mee! the longest date
> Too narrowe is to calculate,

may require a note. *Date* here means "duration" (*OED* 4). Thus the longest duration or period of time is too brief to calculate her hoped for return. He cannot expect to see her until the end of the world, when the earth and all that is in it, including her dead body and his, shall be burnt to ashes.

The belief that the world would be destroyed by fire rests principally upon one of the minor books of the New Testament, 2 Peter 3:10. The King James version, which is presumably the one that Bishop King used, reads as follows: "But the day of the Lord will come as a thief in the night; in the which the heavens shall pass away with a great noise, and the elements shall melt with fervent heat, the earth also and the works that are therein shall be burned up." In lines 53-54 the speaker tells us that a "fierce Feaver" brought about the death of his wife, and he now makes plain that such a fever will, in the last days, bring to an end the life of the world itself. Thus, the fate of Anne as microcosm anticipates the similar fate of the macrocosm. He calls his wife in line 55 "My Little World."

Yet, once this "fitt of Fire" (line 55) is over, the mourner and his wife will rise phoenix-like from their ashes. (Though King does not directly invoke the phoenix image, it clearly underlies the passage.) Moreover, the action of the fire will be cleansing and purifying, for they will arise from their dust and look upon each other with "cleerer eyes" in a realm of everlasting day in which "no Night / Can hide [them] from each other's sight" (lines 59-60).

Though King does not spell out the precise way the dead will arise from their graves, he apparently believes the grains of dust or ashes will be reconstituted to become the resurrected body. Such a view was common in the period. King's friend, Izaac Walton, expressed the same belief in his life of another friend of King's, John Donne. The last sentence of Walton's "Life of Donne" reads: "He is now a handful of Christian dust, but I shall see it reanimated." In short, King's conception is not at all that envisaged in Shelley's line "Like a ghost from the tomb," but a literal reading of the Apostles' Creed: "I believe . . . in the resurrection of the body."

At line 61 the speaker, with a distinct shift in tone, now addresses the earth, which with the lowering of Anne's body into the grave, will take possession of it. But not forever. The speaker reminds the earth that it will someday be required to

> yeeld Hir back againe by weight;
> For thou must Auditt on thy trust
> Each Grane and Atome of this Dust.
> (lines 74-76)

The tone of his admonition to the earth lies somewhere between resignation and bitter reproach. It is the tone of a man who through some mishap or turn of fortune has had to give up a precious possession into the hands of another. Bitterness is uppermost in "Much good / May my harme doe thee" (lines 61-62); resignation in "I give thee what I could not keep" (line 68); and a touchingly desperate appeal to the new possessor's unlikely good nature in "Be kind to Hir" (line 69).

The last tonal shift is to a note of grim warning. God has merely lent, not given, the beloved body to the earth, and on his great day, he will demand a strict accounting of his property and a full return of every particle of it. The phrase "thy Doomsday book" (line 70) is very effective. The detailed inventory of all the land and real property in England ordered in 1086 by William the Conqueror had long become a byword for any thorough and detailed accounting. The great inventory was known as the Domesday Book because it provided the final judgment (doom) on all matters within its scope of reference. In King's time "doom's day" had, of course, also come to mean the last great judgment day, in which the Lord shall raise the dead and utter His final judgment on every human being.

The phrase "my deare Monument" in line 78 may mislead the modern reader. The husband's words seem to refer to his wife's tomb or to a marble effigy of her, but at this time she has not yet been buried, for in the very next line the husband orders the grave closed (line 79). "Monument" must then refer to the wife's dead body. It resembles a life-sized effigy of herself, as motionless and cold as a marble statue.

At line 80 the grave is evidently closed. The husband describes the placing of the earth about his dead wife as a drawing of the bed curtains in the ancient ceremony of the bedding of the bride. The use of this metaphor to describe the placing of a young woman in the grave is a familiar one. It can be traced from the Middle Ages down to A. E. Housman's "Bredon Hill." But here it is given a fresh application. The bridegroom in this instance is not death but the bereaved husband himself. Though she lies in her bed to await the coming of the bridegroom, their final joining of bodies may be long postponed, for that must await his own burial in her grave. Their final and absolute marriage will occur only when he "must / Marry my Body to that Dust / It so much loves" (lines 85-87).

With line 81 the husband begins his concluding address to his dead wife, the long farewell that closes the poem. In his imagination she once more becomes a sentient being who can hear the promise he makes to her as he speaks his "Last Good-night" (line 83). He insists that some day he will return to "fill the roome / [His] heart keepes empty in [her] Tomb" (lines 87-88), for eventually he will be placed beside her in "that hollow Vale," the grave. The rest of the poem consists of elaborations on this pledge.

Line 89 is the boldest in the entire poem. He implores (commands?) his wife to "Stay for mee there," as if the poor, dead body could do anything else. By stating matters as he does, he converts mere fact into a solemn tryst. The body is seen not as mere clay, however dear, but as needing to be conjured to keep the tryst. As for himself, the very indications of his own inevitable dissolution become proofs of his invincible determination to meet her at the elected trysting place. His passive waiting for his own end becomes, as he describes it in the poem, an active journey toward a sought for goal.

Lines 92-114 of the poem are dominated by images of the journey, the husband's steady progress toward the death that will bring the pair together at last. The journey is first treated as a sea voyage in which the bereaved husband sails steadily toward his "West / Of Life." His progress is indeed as steady as a ship sailing west across the Atlantic. Just as the traveler aboard ship does not have to stop at some wayside inn for a night's rest, so the husband each morning when he wakes is truly eight hours closer to his goal than when he went to sleep. Even in sleep the body's process of dying goes on uninterruptedly.

In line 95 — "Each Minute is a short Degree" — the word *minute* does double duty. It carries a spatial as well as a temporal reference. In calculating the longitude and latitude of a point on the globe, we measure distances in degrees and minutes. Sixty minutes make a degree; 360 degrees, the full circle. Since the sun requires 24 hours to make its apparent circuit of the earth, 15 degrees represents one hour's difference between points of high noon on the earth's surface.

The word "Bottome" in line 102 refers to the speaker's fancied vessel. The word is still used in this sense today in maritime commerce. Thus, the husband voyages steadily westward "from the Sunne" (line 101) toward the realm of darkness and death. Having in mind the references to a sea voyage, most readers will also assume that the "Compasse" mentioned in the next line is a mariner's compass. If so, what can possibly be meant by "my Daye's Compass downward beares" (line 102): The magnetized needle of the compass swings horizontally on its axis; it cannot bear downward. The needle of the dipping-needle compass can be said to bear downward, but this instrument of navigation had not been invented in King's era.

The *OED* clears up the mystery. "Compasse" (*OED* 6) means, "A circular arc, sweep, curve." An example of this usage occurs in Captain Smith's *Seaman's Grammar* (1627): "Here doth begin the compass and bearing of the ship." The compass (arc) of the poet's imaginary ship follows the curve of the globe. It takes him below the horizon and on downward until it will reach his antipodes. Since the tide of life itself takes him toward death, the destination of all mortals, the bereaved man has no desire "to stemme [that] Tide" (line 103). Because it carries him toward his beloved wife, he welcomes it.

With line 105 the figure shifts from a journey by sea to a journey overland, the march of the rear guard of an army hastening to unite with the vanguard, which has already joined battle with the enemy and gained a victory. Any Christian communicant of King's time, let alone a bishop, would remember St. Paul's "O death where is thy sting? O grave where is thy victory?" To die in the Lord is to insure admission into eternal life—and reunion of the devoted man and wife. It is this conviction that allows the speaker to tell his wife in the closing lines of the poem that he is content to wait upon his own "dissolution / With Hope and Comfort" (lines 116-117), though he feels obliged to ask her pardon for finding any comfort at all while still living apart from her.

Lines 111-114, recounting the march of the rear guard to rejoin the now victorious vanguard, are probably the most powerfully resonant lines in the poem. The speaker's own pulse is the drum to the beat of which his military corps marches to join hers. The march may be slow and take years to accomplish, yet nothing can stop him, he assures her.

> And, slowe howe're my Marches bee,
> I shall at last sitt downe by Thee.
> (lines 113-114)

So much for this brilliantly conceived and executed poem. Some years later King wrote a poem entitled "The Anniverse," which, like "The Exequy," is an elegy on the death of Anne King. It begins with a tender address to the "Poore Earth, once by my Love inhabited." After this pityingly affectionate opening it degenerates into a self-pitying whining over King's sorrowful plight. Before the poem ends he even goes so far as to describe himself as bound alive to a corpse. The image of decay that this downright grisly expression invokes is thoroughly self-serving: poor fellow, to be expected to endure this horror. The failure of the poem requires no belaboring. Taken as a biographical document, however, it is interesting. It makes one wonder whether King was not, after six years, finding the widower's lot a truly unhappy one. One might even conjecture that it presages a second marriage.

Lawrence Mason, King's most thorough and conscientious biographer,[1] believes King did marry a second time. He is properly cautious on this subject. In fact, he is plainly reluctant to accept the possibility that the author of "The Exequy" could prove disloyal "to [Anne's] memory," or, worse, "write about, woo [and] even win a second wife." But Mason as an honest scholar is forced to conclude that King did make a second marriage. Though there is no record of it, the evidence is in King's poems.

One of them, of indeterminate date, is entitled "The Short Wooing." It is a wittily perfunctory proposal of marriage. The suitor does not wish a long probation. He wishes to hear the verdict at once. He reminds the lady that she is the sole mistress of herself. The decision to accept or reject him is hers. The lady might, of course, be Anne Berkeley herself, but if not, the poem would indeed suggest a second wooing. In any case it scarcely seems the utterance of an impassioned lover. In itself, however, the poem gives us little help with our question.

A second poem, "The Legacy," also of indeterminate date, is addressed to the speaker's wife. The poem is a reasoned justification of second marriages. If he should die first, it is the speaker's wish that his widow remarry. Among other things, he says

> Those were Barbarian Wives that did invent
> Weeping to Death at th' Husband's Moniment.
> (lines 49-50)

Was this poem perhaps addressed to King's first wife, Anne? It may have been, since we have no clue as to the date of its composition. Or is the poem simply a speculative exercise? In any case, does it represent the bishop's true opinions about second marriages, and if so, how do we square it with the implications of "The Exequy"?

As to whom "The Legacy" was addressed, we do not know. As to whether it expresses King's true feelings about second marriages, we must remember that poems are not sworn affidavits presented at a court of law. Men do change their minds, and what was written during a period of wracking grief does not necessarily represent the emotions of a later period. "The Legacy" would at least suggest that King was not of that monogamist cult of which Goldsmith's Vicar of Wakefield was a fanatic member. As the historian will tell us, second and third marriages were frequent and even usual in the seventeenth century.

One passage in "The Legacy," stands out, however.

> My Bodye's pamper'd care
> Hungry Corruption and the Worme will share,
> That mouldring Relick which in Earth must ly
> Would prove a guift of horrour to thine Ey.
>
> (lines 15-18)

It recalls "If thou wilt bind mee Living to a Coarse" in "The Anniverse," a poem certainly written about King's dead first wife, and it looks forward to a variation on the same gruesome image in our last piece of evidence, a poem entitled "St. Valentine's Day." The relevant lines in that poem read:

> Henceforth I need not make the dust my Shrine
> Nor search the Grave for my lost Valentine.
>
> (lines 29-30)

"St. Valentine's Day" can only be read as a poem by a widower proposing marriage to a prospective second wife. It simply makes no sense otherwise. The poem begins with a reference to one of the customs of Valentine's Day. As the *OED* describes it, "A person of the opposite sex [was] chosen, drawn by lot . . . as a sweetheart, lover, or special friend." The speaker of "St. Valentine's Day" tells the lady that he "could have wisht for your own sake / That Fortune had design'd a nobler stake / For you to draw." A few lines later he goes on, "Yet since you like your Chance," and then in line 25, "Hail then my worthy Lot." Though this is spoken to the lady gallantly enough and with much self-deprecation, there is certainly no passionate commitment, stated or implied. His future attachment to her has come about by the workings of fate. This scheme of fatal action is reinforced by references elsewhere in the poem to his "cross Starres and inauspicious fate," which have for years "Doom'd [him] to linger here without [his] Mate."

The argument of the poem amounts to this: though I wish that fortune had provided you with a "nobler stake" than I am, fortune has been most kind to me in rescuing me from my residence in a tomb where I

> Like to a dedicated Taper lay
> Within a Tomb, and long burnt out in vain
> Since nothing there saw better by the flame.
>   (lines 16-18)

This last figure has its own brilliance. It even reminds one a little of Donne, King's good friend for whom King served as literary executor. A votive candle placed inside a tomb provides a light useless to the corpse within, and no light at all to anybody else.

The restiveness and unhappiness perhaps hinted at in "The Anniverse" have become defined and realized in "St. Valentine's Day." The speaker of this poem, long bereaved, has resolved to give up living with his fruitless grief. There is a perceptible note of relief in the concluding lines, which tell of his discovery that "I need not make the dust my Shrine / Nor search the Grave for my lost Valentine."

John Sparrow, who published an edition of King's poems in 1925,[2] thought that the fact of a second marriage had been proved and referred to the closing line of "St. Valentine's Day" as an "ignoble sequel to 'The Exequy.'" Whatever the poem may or may not tell us about King's own life, on its own terms it is a sadly inept poem. For how can a lady welcome a lover who comes to her with hands confessedly grimy from scrabbling through the dust of his first love's grave?

Mason presents one more bit of evidence, an unsigned poem in Harleian MS 6917. Mason believes it was written by King and that it demonstrates that King was remarried by 1 January 1631. Margaret Crum, King's most recent editor (1965), argues that the author of this poem was not Henry King but his brother John. This bit of evidence for a second marriage collapses.

Miss Crum's edition of King's poems[3] has had the benefit of the discovery of certain manuscripts not available to Mason and Sparrow. She is an excellent textual scholar and I am grateful that I can quote from the texts of King's poems as she has established them. But in disproving Henry King's authorship of the poem in Harleian MS 6917 she has not disposed of the possibility of a second marriage by King. What about the other poems: "The Anniverse," "The Short Wooing," "The Legacy"? Most of all, what about "St. Valentine's Day"? That strange poem is a veritable lion in the path.

Yet, interested as I am in biography and history, I am more interested in the bearing of historical fact on aesthetic judgment. Let us suppose that some scholar should come upon definite evidence that Bishop King had remarried. Ought we in that case to think less of "The Exequy"? My answer is that this magnificent poem stands apart from all the vicissitudes of King's personal life. I grant that the poem came out of a mind shaped by certain social and intellectual influences, and that if we want to enter fully into the poem we have to become acquainted with the language and culture that formed that mind. But the umbilical cord connecting poem and poet has been severed. The poem now enjoys a life of its own, not to be affected by what subsequently happened to its author or what he caused to happen.

Let me be more specific. Ought our appreciation and enjoyment of "The Exequy" be affected by a subsequent reading of "St. Valentine's Day"? The latter poem and the related poem, "The Short Wooing," incidentally, occur in only one manuscript, Phillips MS 9325. Suppose that that manuscript had never been discovered. Would readers find "The Exequy" a more moving and sincere poem for never having read "St. Valentine's Day"? The hoped for answer is no — and not merely on the principle that what you don't know won't hurt you.

A fair evaluation of "The Exequy" does not depend upon an ignorance of the later poems, but on an accurate sense of the nature of poetry and the relation of poem to poet. Surely a good poem is not so fragile that it can be damaged or destroyed by our knowledge of later (or earlier) events in the poet's life. "St. Valentine's Day" is an inept poem because of its own internal defects, not because King could not live up to something he may earlier have pledged to do. A truly good poem is not tarnished by its author having written a bad poem or two dozen of them, or even having lived a bad life. An authentic poem is not inextricably attached to its author so as to be affected by the author's actions.

The concept of the poet's sincerity as a norm for evaluating his work simply constitutes another way of tying the poem too closely to the poet. In real life, sincerity is not easy to determine. In the work of poets like King, about whom we know so little, it is almost impossible to determine. Such evidence as there is amounts almost wholly to what may be gleaned from the very poems to be judged. Thus, the argument is hopelessly circular: we read the poem and find it truly moving and so argue that it represents the author's sincere expression of his feelings. Then we proclaim that because the poet was sincere his poem is tender and moving. The term *sincere* is superfluous and may be profitably discarded. In their *Theory of Literature,* René Welleck and Austin Warren put the case against sincerity very well.

There is no relation between "sincerity" and value as art. The volumes of agonizingly felt love poetry perpetrated by adolescents and the dreary (however fervently felt) religious verse which fills libraries, are sufficient proof of this. Byron's "Fare Thee Well . . ." is neither a worse nor a better poem because it dramatizes the poet's actual relations with his wife, nor "is it a pity," as Paul Elmer More thinks, that the MS shows no traces of the tears which, according to Thomas Moore's *Memoranda,* fell on it. The poem exists; the tears shed or unshed, the personal emotions are gone and cannot be reconstructed, nor need they be.[4]

Apparently Bishop King's dust was never mingled with Anne's, nor with that of any second wife, if ever there was such. Anne was buried in London in 1624. Henry King died 30 September 1669 and, as bishop of Chichester, was buried in the cathedral. But what difference does it make? We have "The Exequy," and that poem is still very much alive. It is recoverable for any reader who will take the trouble to appropriate it for himself.

NOTES

1. "The Life and Works of Henry King, D.D.," *Transactions of the Connecticut Academy of Arts and Sciences* 18 (1913-15): 227-289.

2. *The Poems of Bishop Henry King* (London: Nonesuch Press).

3. *The Poems of Henry King* (Oxford: Clarendon Press, 1965).

4. *Theory of Literature,* 2d ed. (New York: Harcourt, Brace, and Co., 1956), p. 68.

II

"THAT SOBER LIBERTY": MARVELL'S CROMWELL IN 1654

Derek Hirst

Marvell scholars have long recognized that familiarity with political context is essential to a full appreciation of the Cromwell poems. Unfortunately, not all scholars have examined the material with the scrupulous attention that John Wallace gave to the "Horatian Ode." The result has been a remarkable divergence in interpretations of Marvell's politics. That divergence is greatest of all over "The First Anniversary," the longest and thematically most complex of the three.[1] Were we to follow any one of the major arguments of recent years, we could, with Wallace, see Marvell urging the crown on the lord protector; with J. A. Mazzeo, herald Marvell's vision of Cromwell as a Davidic king (although where such a figure would lead is not quite apparent); with Steven N. Zwicker, see Cromwell cast not as king but as Old Testament judge, guarding the Israelites from sin and from their enemies; with A. J. N. Wilson (if I read him right), watch Marvell saluting Cromwell as Augustus; and with Annabel Patterson, admire the dexterity and perspicacity with which Marvell balances all these models and finds them inadequate in comprehending the protector.[2] A mere historian would be rash in seeking to teach such a distinguished assembly its business, or in attempting a complete reading of the poem. But it is open to the historian to

17

point to features of Cromwell's career in 1654, and of the politics of that year, which might provide a means to reconcile some of the various readings, and to explicate more clearly the political and ideological thrust of the poem.

Disagreement about Marvell's meaning is of course inevitable given the nature of his work. No other writer is so ready to view a problem from all angles and all levels, or suddenly to stand back and scrutinize himself and his own motives. But "The First Anniversary" should be capable of a more or less coherent political interpretation. Unlike the "Horatian Ode," it was published in short order, and by the government's own printer to boot, with an advertisement for it in the government's own newspaper.[3] That is not to suggest that "The First Anniversary" is merely a piece of government propaganda, but it is to suggest that perhaps Marvell and certainly others expected it to be understood in a certain way.

Redundant though the exercise will be for most readers, the broad political context of the poem needs first to be established. The army's revolution of the winter of 1648-49, which brought with it the trial and execution of Charles I, established a rather uneasy republic, popularly, or unpopularly, known as the Rump. Striving hard for respectability, the only justification for its existence it could come up with was the argument that obedience should be paid to the de facto power, or, in a slightly different guise, to the power that was providentially decreed. As John Wallace and Quentin Skinner have convincingly demonstrated, the question of the legitimacy of a state served wonderfully to concentrate the minds of brilliant men, and it is in this context that both Marvell's "Horatian Ode" and Hobbes's *Leviathan* should be read.[4] The quest for respectability was not, however, conducted solely in the woods and thickets of the printing presses. That quest also drove the Rump into political immobility as, desperate to be accepted by the local gentry, it forgot the practical reforms that had been urged on it by the army and moved ever more slowly to create a new and more permanent constitution. Fresh from its final triumph at Worcester in 1651 over the Anglo-Scottish royalist forces of the young Charles Stuart, the army watched increasingly impatiently as the Rump did less and less. Cromwell had long tried to reconcile the conflicting forces of conservatism and reform, but he was at last in April 1653 driven from behind by the army, as much as by his own anger, to eject the Rump.[5] There followed two and one-half months of rule by the more or less naked sword, until in July 1653 Cromwell and reformist army officers called together that anomalous body in English history, the Barebone's Parliament. The reformist zeal and internal fractiousness of this assembly quickly proved as tiresome to Cromwell the country gentleman as the inertia of the Rump had been to Cromwell the saint. On 12 December he gladly acquiesced in a parliamentary coup that drove Praise-God Barebone back to his leather selling business.[6] More prepared this time, the army officers had no need for an embarrassing period of military rule. On 16 December Cromwell's protectorate was established (the passive voice accurately reflects the discreet impersonality of the official account[7]) under the Instrument of Government, after Cromwell had rejected the suggestion of some officers that he take the crown. It was of course the anniversary of the Instrument which Marvell's poem celebrated.

Those in power made little secret of the fact that the English body politic had not reached its final home in December 1653. Just as in the summer of that year Cromwell had turned to a nominated assembly in the hope that the English people could gradually be won to godliness by good examples and reform, so the Instrument was visibly something of a halfway house to a reformed parliamentary constitutionalism.[8] Until the first parliament under the Instrument, scheduled for September 1654, the protector and his council were to have untrammeled legislative power, probably again in the hope that the nation could be won over by the pattern of godliness. Accordingly, in its first nine months the council established a fairly impressive record of reform.[9] As a further sign of the intermediate status of current arrangements, royalists and other delinquents were only to be debarred from the parliamentary franchise for a period of years.

Not surprisingly, some spectators were suspicious of Cromwell's plans for the future.[10] Such fears were not wholly unfounded, for a sizable minority of members of the first protectorate Parliament tried in October to reconstitute the elective protectorate of the Instrument on a hereditary footing, and two months later a much smaller group moved that Oliver become king. The aim of both groups was to provide a succession, and thus some security for the future, in order to break Cromwell's dependence on the military arm, which so many civilians hated; for 1654 saw an

unnerving series of assassination plots. Given the importance of
Cromwell's commanding presence to the survival of the regime —
an importance to which Marvell testifies in his account of the
coaching accident — the success of any of those plots would have
brought disaster to the godly cause and perhaps to the nation too.
As Wallace has rightly pointed out, that uncertain future was a
vital part of the background to the poem. Although Cromwell
himself protested his distaste for the attempts to make his rule
hereditary, a protest that is given some substance by his rejection
of the crown in 1653 and again in 1657, and by other evidence to
be considered shortly, there were many in England who saw the
question of the succession as central to politics. Thus, several
published works in the summer and autumn of 1654 focused on
the matter.[11] Those anxious for stability — and by no means all
were covert royalists pragmatically settling on Oliver faute de
mieux — dreamed hereditary dreams, whereas republicans and
radical saints saw any move to give substance to those dreams as
either a betrayal of the ideals of their revolution or a tampering
with forms against which God had witnessed.

A consciousness of the urgency of the problem of the future
shape of the government, and of the recurrence of discussion of
that problem throughout the nearly five years of Cromwell's protectorate, has been a major factor in shaping some of the leading
interpretations of Marvell's poem. Wallace looks to the sun imagery applied to Cromwell, imagery that had undeniably earlier
been put to monarchical use, and to some of the biblical types,
and sees in them a recommendation of the crown. In likening
Cromwell to Noah, Marvell referred to perhaps the most common source for scripturalist interpretations of the origins of kingship, so recently deployed in the most coherent royalist defense of
all, Sir Robert Filmer's *Patriarcha*. And in Marvell's assimilation
of Oliver to Elijah, after the coaching accident had so nearly terminated the protector's life, Wallace detects strong regret that
there was none to emulate Elisha, picking up the protector's
mantle intact. By contrast, Zwicker focuses on the figure of Gideon, to whom Cromwell is likened in his expulsion of the Rump
and in his victory over two kings (Charles I and his son).[12] As Marvell emphatically reminds us, "Yet would not he be Lord, nor yet
his Son" (1.256). Is this a case of blithe if eloquent incoherence,
an incoherence that encourages scholars to take up their cudgels
yet more blithely?

The historical record provides grounds for resolution. Some contemporaries, as well as some historians, certainly detected a drift toward kingship over the months of 1654. But looked at carefully, the evidence, in particular the ceremonial of the protectorate, points another way. Ceremonial was in effect the public image of the regime: state occasions were not just for locals to gawk at but were carefully reported in newspapers that were for the most part government controlled. These occasions were not regal. Accounts of the great state occasions of the early protectorate repeatedly contrast the grandeur of the occasion with the simplicity of the protector's conduct. Time after time, he was reported to have remained standing, hat in hand—rather than with hat on as his dignity might be thought to demand—and clad in plain black.[13] It was the regime, rather than the personality, that was being celebrated in these affairs. And Oliver himself gives some clues to his own feelings. In an angry piece of self-justification to Parliament on 12 September, he recounted the establishment of the protectorate and observed, "When I had consented to accept of the government, there was some solemnity to be performed."[14] It is hard to imagine a smaller degree of personal involvement in the display which the Tudors had made so much a part of the business of kingship.

The notoriously ungrandiose scale of protectoral entertaining, of which royalist scandal-mongers made so much, may owe less to the alleged niggardliness or boorishness of Mrs. Cromwell than to Oliver's own tastes and his own conception of his position. True, considerable energy was expended in 1654 in regaining for the protector's use the royal palaces disposed of after Charles's execution; it may be to this that Marvell refers when he speaks of Amphion's sweeter touch creating marble palaces (11. 61-62). But what went on in them was hardly the court life of old. It has indeed been argued that Sir Oliver Fleming, Cromwell's master of ceremonies, modeled the protector's ceremonial on that of the Swiss cantons, which are not usually thought of as the home of regal style.[15] Reflecting this posture, one newspaper reported in unusual detail the reception in 1654 of a delegation from the insignificant Surrey town of Guildford, at which Oliver remained standing throughout, "and then dismissed them . . . with so much courtesy and respect as . . . persons who may justly call themselves somebodies might be well pleased with."[16] Bluff King Hal might conceivably have acted in such a fashion on occasion and wished to broadcast it to the world, but few other kings would. Cromwell at home was indeed "a Subject on the equal Floor" (1. 390).

There is, however, an important qualification. From the very beginning of the protectorate, the Oliver who faced the potentates of Europe was a different figure from the Oliver who faced his fellow Englishmen. Ambassadors receiving audience from the protector in his "cabinet" had to pass through four sets of apartments with closed doors on their way to the inner sanctum.[17] In other words, the protector's reception line resembled strongly that of any European prince. Furthermore, Oliver was as much a stickler about diplomatic precedence and modes of address as were the princes with whom he had to deal, and he manifestly had the power to uphold his claims. Marvell has, I think, exactly caught Oliver's posture in 1654 in the words of the wondering prince at the end of the poem:

> He seems a King by long Succession born,
> And yet the same to be a King does scorn.
> Abroad a King he seems and something more,
> At Home a Subject on the equal Floor.
> (11. 387-390)

The precise congruence between so many aspects of Marvell's Cromwell and the real thing, or at least the real thing as he presented himself, is further apparent in some of the few lines of direct commentary in the poem:

> For all delight of Life thou then didst lose,
> When to Command, thou didst thyself Depose;
> Resigning up thy Privacy so dear,
> To turn the headstrong People's Charioteer;
> . . . .
> Therefore thou rather didst thy Self depress,
> Yielding to Rule, because it made thee Less.
> (11. 221-224, 227-228)

Compare that with Cromwell's angry expostulations, to Parliament on 12 September, of his honesty and good intent — expostulations that were of course promptly published:

I called not myself to this place. I say again, I called not myself to this place; of that, God is witness . . . I was by birth a gentleman, living neither in any considerable height, nor yet in obscurity. I have been called to several employments in the nation . . . [and] having had some occa-

sions to see . . . a happy period put to our sharp wars and contests with
the then common enemy, hoped, in a private capacity, to have reaped
the fruit and benefit, together with my brethren, of our hard labours
and hazards: to wit, the enjoyment of peace and liberty, and the privileges of a Christian and of a man . . . That which I drive at is this; I say
to you, I hoped to have had leave to have retired to a private life. I
begged to be dismissed of my charge; I begged it again and again. And
God be judge between me and all men if I lie in this matter![18]

And so he goes on, in a typically Cromwellian multiplication of
emphases.

But Cromwell's acquiescence to office went beyond taking
away the "delight of life" to which Marvell testified. As the protector repeatedly pointed out in that same speech, the interval
between the expulsion of the Rump and the promulgation of the
Instrument had left his power absolute. "My power . . . was . . .
boundless and unlimited . . . all things being subjected to arbi-
trariness, and [myself] a person having power over the three
nations boundlessly and unlimited. . . . I was arbitrary in power,
having the armies in the three nations under my command, and
truly not very ill beloved by them."[19] In a very real sense, to be
mere "*Cromwell* was a greater thing, / Then ought below, or yet
above a King" (11. 225-226), and the captain-general of the
forces of the commonwealth did indeed, as he stressed, yield up
raw power when he agreed to rule as protector under the Instrument of Government. It was one more element in Cromwell's central theme in that great speech, of his humility and self-abase-
ment, as well as of his honesty of intent. Marvell was not just
drawing elegant parallels with Cincinattus and Roman *virtu*; he
was also painting Cromwell as the man said he was.

Marvell was not alone in his choice of features to highlight.
Patterson has pointed to Marvell's debt to Milton's *Second
Defence*,[20] but she and others have overlooked the degree to
which Marvell articulated arguments common among the protectorate's supporters and propagandists. Marvell's suggestion that
Cromwell's position transcended that of a mere monarch has
caused some controversy among critics. Yet that thought was part
of the common stock of estimates of the protectorate, that it was
sui generis. That it should be so might not have bothered Englishmen, who saw their history as the providential doings of God's
chosen people. Thus, on the second of the three great state occasions of the early protectorate, Cromwell's ceremonial entry into

the City of London, the recorder of the City greeted him—in a speech that was immediately printed in the government's newspaper—as a purely providential ruler, the remarkable product of "this age and land of wonders." He then dismissed any thought of categorizing Oliver's authority: "leave it to other nations to salute their rulers and victorious commanders with the names of *Caesares* and *Imperatores.*"[21] On the same occasion the same government newspaper—whose editor, Marchamont Nedham, we now know to have stood very close to Marvell at the time of the "Horatian Ode"—printed a Latin poem which begins:

> Let the barbarian greatness of Caesar's Rome fall silent.
> A greater Caesar is at hand. Like a new star in the sky.
> Greater than Caesar because he did not want to be greater.
> Let others seize upon a crown. Enough that he could have done so.[22]

One of the Oxford panegyrics on the summer's peace with the Dutch concluded in a manner still more reminiscent of Marvell's account: "For thus of you must following ages tell / You are Your Selfe; without a Parallel."[23] And most tellingly of all, there was Milton in the *Second Defence,* who greeted Cromwell as

the greatest and most glorious of our citizens, the director of the public counsels, the leader of the bravest of armies, the father of your country. . . . Other titles, though merited by you, your actions know not, endure not; and those proud ones, deemed great in vulgar opinion, they deservedly cast from them. For what is a title, but a certain definite mode of dignity? Your achievements surpass every degree even of admiration, and much more do they surpass every title;—they rise above the popular atmosphere of titles, as the tops of pyramids hide themselves in the clouds. But though it can add nothing to dignity, yet as it is expedient, for virtues even the most exalted to be finished and terminated by a sort of human summit, which is counted honour, you thought it right, and suffered yourself, for the public benefit, to assume something like a title, resembling most that of *pater patriae,* the father of your country; you suffered yourself not to be raised indeed, but to descend so many degrees from on high, and to be forced as it were into the ranks; despising the name of king for majesty far more majestic.[24]

That England did not fall readily into either of the forms of government, monarchy or republic, evidently did not deeply perturb some of those who looked admiringly on the figure of Cromwell. Marvell's state of mind, and his antipathy to further consti-

tutional change, seem not to have been dissimilar. At the end of
the poem, the poet suddenly resigns from the debate about the
meaning of Cromwell since no title can do him justice: "I yield,
nor further will the Prize contend" (1. 397). Indeed, Marvell's last
words cast the protector as "the Angel of our Commonweal" (1.
401), which, it need hardly be said, is no civic office.[25]

To point to Cromwell's distancing of himself from the splendor
and paraphernalia of kingship and to the apparent happiness of
some of his supporters, including Marvell, with the anomalies of
the protectorate, does not of course dispose of all the tension in
"The First Anniversary." Oliver's stance, both quasi-republican
and quasi-imperial, was extremely congruent with much of the
language of the poem. Yet the Noah figure remains, seeming to
underline some genuinely monarchical trappings that Oliver took
on in the course of 1654, most notably the increasingly regal style
of his proclamations and the elaborate state funeral in Westminster Abbey which he accorded his "saint-like mother."[26]
Annabel Patterson takes a sensible course by suggesting that Marvell may have introduced various figures and images in a process
of deliberation, in a very self-conscious attempt to interpret the
meaning of Cromwell.[27] Another and not altogether incompatible response might be to stress the very anomalies of the protectorate, of single-person rule within a commonwealth. If one were
writing a celebratory poem about Cromwell, above all people, at
any time in his career, it would be very difficult to echo Martin
Luther and say, "Here I stand. I can no other." For one could
never have known precisely where one, or rather Oliver, did
stand. To paraphrase Patterson's argument,[28] not only did Cromwell outwing the wind but he also outwinged the poet. Or, as a
well-informed English correspondent of Cardinal Mazarin complained of Cromwell in late September, "His enterprises are only
known to himself: he doth . . . as he did with his business in Scotland and Ireland: he did his work and spoke afterwards . . . Certainly we are led into the clouds; we know no longer what to
believe. There is no body hardly can judge aright of the intentions of our superiors, no more than a blind man can of colour."[29]
If then the poet were to celebrate Cromwell's rule and his policies,
it might make sense for him to leave his options open, for he could
not have known which way the protector was about to jump. The
suggestion helps make sense of the openly regalist character of

Marvell's 1657 poem on Blake, for by that time Cromwell seemed to have made his course clear.[30]

Such an argument for "The First Anniversary" depends, however, on Marvell's balancing of kingship and commonwealth, and it is not clear that Marvell does that. Wallace's argument that certain passages in the poem seem to recommend the crown is open to question. The most signal of these is the reference to Noah:

> Thou, and thine House, like Noah's Eight did rest,
> Left by the Wars Flood on the Mountains Crest:
> And the large Vale lay subject to thy Will,
> Which thou but as an Husbandman wouldst Till:
> And only didst for others plant the Vine
> Of Liberty, not drunken with its Wine.
>
> (11. 283-288)

The references to Cromwell's house and to the subjection of all things to his tutelary care seem undeniably monarchical in drift. Yet if Noah is to stand for patriarchal kingship, as he did in conventional royalist argument, then a reference to the succession might be expected at this point in the poem. It is not to be found. Instead, the more obvious reference to the succession appears with the ascent of Elijah, at the end of Marvell's elegy for Cromwell after the coaching accident:

> We only mourn'd our selves, in thine Ascent,
> Whom thou hadst left beneath with Mantle rent.
>
> (11. 219-220)

But even this does not quite serve the turn. True, the rent mantle does point at the dissension that would beset England/Israel at this moment when there was no Elisha to pick up the intact mantle of Elijah's authority. But greater force seems to attach to the criticism of the self-interest of the bereaved watchers: "we only mourn'd our selves." The obvious unspoken contrast is with Elisha's lament, which was both for Israel and for his father; the spoken contrast is with the lines that immediately follow, lines that pay tribute to Cromwell's self-denial, beginning "For all delight of Life thou then didst lose" (11. 221-228). We seem to return here to the great apocalyptic passage, with its castigation (at l. 156) of the unconcern and sinfulness of the nation which jeopardizes Cromwell's prophetic role.[31] Perhaps significantly, one of Oliver's most deeply felt regrets about the English was their fondness for "self-ends."[32]

What significance is there in the Noah passage if not patriarchal kingship? The suggestion of A. J. N. Wilson is well taken, that Noah is introduced to jibe at the "Chammish issue," the Fifth Monarchists, Ranters and other exotic sectaries, rather than to emphasize Noah himself.[33] For while Noah receives a paltry six lines, the abuses of his issue have a full thirty-five devoted to them, and the threat they represent is central to much of the latter part of the poem (11. 283-288, 289-324).

There is indeed considerable justice in Marvell's treatment of this episode. The Fifth Monarchists were in a very real sense Cromwell's own "Chammish issue." He had been directly responsible for the establishment of the Barebone's Parliament, the main hope of the Fifth Monarchists and "a story of my own weakness and folly" as he himself later confessed.[34] Noah therefore seems introduced as a device for commenting on Cromwell's career, rather than as a recommendation for the future.[35] Such a device was all the more necessary in that the Fifth Monarchists repeatedly and uncharitably reminded the nation that very autumn of 1654 of Oliver's emphatically millennial opening speech to the Barebone's Parliament.[36] The paternity of the Barebone's, an episode against which Marvell fulminates in the poem and against which Oliver fulminated in his opening speech to the 1654 Parliament, was therefore embarrassingly clear. It needed explaining away, and likening the zealots to the "Chammish issue," and thus casting Oliver as Noah, must have seemed one of the few ways of doing it which would not bring scorn down on the protector's head. This strategy of deflecting blame and exalting Cromwell's past career is one we shall see Marvell employ elsewhere in the poem.

The other apparently monarchist images can be quickly disposed of. Granted, certain language had traditionally been used as a metaphor for kings, but kings were now no more in England, and language had to be put to new uses. Thus, the anointing oil of the olive (1. 260) has been taken as a deliberate reference to the unction used in the coronation of kings and therefore as counsel to Cromwell. Yet in an attack on Oliver in October 1654, the decidedly antimonarchist Fifth Monarchist John Spittlehouse

called for the casting down of all earthly rule and prayed that
God "would give us Magistrates as at the first, and Rulers as at
the beginning; viz. Ministers of the Unction and Magistrates of
the Unction; such as fear God, and hate covetousness."[37] To Spittlehouse, clearly, the oil of unction was purely spiritual. Similarly, the once royal image of the sun now figured uncontrover-
sially in rhetoric about republican government. The Smectym-
nuan William Spurstowe argued in a sermon to the newly elected
lord mayor of London that any magistrate was a sun, "the pub-
lique servant of light unto the world, and shines not for it self, but
others."[38] All the more open to question are the royal implications of *concordia discors*. Perhaps the clearest constitutional
assertion of the Instrument of Government was of division and
balance, between executive and legislative powers. As the semiofficial *True State of the Case of the Commonwealth*—eagerly
parroted afterwards in the newspaper—put it:

Here we see, our friends have taken in the good of all the three sorts of
government, and bound them in all one. If war be, here is the unitive
virtue (but nothing else) of monarchy to encounter it; and here is the
admirable counsel of aristocracie to manage it: If peace be, here is the
industry and courage of democracy to improve it. And whereas in the
present constitution, the legislative and executive powers are separated:
the former being vested in a constant succession of parliaments elective
by the people; the latter in an elective Lord Protector, assisted by a
council; we conceive the state of this commonwealth is thereby reduced
to so just a temper.[39]

The dismal account of the state of England in the first night at
the end of the first day is unlikely to be the sign of Marvell's
monarchical preferences that Wallace has claimed.[40] Its position
in the apparently chronological arrangement of the latter part of
the poem would alone argue against its being a reference to the
horror that greeted the execution of Charles I. At first glance it is
hypothetical, predicting the likely "screeching noyse" (1. 333)
from Feake, Simpson, and the other Fifth Monarchist "locusts"
had Cromwell actually died in the coaching fall. But as Wallace
points out, such a limited reading makes nonsense of the succeeding passage, in which the foreign prince is amazed at Cromwell's
swift creation of the state after he had risen from apparent death.
Certainly the passage does seem to look backward, but not to
1649. Cyclical language opens and closes it: Cromwell, to end the
Chammish episode, "returning yet alive / Does with himself all

that is good revive" (11. 323-324); and at the end, the sun rises again (11. 341-342). There appear to be two periods of Cromwellian rule, sandwiching a cacophonous interlude. The year 1654 certainly fits the bill, albeit inadequately,[41] with the interruption of Cromwell's near death in the fall. The only other contender is 1653. And what could be more appropriate than that an anniversary poem of 1654 should reflect and comment on the previous year? For 1653 had indeed seen two periods of rule by Cromwell, the first when he took the helm out of the hands of the "artless Steersman" (1. 275) of the Rump, only to surrender it two and one-half months later to the Barebone's Parliament; and the second beginning with the inauguration of the protectorate in December. It was 1653 rather than 1649 which heard a surfeit of "screeching noyse" from Feake and Simpson, the spiritual guides of some of Barebone's colleagues, in their Blackfriars pulpits. The poem manifestly advocates rule by Cromwell, but its preference seems to be for that rule as it now stands rather than in any different guise.

If "The First Anniversary" is no clarion call to monarchy, is it then a celebration of rule by prophet and judge, the form of government peculiar to Old Testament Israel which foreshadowed Puritan England? There were certainly those in 1654 who thought in such terms, underlining the plausibility of such an interpretation of Marvell's poem. One progovernment account of the discovery of a royalist plot criticized the presumption of Oliver's enemies, "seeing that we are but as the first ripe fruit to this flourishing harvest, wherein the sickle of providence will be put into the hands of our present governors, to accomplish that glorious prophecie, of Gods cutting down monarchs, his adversaries, and making way for restoring of his judges as at first, and his councellors as at the beginning."[42] And a number of tracts published in defense of the regime saw Cromwell as variously Joshua, Gideon, and most especially Moses.[43] Such a characterization of the protector had much to recommend it in his early stress on his government's concern for justice.[44] Of course, a judicial mission did not have to be conceived of in terms of the Hebrew judges. The claim that justice, the protection of *meum et tuum,* was the chief business of a king was an old one in English history. Nevertheless, Oliver's public addresses to the nation seem without any doubt to be those of an Old Testament prophet.

On three occasions in 1654 Oliver spoke to his people through press and pulpit. Following in the footsteps of his parliamentary predecessors in government, he sought to enlist God's aid for the nation by calling, in March and September, for days of fasting and humiliation; in May he proclaimed a day of thanksgiving to the Lord for the peace with the Dutch. While Cromwell's behavior was not peculiar to himself, since the leaders of the Long Parliament had equally seen themselves as custodians of the ark of the new covenant, a sampling of the language of Oliver's calls on the nation shows just how appropriate was a characterization of the protector as virtually any of the Hebrew prophets or judges. Oliver's declaration on 9 September of a day of humiliation was closest to the date of composition of Marvell's poem. The declaration demanded:

Who is such a stranger in our Israel that hath not taken notice of the great things God hath brought to pass amongst us by his outstretched arm? What nation is there who hath God more nigh unto them, than the Lord our God hath been to us, in all things we have called unto him for? Ask of the daies that are past, which have been before us, in these later ages, whether there have been any such things as those many blessings and signal deliverances vouchsafed to us from his own hand, in answer to the voice of tears and blood that have been [sic] powred forth.

In response, the English had shown only unthankfulness, and Oliver therefore devoted the bulk of what can only be called this sermon to chastising his countrymen for their "general ignorance, unthankfulness, and unfruitfulness, under all those dews of grace and gospel mercies."[45]

That last clause has important resonances in the poem, in the figure of Elijah. Oliver's first call, in March, for a day of humiliation had not been merely a prayer for an end to the spiritual pride that was causing such deep dissension among the godly; it was also a prayer for rain. As he pointed out in the very beginning of that declaration,

The common and notorious sins so boldly and impenitently practised amongst us, notwithstanding all our deliverances and mercies, together with the present rod of an exceeding and an unusual drought, which hath layen upon us for some years, and still continues and increaseth upon us, threatning famine and mortality, are no less than the voice of God, calling aloud in our ears to fasting and mourning, and great abasement of soul before him.[46]

And what was most remarkable, Cromwell's call worked; or at
least, the rains came, a sign that was taken by some of his supporters as proof of God's good will. Oliver's declaration of a day
of thanksgiving in May was therefore for more than peace with
the Dutch; it was also "for the late seasonable rain."

Was not the earth lately so unusually parcht up, that it threatned famin,
and did cause the beast of the field to mourn for want of food, and
water to sustain it? And hath not the Lord so watered the earth that he
hath turned those fears into the expectation of the greatest plenty that
ever was seen by any now living in this nation?[47]

It therefore seems possible that Marvell introduced the figure of
Elijah because of the singular aptness of a prophet who "pow'rdst
the fertile Storm" (1. 236), and not simply because he wished to
talk about the fate of the mantle on Elijah's death. As in the cases
of Noah and of the setting sun at the end of the poem, the intention seems celebratory rather than recommendatory, as Wallace
would have it, or even deliberative, as Patterson claims.

A similar argument can be advanced for the figure of Gideon,
which caused some problems for both Wallace and Patterson. To
Wallace, Gideon's scourging of the elders of Succoth and his
destruction of the tower of Penuel, taken in conjunction with
Marvell's reference to the silence of watching Israel, indicates the
poet's "criticism of Cromwell's high-handedness," and thus sub-
verts the force of Gideon's refusal of the crown. To Patterson the
episode and Cromwell remain "ambiguous."[48] Yet once again,
the exact congruence of the figure to aspects of Cromwell's career
makes it questionable how far complex value judgments can be
read into it. Marvell may merely have deployed Gideon because
Gideon fit the facts. Not only did Gideon refuse the crown, judge
his people, and lead them out to war but even the every punishment of Succoth and Penuel pointed in a direct way to Cromwell's own history. Of course, it is generally recognized that the
episode is a reference to Cromwell's expulsion of Parliament-men,
particularly of the Rumpers. But Gideon turned on the elders for
their refusal to provide supplies for his army. The general cause
of Oliver's expulsion of the Rump was its reluctance to give political support to the army, but a major element in that intransi-
gence was material. The Rump had persistently dragged its feet
over meeting the soldiers' material demands, especially for in-

demnity and for pensions for widows and orphans. The Barebone's Parliament had carried that hostility to the military even
further, and there had been determined attempts to diminish the
army's size and pay.[49] If a writer wished to legitimate actions
taken by a successful military leader against the apparently legal,
but ungrateful, representatives of the people, what better way
than through the figure of Gideon?

Furthermore, the silence with which Marvell has Israel watch
the act of retribution can hardly be taken as a sign of his distaste,
or even, as Zwicker sees it, as evidence of the nation's realization
that its turn might be next.[50] In the first place, that silence
merely recapitulates Cromwell's own words. When on 12 September 1654 he described the dissolution of the Rump he noted that
"there was not so much as the barking of a dog, or any general
and visible repining it." Secondly, and more importantly, Cromwell did not see the nation's silence as a sign of its disapproval. It
had not protested at his use of force against its representatives,
and to him, as his speech makes abundantly clear, silence
equaled consent and conveyed legitimacy.[51] There is no reason to
suppose that Marvell thought any differently.

In other words, Marvell uses the figure of Gideon to legitimate
Cromwell's use of force in politics, just as he uses Elijah to elevate
the protector's moral stance vis-à-vis the nation and the figure of
Noah to give an exalted significance to an otherwise embarrassing
episode in Oliver's career (indeed, we can see Elijah filling the
same role in Marvell's attempt to make the best out of another
embarrassing incident, the fall from the coach). Examination of
Marvell's deployment of scriptural types reveals a brilliant exercise in casuistry.

A similarly pointed eclecticism is evident throughout the
poem. It makes it impossible to see the poem as *doing* a single
thing, other than celebrating the complex figure of Cromwell.
Just as "The First Anniversary" does not advocate the crown, so it
does not simply pin on the protector the role of prophet or judge,
shunning the crown while keeping the nation strong in the ways
of the Lord. The latter interpretation not only does not cope with
the explicitly millennial passage beginning "Hence oft I think"
(1. 131), to which we shall turn shortly, but it also ignores the
classical motifs and classicist tone of much of the poem. The classicism of the poem extends far beyond the rhetorical structure by

reference to which John Wallace explains much of the complexity of the work (as he of course recognizes). Equally it goes beyond the conventions of the *occasional* poem to which Annabel Patterson draws notice (as she too appreciates).[52] The classicism of "The First Anniversary" is a matter of content and theme as well as structure. It is when we come to the difficult problem of the relation between classicism and scripturalism that we have most need of careful balance.

Various solutions have been advanced, with varying degrees of appropriateness. A. J. N. Wilson argues that it is the classical tropes which stand out clearest, particularly in the long final peroration by the European prince (11. 349-394), with its unmistakably Augustan resonances. But of course, that source is damned from its own mouth, for the princes are congenitally incapable of comprehending Cromwell. Wilson's other claim, that the classical motifs are more carefully woven into the poem than are the scriptural ones, seems dubious.[53] As we have seen, several of the scriptural themes are unavoidably appropriate to Cromwell. And if we take a crude, quantitative measure, there are precisely as many lines in the apocalyptic passage, lines 105-158, as there are in the most overtly classical section, which starts at line 45 with the introduction of the Platonic-Pythagorean theme of Cromwell's education in the music of the spheres, goes on through the likeness to Amphion and the long architectural excursus, and concludes at line 98. A more exact balance between the political languages of scripture and classics could not be found.

The classical material needs to be taken fully as seriously as does the scriptural, for it is equally carefully applied to the figure of Cromwell. The wordplay with the Instrument of Government is obvious, as are the barbs at the statesmen of the Rump (11. 67-72). Further, Patterson skillfully points to the important political and religious distinctions that need to be made between Marvell's use of the Amphion legend and his source. Yet even she has not established more than a general relationship between the poem and Cromwell's career. Marvell of course drew not just on classical myth and on the scriptural history of Solomon's Temple but also on Edmund Waller's poem celebrating Charles I's rebuilding of St. Paul's Cathedral in the 1630s. Whereas Waller had praised Charles for piously continuing his father's project of restoring the

great church, Cromwell builds anew. The adaptation of Waller
thus allows Marvell to make his brilliant and telling contrast between the laborious work of kings and Cromwell's dynamic crea-
tivity, as Patterson points out.[54] But there was more than that in
Waller's poem to attract Marvell. The building of the temple was
an appropriate motif through which to celebrate Cromwell in
1654, since the protector's ordinances establishing the triers and
ejectors had at last provided the framework for the loosely structured national church of which Puritans had dreamed for so
long. Most of all, though, Waller's vision of the 1630s was in 1654
the perfect foil. The newspapers that year were full of the pro-
gressive collapse of Charles's cherished cathedral, and of the
plans of Cromwell's council to knock the whole thing down as
dangerous as well as redundant. The immediate physical demise
of Charles I's church, and not just its institutional demise some
years before, made the irony of Marvell's appropriation of Waller's Amphion sharply pointed.[55]

Throughout the poem there are so many direct glances at
Cromwell that Marvell's purpose appears more panegyric than is
often thought. A suggestive instance is the part of the Amphion
passage where the great builder "ere he ceas'd, his sacred Lute
creates / Th' harmonious City of the seven Gates" (11. 65-66).
The seven-gated city was indeed Thebes; but it was also, not the
new Jerusalem, which the prophet Ezekiel informs us will have
twelve gates,[56] but London, with its seven major gates.[57] One of
the few concrete achievements for which the poem can already
give Cromwell credit is the distinctly nonmillenarian one of building a harmonious city—harmonious in contrast even to Thebes,
which became a byword in antiquity for the city of strife.[58] The
harmonious city may be a shorthand for the nation as a whole,
but that passage and the reference to the "animated city" twenty
lines later (1. 86) pay tribute to a major theme in Cromwell's
early rule, the appeal to London for Support.[59] When at last Oliver turned to justify himself in his angry speech to Parliament on
12 September, before imposing the Recognition, acceptance by
the City was one of his few signs of a "call" from the people.[60] Yet
again, celebration in fairly direct terms seems to be the poet's
order of the day.

If the classical language connects as closely with Oliver's career
as does the scriptural, how can we achieve a balance between the

very different visions of authority they signify? Annabel Patterson's subtle answer is that Marvell presents various models in order to invite deliberation, in an attempt to determine which model best fits the enigma of Cromwell. It is an attractive suggestion, but it does not provide a full understanding of the politics of the poem. In the first place, there was probably no "either/or." Cromwell repeatedly testified that his duty was to rule over "Christians as Christians and men as men," and he once averred that, "He sings sweetly that sings a song of reconciliation between these interests."[61] Had he seen his mission as anything other than a dual one, building Jerusalem and keeping the peace over stubborn, conservative Englishmen, his lot might have been easier. He was ultimately to find the two causes incompatible, although he strove as hard as he could to reconcile them in his own person, as a university-educated, music-loving country gentleman and yet a zealous saint. That there should be tension between the scriptural and the secular in Marvell's poem is of a piece with the nature of Cromwell's rule.

In the second place, Patterson's argument that the poem is a deliberative work does not adequately address its millennialism. She, like many other commentators, has assumed its millennialism is guarded, and that, with the lines "But a thick Cloud about that Morning lyes, / And intercepts the Beams of Mortal eyes" (11. 141-142), Marvell withdraws the possibility that he had earlier raised in the lines beginning, "Hence oft I think."[62] On the contrary, what is striking about the passage is the vividness of its millennialism. Even textually its apparent doubts are close to the language of the book. In Daniel's dream of the apocalypse, the Son of man comes "with the clouds of heaven" to the Ancient of Days.[63] And if we look at what saints who were not rabid Fifth Monarchists were saying, Marvell does not seem at all backward. Scholars have too often overlooked the cardinal methodological principle of Quentin Skinner and John Pocock, that if we are to comprehend a text we must familiarize ourselves with its linguistic context.[64] In this connection it is significant that Oliver himself, in his highest of times when he was addressing the newly assembled Barebone's Parliament in the summer of 1653, sounded almost like a paraphrase of Marvell. After enthusiastically avowing that "this may be the door to usher in the things that God hath promised," he checked himself and confessed,

"But I may appear to be beyond my line; these things are dark."[65] Marvell's hope that one day the English might prove to be "a seasonable People" (1. 133) echoed Cromwell's own conviction, repeated in his first speech to Parliament on 4 September 1654, that Christ's kingdom would only be established when the hearts of men were changed.[66]

Marvell was in fact talking the language of Cromwell's godly party when he threw clouds around "the latest Day" and regretted that men were "unprepar'd" (11. 140-141, 150). A congratulatory address to Cromwell from the godly on Newcastle's corporation, printed in the government's newspaper in April 1654, reported that the saints had gone to their watchtowers

to see if they can discover what hath been the eminent design of the Lord in these latter days. For the all-wise God hath of late visibly bin out of his common-road of providences his paths have been in tempests and thick darkness.

Another declared that "to see through these clouds" that enveloped God's providential plan was "the great desire" of the godly.[67]

Some at least of the millennial language of "The First Anniversary" therefore falls in the mainstream of the rhetoric of the godly party at this point in the history of the English Revolution, and there is no reason to believe that Marvell was expressing unusual doubts about the applicability of God's design to England. He was merely articulating a widely shared uncertainty about the future of the English Jerusalem. But to restore the millennial dimension to Marvell's poem brings us back again to the problem of relating a now more urgent scriptural argument to the praise heaped on Cromwell's achievement of founding merely "the harmonious city." For Augustine's city of God and the earthly city were diametrical opposites, and Marvell's task was therefore a more complex one than merely celebrating the dual aspect of Cromwellian rule. It is in the reconciliation of those apparent opposites that we discover the inadequacy of any characterization of Marvell as mere publicist for the Cromwell of 1654. Despite the very different cast of the poem, and despite the panegyric contemporary references, there are echoes in "The First Anniversary" of the "Horatian Ode."

Machiavelli provides the key to the conundrum. In a series of trenchant works J. G. A. Pocock has reminded us of the vitality of

English Machiavellianism in the 1650s.[68] Long ago Mazzeo found in the "Horatian Ode" evidence that Marvell was, in 1650 at least, a disciple of the great Florentine political theorist. His insights have since been confirmed by Blair Worden, who has shown how close Marvell stood in 1650 to Marchamont Nedham, editor of the government's newspaper *Mercurius Politicus* and at that point England's leading Machiavellian theorist.[69] If the "Horatian Ode" presents Cromwell as the Machiavellian hero, it is a predictive account: Cromwell may have the requisite *virtu* and favor from fortune, yet he has still to build the new state. By 1654 the potential has been realized. Cromwell in "The First Anniversary" still possesses all the vigor of the Machiavellian hero, far outdistancing the leaden-footed mere hereditary monarchs, hurling "the World about him round" and, as the fearful prince at the end of the poem recognizes, animating the nation (11. 100, 380). By this point Cromwell as Amphion has also, by his own creative force, founded the new state. And just as the great man with *virtu* who founds the new state in Machiavelli's *Discorsi* provides the laws and institutions of a republic and refrains from taking the crown, so Marvell's Cromwell distances himself from that bauble.

Mazzeo's definition of the Machiavellian prince in his essay on the "Horatian Ode" is strikingly relevant to "The First Anniversary." Such a prince is

the man of *virtu* who creates a state from chaos, the central figure of *Il Principe,* and the legally self-binding new ruler of the *Discorsi,* who, having consolidated his power tries to establish the rule of good customs enforced by good arms.[70]

Not only did the Cromwell of "The First Anniversary" "still refuse to Reign," but Marvell also sees him as "first growing to thy self a Law" (11. 258, 263). He is indeed the legally self-limiting ruler, who imposed the Instrument *on himself.* Furthermore, as Mazzeo recognized, the goal of Cromwell's state was, in an important sense, liberty. According to Marvell, Cromwell "didst for others plant the Vine / Of Liberty," he "knows to lay" the limits of "Freedome" and "Tyranny," and he provides for "That sober Liberty which men may have" (11. 279-281, 289). These are thoroughly Machiavellian qualities. The Machiavellian ideal is also perfectly congruent with the constitutional structure under Cromwell. The protectorate was a commonwealth, that is, a republic, ruled over by a single person whose successors were to have less power than he. Thus, the Instrument provided for a diminution in both the size of the army and in the protector's legislative power after the current emergency was ended.

Furthermore, the Machiavellian thrust fits the long, horrified account of the catastrophe that would have beset England had Oliver died in the coaching accident. The future of the republic established by Machiavelli's new ruler of the *Discorsi* could only be secure once the people were united in *virtu*. The rent mantle left to the self-regarding nation on Oliver's "ascent" pointed graphically to England's lack of collective *virtu* at this juncture. The passage is an unconcealed warning to Englishmen to think on the future, and to mend their ways.

The manifest Machiavellianism of the poem still leaves us with the problem of the role of scripture. Here we must turn again to Pocock, who has brilliantly pointed to the problem of the legitimation of such a new state; legitimation was, of course, the most urgent goal of all the parliamentarian regimes after the execution of Charles. As Pocock observes, Machiavelli himself was crucially aware of the difficulties facing the rule of the new state; those difficulties are the concern of *The Prince*. Machiavelli saw the advantages to a new ruler of harnessing a divine mandate, and he remarked, perhaps wistfully, perhaps jestingly, on the assets Moses possessed. Pocock deploys this insight superbly to interpret the greatest English Machiavellian work of the 1650s, Harrington's *Oceana*. As he demonstrates, Oceana derives its stability not just from the constitutional forms provided by Harrington, or rather by the Lord Archon, a thinly disguised Oliver Cromwell, but also from its millennial role. In other words, it is the part the new republic plays in hastening the apocalypse which enables it to transcend the cyclical history dictated by the operations of *Fortuna*.[71] In a short but perceptive paragraph, Pocock suggests that "The First Anniversary" should be read in the same ideological context as *Oceana*.[72]

We can now see in detail how the prophetic dimension legitimates the Machiavellian founder of a new state. If there is a problem with Cromwell's brutally military eruption into politics in 1653 — and clearly there is in a nation so preoccupied with the "ancient rights" Marvell recognized in the "Horatian Ode" — then the figure of Gideon provides the answer.[73] In the lines on

Gideon, Marvell uses a phrase charged with Machiavellian dynamic: "No King might ever *such a Force* have done" (1. 255).[74] Similarly, if the Barebone's episode proves politically embarrassing to Cromwell, now lord protector and no longer mere captain-general, then Noah and his "Chammish issue" take the blame off Cromwell and instead exalt him. Cromwell's role as the "prophet armed" transforms actions that might have had negative political significance.

But "The First Anniversary" is not simply a panegyric. Exaltation of the new ruler did not require such explicitly millennial language as Marvell uses. Had Marvell merely been concerned to claim greater legitimacy for the new Cromwellian republic by imparting to it a religious aura, there would have been other models available to him. He could even have clung to the classical forms that Annabel Patterson and, to a greater extent, A. J. N. Wilson see as central to the poem. Thus, Marchamont Nedham (assuming it was he who wrote the Machiavellian Latin poem on Cromwell's entry into the City), after insisting that Cromwell's modesty made him greater than Caesar, predicted:

He will also be a second Caesar, if omens have any power, for he will attack your gods, O profane Rome. Hence I also predict that he can now scale your citadels and subdue your neck to the British yoke, and thus tame the three-headed tyrant. So trembles the triple crown of the Italian Jupiter.[75]

The similarity of the theme to Marvell's account that begins with the "holy Oracles" and has Cromwell hunting the beast to its Roman lair is apparent (11. 107-130). Nevertheless, Marvell goes far beyond any mere attack on the Whore in the succeeding lines, and in this connection it is pertinent to think about one dog that failed to bark in Marvell's night.

As Pocock pointed out, Machiavelli recognized the greater chances for success of the "prophet armed," the new ruler who gave laws with divine assistance and inspiration. The classic example of this type, the first and greatest in the famous sixth chapter of Machiavelli's *The Prince,* was Moses. Yet among all the prophets Marvell deploys as likenesses for Cromwell, Moses does not appear. The puzzle is the greater since Moses was the figure most commonly seen in 1654 as the pattern or type of Cromwell.[76] For someone wishing to argue the duty of obedience to Cromwell, Moses provided the obvious answer to the dangerous question "Who made thee a ruler or a judge?"[77] Moses was also a divine lawgiver, a not inconsiderable factor since Cromwell prided himself, as in his first speech to Parliament in September 1654, on his legislative activities. And Moses led the Israelites out of the wilderness and toward the promised land. For all these reasons, Moses appealed to mainstream Cromwellians such as the great Independent divines John and Thomas Goodwin, the recorder of the City of London, and the anonymous author of *Protection Perswading Subjection*. Not least, Moses had enormous meaning for Cromwell himself, for in his opening speech to Parliament in September, the protector repeatedly dwelled on the history of the Israelites on their journey toward the promised land.[78] Given the attractions of Moses for both Machiavelli and the Cromwellian camp, the decision of Marvell the Machiavellian to avoid him when he sought to legitimate the new ruler seems odd. But for whatever reason (and as we shall see the reason is unlikely to be strategically insignificant), Marvell upstaged the prophet in a remarkable assimilation of Cromwell to Christ.

Pocock's references to the prophetic quality of the poem, or rather, of Cromwell, halt at line 130, and he fails to mention the very different tone of the lines from 131, beginning "Hence oft I think."[79] Up to line 130 Cromwell can be seen as a Hebrew prophet or judge. Thereafter, he shadows Christ, for there is only one great captain in Revelation. Granted, a certain amount of Christic imagery was probably essential in order to correct those misled by *Eikon Basilike* into believing that Charles I was the real suffering servant of his people. A lament for Cromwell like that at line 174, "Our Sins endanger, and shall one day kill," may have been par for the course. But Marvell went much farther than such a strategy demanded. Apart from Steven Zwicker,[80] no scholar has caught the Christic significance of the last two lines of the poem:

> And as the *Angel* of our Commonweal,
> Troubling the Waters, yearly mak'st them Heal.
> (11. 401-402)

As Cromwell's own chaplain, Nicholas Lockyer, stressed in November 1654 in a work of impeccably governmental associations, "Twas Christ, the Angel of the Covenant, that stirred those Waters of Bethesda."[81] Yet even Zwicker did not note the full significance of Marvell's words. The force of "heal" is ambiguous: do the waters heal, or are they themselves healed? If the waters, besides healing others, are themselves healed — and the fondness of defenders of the protectorate for likening the corruption of the long-lived Rump to a standing pond suggests this theme was likely to have been on Marvell's mind[82] — then Marvell ties together the figure of Christ at Bethesda in John, chapter 5 with the vision of the healed waters of the new Jerusalem in Ezekiel, chapter 47. In these lines Cromwell does not merely regularly restore the commonweal and thus provide the grounds for a graceful anniversary tribute; in Marvell's likeness of Cromwell we find Christ and the apocalypse.

That Marvell should have flown so high may seem remarkable. Cromwell, after all, did not share such visions. Although he acknowledged in his opening speech to Parliament on 4 September that it was "A notion I hope we all honour, wait, and hope for, that Jesus Christ will have a time to set up his reign," that reign was to be "in our hearts": Christ's kingdom was to be a spiritual one.[83] The characteristic Independent, or Cromwellian, position was adumbrated in the autumn of 1654 in the major *Sermon on the Fifth Monarchy* by Thomas Goodwin, who also preached the opening sermon to the 1654 Parliament. Goodwin made it clear that the millennium would only be achieved by an outpouring of Christ's word into the world, not by physical action. Marvell might long for that "happy Hour" when "High Grace should meet in one with highest Pow'r" (11. 131-132), but like Goodwin, Cromwell himself was deeply suspicious of those Fifth Monarchists who would "found *dominium in gratia*."[84] As the semiofficial *True State of the Case of the Commonwealth* put it, Fifth Monarchists who subscribed to "that worn tenet, long since exploded, but now revived . . . That temporal power and authority is and ought to be founded in grace," were "poor deluded souls." The significance of these lines is all the greater, not just for the possibility that their author was Nedham and thus close to Marvell, but because Cromwell himself quoted the *True State* in his 4 September speech to Parliament and cited it approvingly by name in his irate speech dissolving Parliament in January 1655.[85]

The irony of Marvell's performance lies in the degree to which the pot seemed to be calling the kettle black. Whereas Vavasour Powell, the Fifth Monarchist leader, denounced Cromwell and his cohorts who dissolved Barebone's Parliament for delaying the millennium,[86] Marvell paid tribute to Cromwell for hastening forward alone "that blest Day" (11. 127, 155-156). And Marvell's derision for the Fifth Monarchists' hopes "That their new King might the fifth Scepter shake, / And make the World, by his Example, Quake" (11. 297-298) curiously echoes his own thoughts of Cromwell earlier in the poem: Cromwell hurled "the World about him round," others would be "by his Pattern won," the beast would be run to earth at last, and soon "the mysterious Work" "would forthwith finish under such a Hand" (11. 100, 105, 137-138). Despite his fulminations against Fifth Monarchist "locusts," Marvell's language has an oddly Fifth Monarchist flavor.

We saw earlier that Marvell's frustration with the clouds that lay about "that Morning" and his doubts about whether these were "the Times" put him in the mainstream Cromwellian camp. Though that is true, the observation applies much less to the excited lines 131-140. In that passage Marvell speculates about an immediate prospect in a way otherwise peculiar to the Fifth Monarchists. Cromwell had been tempted in that direction in the summer of 1653 when he established Barebone's Parliament, but he rapidly abandoned what he soon came to see as delusions. More to the point, those who before that watershed summer of 1653 had cast Cromwell as the potential hero of the apocalypse had largely been Fifth Monarchists.[87] But by the end of 1653, whereas Cromwell and other Independents were no nearer a confident prediction of the millennial future than they had been, the frustrated Fifth Monarchists were branding him as the horn of the Beast, as Marvell's friend Nedham reported.[88] Indeed, I know of only one other work in 1654 that spoke of Cromwell in anything like the terms Marvell uses, although they had been common enough in certain circles a year or so earlier. An obscure Fifth Monarchist tract by one Mathew Coker prophesied that if Christians remained united and if Cromwell acted with godly zeal, "he may be the introducer of a glorious Monarchry [sic] for him that shall wonderfully succeed him Emperour-like." But apart from that, and despite the upsurge of millennial interest that was to come in 1655-56, in 1654 Marvell was on his own, harking back to the visions of the year before.[89]

What could Marvell have been about? It seems implausible to assume that he did not have strategic reasons for his rhetoric, and indeed we can find them in the doings of the Fifth Monarchists. The apocalyptic onslaughts on Oliver made it easier for Marvell to turn the coin and accord the protector the opposite eschatological significance. They also made it all the more important to do so.

Oliver's summons of the Parliament of 1654 generated widespread suspicions in radical circles that he would use the occasion to take the crown. His establishment of the triers and ejectors, the prerequisites for his loosely structured national church, also aroused fears among the extremer saints of a new papalism. Accordingly, the autumn of 1654 saw an upsurge of Fifth Monarchist publications and activity, ominously directed not just at Parliament but also at the army.[90] The petition of the three radical colonels, the commonwealthsmen Okey, Alured, and Saunders, that autumn suggested that the strong millenarian sentiments still present in parts of the army might come to a dangerous head.[91] Intelligence reports brought news of mutterings in the radical churches and of stirrings in the army in Scotland; the attitude of the army in Ireland was more than ever an unknown quantity. The Fifth Monarchists' hopes of the soldiers are evident in an appeal by one of Marvell's bêtes noires, Christopher Feake, to the soldiers in early December: "By the Powers in Being, I understand the Army as Supream, and all those who joyne with them to carry on the work of justice."[92] Others were plainly worried. That autumn Marchamont Nedham founded yet another newspaper, *The Observator,* specifically to counter the threat of a radical alliance linking the Fifth Monarchists and the army. He began his second issue with the warning that "The single-sheeted Incendiaries walk now in state, and toss Granado's without control into the heart of the Army"; and those he singled out as the chief arsonists were the Fifth Monarchist leaders. He then addressed thirty pages of advice to the soldiers to help them see through the wiles of the variegated enemy.[93] Others took a more practical course. Over Christmas Oliver doubled the guards in and around London, and in a characteristic ploy of trying to win over the enemy, he held meetings at Whitehall in December with Feake and Simpson—the same Feake and Simpson whom Marvell viciously attacks in the poem.[94] It is too easy to assume that the opposition that Cromwell faced at this point was that of the constitutionalist gentry in the Parliament which he was shortly to dissolve. There were also threatening shapes of unknown dimensions on the other side.

Cromwell's sense of his mission was of course a dual one, to rule over "Christians as Christians and men as men." We have already noted how the poem can be seen as a tribute to that stand. That central piece of propaganda of 1654 *The True State of the Case of the Commonwealth* likewise addresses the ultimately incompatible concerns of the army and of the constitutionalist gentry. But in the unease of the winter of 1654 Marvell may have been trying to do something rather more pointed than that. As we have found, Marvell's rhetoric is exactly pitched to the political realities of the moment. The nature and excited state of his audience give a clue to his strategy. On the one hand, the poem tells constitutionalist readers that Cromwell was creating something better and greater than that which he had destroyed, and that his use of force must be comprehended in scriptural terms. And on the other hand, Marvell attempted to limit potential damage by reclaiming the high religious ground for the protector, warning the radical saints that they had got the meaning of the "holy Oracles" all wrong and that they should abandon their hostility, for Oliver was still the great captain. It was as part of this gambit that Marvell drew notice at lines 115-116 to Cromwell's forwardness in the intensely topical matter of converting Indians and Jews.[95] The general strategy was hardly outlandish: even as nonreligious and probably time-serving a figure as Nedham could in *The Observator* strive to teach the soldiery the correct meaning of Revelation in order to lessen the damage done by the Fifth Monarchists.[96] The strategy furthermore explains Marvell's eschewal of the figure of Moses in the poem, for the Fifth Monarchists, and Spittlehouse in particular, had been deluging the new Parliament that autumn with calls for the introduction of the Mosaic code.[97] For Marvell now to have typed Cromwell as a second Moses would have been to play into their hands.[98]

Such an argument, that Marvell was deliberately deploying millenarian language against the Fifth Monarchists, reduces him again to the role of publicist for the regime, albeit a publicist of unique perceptiveness. The poem's panegyric tone and its contemporary references make it clear that the construction of a public defense was at least a part of his purpose; and few would question that Marvell was uniquely perceptive. But alternative explanations can be offered for the millenarian passage. We cannot exclude the possibility that Marvell himself may have been a fervent millenarian by this juncture, although most readers have understandably found such a conjecture hard to reconcile with his supremely detached stance of 1650.[99] Another, more plausible, solution centers on the role of the poet, and in so doing provides the vital link with the "Horatian Ode."

There is some difficulty in assuming that "The First Anniversary" was simply commemorative and defensive, as its publication, or at least, the advertisement for it, missed the anniversary rather badly.[100] That fact increases the possibility that Marvell may have had in mind another reader, a man who, as constitutionalist gentleman and radical saint, embodied both his audiences, and a man who had yet to make his position clear on the rival activities of "kinglings" and saints. If Marvell did aim to address Cromwell as well as a wider audience, that may help to explain both the rhetorical posture of the poet and the content of the poem. As did Augustus of Horace, so the commanding figure of Cromwell required humility of Marvell, hence the acknowledgment at line 400 that Cromwell remains "As far above" the praise of the poet as above the malice of the uncomprehending princes. But Cromwell, like any ruler, needed counsel. As those who had ascended to their watchtowers could testify, the future was shrouded with clouds. One bid to crown Cromwell had failed, but others might be mounted and might meet a warm reception from a man who so valued "healing and settling." An Horatian counselor of a Machiavellian bent must have felt that protector as well as nation needed convincing of the virtues of "unkingship."[101]

Marvell must also have known that Cromwell might equally be knocked off course by an assault of quite another kind. Cromwell's ability to talk to Feake and Simpson at this juncture shows that he still spoke their language; in fact, to the end of his life he took it seriously. Oliver was notoriously vulnerable to voices sounding on his conscience. In the kingship crisis of 1657 and again in his early 1658 confrontation with Major Packer and the captains of his own original regiment, he was reduced to paralysis and near emotional breakdown by the cries of the saints that he had betrayed them and the cause of Christ and sought instead

"self-ends."[102] Might it not have been to a doubting Cromwell—
as well as of Cromwell—that Marvell reassuringly said,

> And well he therefore does, and well has guest,
> Who in his Age has always forward prest:
> And knowing not where Heavens choice may light,
> Girds yet his Sword, and ready stands to fight.
>
> (11. 145-148)

Neither the protest of the gathered churches nor the temptings of those who would offer the crown should deflect him.

As was only appropriate, Marvell as poet did not press his advice. The poem of course concludes with the poet abasing himself and his designs, his "End" (11. 397-398), before the benevolent but mysterious Cromwell—a political posture one cannot help but suspect Marvell felt proper for others.[103] One can only suspect also that, on reading a few days later in the protector's dissolution speech his denunciation of the threats on either hand, Marvell breathed a sigh of relief.[104] If he was a mere publicist, he knew that he had not miscalculated the meaning of the immediate political moment.[105] And if he did hope that Cromwell would, having established a new state, secure the people's liberty, those hopes had not yet been dashed.

NOTES

I am most grateful to John Wallace and to my colleagues Steve Zwicker, Steven Schwarzschild, George Pepe, and Dick Popkin for valuable discussion on this problem, and to John Pocock, Blair Worden, and Steve Zwicker for reading and commenting on drafts of this paper.

1. J. M. Wallace, *Destiny His Choice* (Cambridge, 1968), pp. 69-105.
2. Ibid., 106-144; J. A. Mazzeo, "Cromwell as Davidic King," in his *Renaissance and Seventeenth-Century Studies* (New York, 1964), pp. 183-208; Steven N. Zwicker, "Models of Governance in Marvell's 'The First Anniversary,'" *Criticism* 16 (1974): 1-12; A. J. N. Wilson, "Andrew Marvell's 'The First Anniversary,'" *Modern Language Review* 69 (1974): 254-273; Annabel Patterson, *Marvell and the Civic Crown* (Princeton, 1978), pp. 59-94. This essay was written before the appearance of Warren L. Chernaik, *The Poet's Time* (Cambridge, 1983), with which it has a certain congruence.
3. H. M. Margoliouth, ed., *The Poems and Letters of Andrew Mar-*

vell, 3d ed., 2 vols. (Oxford, 1971), 1: 320. All quotations from the poem are taken from this edition.

4. Wallace, *Destiny,* pp. 9-105; Quentin Skinner, "Conquest and Consent: Thomas Hobbes and the Engagement Controversy," in G. E. Aylmer, ed., *The Interregnum* (London, 1972), pp. 79-98.

5. For all this, see Blair Worden, *The Rump Parliament* (Cambridge, 1974).

6. The definitive history of the whole episode is to be found in Austin Woolrych, *Commonwealth and Protectorate* (Oxford, 1982).

7. See the official proclamation of the protectorate printed in W. C. Abbott, ed., *The Writings and Speeches of Oliver Cromwell,* 4 vols. (Cambridge, Mass., 1937-47), 3: 137.

8. The Instrument of Government is printed in S. R. Gardiner, ed., *Constitutional Documents of the Puritan Revolution,* 3d ed. (Oxford, 1906), pp. 405-417.

9. For a survey of the protectorate's early legislation, see I. Roots, "Cromwell's Ordinances," in Aylmer, *Interregnum,* pp. 143-164.

10. See the unflattering history of Julius Caesar published in the newspaper *Perfect and Impartial Intelligence* in May and June 1654 (Brit. Lib. E735 [17*], E738 [6], and E738 [15], and the barb in the *Weekly Intelligencer,* 16-23 May 1654 (Brit. Lib., E735 [19], 260).

11. See Wallace, *Destiny,* for a penetrating discussion of the kingship question.

12. Ibid., pp. 130-131; Zwicker, "Models of Governance," pp. 1-4, 9-10.

13. See the account in *Mercurius Politicus* (reprinted, London, 1971) for the week of 16-22 December 1653, p. 3053 (all subsequent citations are from this edition); also Abbott, *Writings and Speeches,* 3: 136. See also *Mercurius Politicus,* 31 August-7 September 1654, p. 3743; T. Birch, ed., *A Collection of State Papers of John Thurloe, Esquire,* 7 vols. (London, 1742), 2: 588; *A Perfect Account,* 30 August-6 September 1654 (Brit. Lib., E809 [22]), p. 1527.

14. See the forceful account in T. Carlyle, ed., *Oliver Cromwell's Letters and Speeches,* 2d ed., 3 vols. (London, 1846), 3: 48.

15. M. Roberts, "Cromwell and the Baltic," *English Historical Review* 76 (1961): 411n.; and for Cromwell's court generally, see Roy Sherwood, *The Court of Oliver Cromwell* (London, 1977). Oliver imposed a similar restraint on his family. Although his younger son Henry was perhaps as forceful and competent a character as his father, Oliver endeavored to keep him out of the limelight. He apparently delayed sending him over to Ireland in the autumn of 1654 to take up his duties there for fear of charges of nepotism, and throughout his protectorate he refused to give Henry his full backing but insisted he work for his successes. Oliver's attitude is well revealed in a confidential letter of the summer of 1654 to Richard Mayor, the father-in-law of the young Richard Cromwell. The protector expressed deep misgivings that Mayor, let alone he himself, should act for Richard's material advancement: "But indeed I

am so unwilling to be a seeker after the world, having had so much favour from the Lord in giving me so much without seeking; and so unwilling that men should think me so, which they will though you only appear in it (for they will, by one means or other know it), — that indeed I dare not meddle nor proceed therein." As Marvell again put it so accurately, in reference to Gideon and Jotham, "Yet would not he be Lord, nor yet his Son" (1. 256). For the sons, see the article by C. H. Firth in the *Dictionary of National Biography,* s.v. "Henry Cromwell," and Abbott, *Writings and Speeches,* 3: 280.

16. Quoted in Abbott, *Writings and Speeches,* 3: 244-245.

17. Ibid., p. 153.

18. Ibid., pp. 452-453.

19. Ibid., pp. 454-455.

20. Patterson, *Civic Crown,* pp. 71-73.

21. *Mercurius Politicus,* 9-16 February 1653/4, pp. 3265-3267.

22. Ibid., p. 3270. I am indebted to George Pepe for the translation.

23. *Musarum Oxoniensum* (1654: Brit. Lib., E740 [1]), p. 63.

24. *The Works of John Milton,* 20 vols. (New York, 1931-40), 8: 223-225.

25. I am grateful to Steve Zwicker for stressing this point to me.

26. A quasiregal form, with "O. P." at the head, began to characterize Oliver's proclamations in May 1654 (Brit. Lib., 669f.17 [94 and 95]). The state funeral Oliver accorded his mother was an act of filial piety that jarred with the restraints he imposed on his sons. See Abbott, *Writings and Speeches,* 3: 359, and note 14 above.

27. Patterson, *Civic Crown,* p. 71.

28. Ibid., pp. 69-70.

29. Birch, *Thurloe State Papers,* 2: 606.

30. Not surprisingly, I am unpersuaded by Patterson's suggestion that Marvell could not have written "On the Victory obtained by Blake" because it comes near to an open advocacy of kingship. Patterson, *Civic Crown,* pp. 70-71.

31. The prominent Fifth Monarchist prophet Hannah Trapnel attacked Cromwell and his comrades in just these terms in her major 1654 outpouring: "They are so taken up and wrapt up in their own mantles, that they have no eyes to look up for Elias his mantle." *The Cry of a Stone* (1654: Brit. Lib., E730 [3]), p. 66.

32. See, for example, his call of 19 September for a general fast: *Mercurius Politicus,* 14-21 September 1654, pp. 3777-3779.

33. Wilson, "First Anniversary," 267.

34. Abbott, *Writings and Speeches,* 4: 418.

35. Nor does Noah seem to be introduced to question Oliver's credentials as prophet, or to raise "the question of human inadequacy," as Patterson suggests (*Civic Crown,* p. 82).

36. Abbott, *Writings and Speeches,* 3: 52-66. The speech was anonymously republished in October, presumably by Fifth Monarchists, and was thrown back against Oliver by, among others, John Spittlehouse:

The Lord General Cromwel's Speech Delivered in the Council-Chamber, upon the 4 of July, 1653 (1654: Brit. Lib., E813 [13]); John Spittlehouse, *An Answer to One Part of the Lord Protector's Speech* (1654: Brit. Lib., E813 [19]), pp. 4-6; see also *A Declaration of Several of the Churches of Christ* (1654: Brit. Lib., E809 [15]).

37. Wallace, *Destiny*, p. 131; Spittlehouse, *Answer*, p. 4.

38. William Spurstowe, *The Magistrates Dignity and Duty* (1654: Brit. Lib., E727 [3]), p. 21. Similarly, Noah had other, nonmonarchical, uses: thus Obadiah Sedgwick, ranking the prophets, noted that "Noah was eminent for Uprightness, and Moses for meekness." Sedgwick, *Elisha his Lamentation* (1654: Brit. Lib., E745 [14]), p. 5.

39. Anon., *A True State of the Case of the Commonwealth* (1654: Brit. Lib., E728 [5]), p. 51. The passage is reprinted in *Perfect Occurrences* for 20-27 February 1653/4 (Brit. Lib., E730 [11]), pp. 14-15. The case for *concordia discors* could be applied even more strongly to Oliver's religious policy.

40. Wallace, *Destiny*, pp. 134-135.

41. P. Legouis, in Margoliouth, *Poems of Marvell*, I: 327.

42. Anon., *A Full and Perfect Relation of the Great Plot* (Brit. Lib., E730 [1]), p. 5.

43. For example, Joshua: E. M., *Protection Perswading Subjection* (Brit. Lib., E729 [4]), pp. 19, 21; Gideon: Peter English, *The Survey of Policy* (Brit. Lib., E727 [17]), p. 157, and Trapnel, *Cry of a Stone*, pp. 6, 10, 11; Moses: John Goodwin, *Dissatisfaction Satisfied* (Brit. Lib., E725 [7]), p. 8, and idem, *Peace Protested and Discontent Disarmed* (Brit. Lib., E732 [27]), pp. 27-32, also E. M., *Protection Perswading Subjection*, pp. 2-3, 15.

44. For example, *Mercurius Politicus*, 9-16 February 1653/4, p. 3273; Abbott, *Writings and Speeches*, 3: 439.

45. *Mercurius Politicus*, 14-21 September 1654, pp. 3777-3779.

46. Abbott, *Writings and Speeches*, 3: 225-228.

47. Ibid., pp. 290-291. Newspaper reports of bumper harvests bear out Oliver's claims: *Weekly Intelligencer*, 24-31 October 1654 (Brit. Lib. E814 [3]), pp. 109-110, and *Perfect Account*, 1-8 November 1654 (Brit. Lib., E816 [9]), p. 1600.

48. Wallace, *Destiny*, pp. 130-131; Patterson, *Civic Crown*, pp. 83, 85-86.

49. See Worden, *Rump Parliament*, passim, and Woolrych, *Commonwealth*, passim.

50. Zwicker, "Models of Governance," p. 3.

51. Abbott, *Writings and Speeches*, 3: 453.

52. Wallace, *Destiny*, pp. 136-138; Patterson, *Civic Crown*, pp. 50-94.

53. Wilson, "First Anniversary," pp. 263, 266, 273.

54. Patterson, *Civic Crown*, pp. 74-77.

55. For example, *Mercurius Politicus*, 9-16 March, p. 3332; *The Dutch Diurnall*, 7-14 March 1653/4 (Brit. Lib., E731 [16]), p. 80; *A*

Perfect Account, 8-15 March 1653/4 (Brit. Lib., E731 [19]), p. 1325. The irony was all the greater in that, as Waller conceded, Charles I had been unable to persuade the heavens to send rain: see, 1. 48 of "Upon His Majesty's Repairing of Paul's," in G. Thorn Drury, ed., *The Poems of Edmund Waller* (London, 1890), p. 18.

56. Ezek. 48: 31-34. I am grateful to Steven Schwarzschild for this reference.

57. Aldgate, Bishopsgate, Cripplegate, Aldersgate, Newgate, Ludgate, and London Bridge.

58. I am grateful to George Pepe for this point.

59. See, for example, *Mercurius Politicus,* 2-9 February 1653/4, p. 3262, and *The Weekly Intelligencer,* 7-14 February 1653/4 (Brit. Lib., E729 [9]), p. 159.

60. Abbott, *Writings and Speeches,* pp. 455-457.

61. Woolrych, *Commonwealth,* p. 397, and references there cited; for other examples of the coupling, see Abbott, *Writings and Speeches,* 3: 62, 452, 461.

62. Patterson, *Civic Crown,* p. 69, where she claims that the poet's millenarian hopes "are presented in the most hypothetical terms"; see also Wallace, *Destiny,* p. 120.

63. Dan. 7: 13.

64. See especially Quentin Skinner, *The Foundations of Modern Political Thought,* 2 vols. (Cambridge, 1978), 1: x-xiv; J. G. A. Pocock, *Politics, Language and Time* (New York, 1971), pp. 3-41, 273-291.

65. Abbott, *Writings and Speeches,* 3: 64.

66. Ibid., p. 437.

67. *Mercurius Politicus,* 13-20 April 1654; *The Grand Catastrophe, or, The Change of Government* (Brit. Lib., E726 [12]), p. 1-2.

68. Especially in his *The Machiavellian Moment* (Princeton, 1975), pp. 333-400, and in his edition of *The Political Works of James Harrington* (Cambridge, 1977).

69. Mazzeo, "Davidic King," pp. 166-182; Blair Worden, "Classical Republicanism and the Puritan Revolution," in H. Lloyd-Jones, V. Pearl, and B. Worden, eds., *History and Imagination* (London, 1981), especially pp. 197-198. I am also indebted to Blair Worden for allowing me to read before publication his essay "The Politics of Marvell's "Horatian Ode," *Historical Journal,* forthcoming.

70. Mazzeo, "Davidic King," p. 182.

71. Pocock, *Works of Harrington,* pp. 15-76, and especially pp. 23, 30-31. See also John Wallace's insightful remark that Cromwell alone in "The First Anniversary" functions in linear time, in contrast to the circular movements not just of kings but of all other mortals. Wallace, *Destiny,* p. 138 n. 2.

72. Pocock, *Works of Harrington,* p. 37.

73. Cromwell's subsequent embarrassment at the expulsion of the Rump is vividly rendered in Worden, *Rump Parliament,* pp. 345-363, and Woolrych, *Commonwealth,* pp. 68-102.

74. My italics.

75. *Mercurius Politicus,* 9-16 February 1653/4, p. 3270; again I am indebted to George Pepe for the translation.

76. To the works cited in note 43 above should be added the recorder's speech welcoming the protector into the City, and Thomas Goodwin's sermon at the opening of Parliament: *Mr. Recorders Speech to the Lord Protector* (Brit. Lib., E729 [2]), p. 3, and Abbott, *Writings and Speeches,* 3: 432, 434-435.

77. Goodwin, *Dissatisfaction Satisfied,* p. 8.

78. Abbott, *Writings and Speeches,* 3: 434-435, 442.

79. Pocock, *Works of Harrington,* p. 37 n. 3.

80. Zwicker, "Models of Governance," p. 12.

81. Nicolas Lockyer, "Preface," in Robert Dingley, *The Deputation of Angels* (1654: Brit. Lib., E1505 [2]). The work was dedicated to Cromwell's councillor and friend William Sydenham, to Lord Commissioner Lisle, and to Cromwell's cousin Colonel Robert Hammond, the "dear Robin" of the revealing letters on the eve of the army's revolution of 1648-49.

82. See, for example, *Confusion Confounded* (1654: Brit. Lib., E726 [11]), p. 2, and Dingley, *Deputation of Angels,* epistle dedicatory, sig. A3$_v$.

83. Abbott, *Writings and Speeches,* 3: 437.

84. Thomas Goodwin, *A Sermon of the Fifth Monarchy* (1654: Brit. Lib., E812 [9]), especially p. 12; Abbott, *Writings and Speeches,* 3: 587.

85. *A True State of the Case of the Commonwealth,* pp. 26-27, and the introduction to the reprint by The Rota (Exeter, 1978). Nedham's biographer argues against an ascription to Nedham of the *True State,* but his case is not wholly convincing: Joseph Frank, *Cromwell's Press Agent* (Lanham, Md., 1980), p. 135 n. 83.

86. Information of Marchamont Nedham, *Calendar of State Papers, Domestic, 1653-1654,* pp. 304-308.

87. See the references in B. S. Capp, *The Fifth Monarchy Men* (London, 1972), pp. 53-64; and also in Wallace, *Destiny,* p. 119, with the important correction that John Rogers's *Sagrir* was first published in 1653, not 1654.

88. *Calendar of State Papers, Domestic, 1653-1654,* pp. 304-308.

89. Matthew Coker, *A Prophetic Revelation* (1654: Brit. Lib., E734 [7]), p. 4; for the surge of excitement in 1655-56, see David S. Katz, *Philo-Semitism and the Readmission of the Jews to England 1603-1655* (Oxford, 1982).

90. To the works cited in n. 10 above, add Col. Edward Lane, *An Image of our Reforming Times* (1654: Brit. Lib E808 [11]); John Spittlehouse, *Certain Queries* (1654: Brit. Lib., E809 [14]); *A Declaration of Several of the Churches of Christ* (1654: Brit. Lib., E809 [15]); Jeffrey Corbet, *England's Warning-Piece* (1654: Brit. Lib., E812 [4]); and John Spittlehouse, *An Answer to One Part of the Lord Protector's Speech.* For the importance of the triers and ejectors, see the intercepted letters

in C. H. Firth, ed., *The Clarke Papers* 3 (Camden Soc., 1899), pp. 12-15.

91. See B. Taft, "The Humble Petition of Several Colonels of the Army," *Huntington Library Quarterly* 42 (1978-79): 15-41.

92. Christopher Feake, *The Oppressed Close Prisoner in Windsor-Castle, His Defiance to the Father of Lyes* (1654: Brit. Lib., E820 [10]), p. 2.

93. *The Observator* ran for two issues in October-November 1654 (Brit. Lib., E814 [4] and E816 [4]).

94. S. R. Gardiner, *History of the Commonwealth and Protectorate*, 4 vols. (London, 1903), 3: 233, L. F. Brown, *The Political Activities of the Baptists and Fifth Monarchy Men* (Washington, 1912), pp. 66-68.

95. Katz, *Philo-Semitism,* pp. 127-157. I am grateful to Steve Zwicker for stressing this point to me.

96. That Nedham was willing to contemplate a more regalist reading of Revelation than was Marvell may have been not unconnected to the fact that he was writing before the failure of the attempt in Parliament to crown Cromwell.

97. See, for example, Spittlehouse, *Answer,* pp. 9, 18, 23-24, the jibes of *The Observator,* 24-31 October (Brit. Lib., E814 [4]), pp. 2, 8-10, and in particular Oliver's criticisms in his opening speech to Parliament, Abbott, *Writings and Speeches,* 3: 438. Moses might also have seemed inappropriate as a model in a celebratory poem for Cromwell since the prophet was left outside the promised land; furthermore, when Marvell had already celebrated the protector as eloquent Amphion, to liken him to the tongue-tied Moses, for whom Aaron acted as spokesman, might seem contradictory. (I am grateful to Steve Zwicker for the latter suggestion.)

98. Marvell's strategy may at first glance seem to have been doomed. Surely the members of Feake's or Spittlehouse's churches would have been unlikely to have read such a text as "The First Anniversary." But the Fifth Monarchist ranks also included men like the eminently witty ex-colonel Edward Lane, whose *Image of our Reforming Times* appeared in August. And more frightening was the openness to their appeal of men like Col. Robert Overton, whom Milton celebrated.

99. That Marvell may indeed have been a millenarian is suggested by the almost complete seriousness of the key passages, which reveal little of the ironical touch so characteristic of Marvell elsewhere. The only possible exception to this assertion comes at line 124, where Marvell speaks of himself as "Winding his Horn." It is open to question whether someone, and particularly someone as sensitive to language as Marvell, writing in high earnestness a commentary on the apocalypse, could in the same breath speak of himself as possessing a horn, when the single constant of those tortured books Daniel and Revelation is that horns are the peculiar property of the anti-Messiah. Perhaps as likely might be the sight of the Rev. Jerry Falwell driving down the highway with a personalized license plate reading "666." A further piece of distancing may

occur at line 116, where Marvell blames the foreign princes for their failure to "teach" the Jews. Someone moving in the more excited circles in 1653-55 might have been expected to refer to the conversion, not the teaching, of the Jews: see Katz, *Philo-Semitism,* passim.

100. I am most grateful to Blair Worden for stressing this point to me, and to him and Steve Zwicker for helpful discussions on the argument of the following paragraphs. "The First Anniversary" was advertised in *Mercurius Politicus* for 11-18 January, 1654/5, just over a month after the anniversary.

101. The term is John Evelyn's, commenting on the awkward establishment of the republic, and it could be appropriately applied to the ambiguities of the protectorate. E. S. DeBeer, ed., *The Diary of John Evelyn,* 6 vols. (Oxford, 1955), 2: 555.

102. See the degenerating syntax of Cromwell's speeches in the kingship crisis: Abbott, *Writings and Speeches,* 4: 442-446, 453-455, 456-461, 467-474, 480-483, 484-497; also, D. Underdown, "Cromwell and the Officers, February 1658," *English Historical Review* 83 (1968): 101-107.

103. I am indebted to Steve Zwicker for stressing this point to me.

104. The ill-tempered breach with Parliament was unlikely in itself to have perturbed Marvell unduly. The condescending tone in which he refers to Parliament-men at lines 87-96 seems characteristic of one who views matters from the government's perspective. It reminds one of nothing so much as the remarks in 1523 of that other great Cromwell, Thomas, soon to be Henry VIII's greatest servant. To such a mind Parliament may have been a fact of life, but it was one that had at times to be borne with in patience. See G. R. Elton, ed., *The Tudor Constitution* (Cambridge, 1960), p. 236.

105. As Nedham miscalculated it when he published *The Excellencie of a Free State* in 1656. See Frank, *Cromwell's Press Agent,* 93-102.

III

DRYDEN IN 1678-1681: THE LITERARY AND HISTORICAL PERSPECTIVES

Phillip Harth

My subject deals in about equal proportions with literature and history, the topic of this series. It is the question of Dryden's participation in English political affairs during 1681 and the three years preceding that important date in English history. In particular, I want to reexamine the view, widely held today, that *Absalom and Achitophel,* published 17 November 1681, was not one of Dryden's earliest literary productions occasioned by the long-standing Exclusion Crisis, but the culmination of a series of literary sorties he had been carrying out against the Whigs, and particularly the earl of Shaftesbury, since the beginning of the crisis and even earlier. I shall argue that this view is a myth largely fashioned in recent years by Dryden's twentieth-century biographers to replace the account accepted until our own era.

In simple outline, the details of Dryden's career during the reign of Charles II which had passed down to his nineteenth-century biographers were these: for the first seven years following the Restoration he was both a playwright and a poet, most of whose poems were overtly political, supporting the crown and the Restoration Settlement; during the next fourteen years, from 1667 to 1681, he abandoned politics and nondramatic poetry for a career in the theater writing plays and dramatic criticism;

finally, beginning with *Absalom and Achitophel* in the latter part of 1681, he stopped writing tragedies and comedies to return, for the remainder of Charles's reign, to political authorship, this time in a variety of genres.

Dryden was not wholly silent on politics, however, during his fourteen-year interlude as a playwright and critic. In March 1678, in his dedication of *All for Love* to the earl of Danby, the lord treasurer, he warmly defended the King's chief minister, supported his administration, and assailed his opponents. But that was three and a half years before *Absalom and Achitophel* appeared, a turbulent interval in which more than one political allegiance shifted. In Dryden's case, questions about his political consistency were inevitably raised by his choosing to write, as his last play before abandoning the theater, *The Spanish Fryar,* which mercilessly ridiculed the Catholic priesthood at a time when the outcry over the Popish Plot was serving Whig interests. Furthermore, as if to emphasize the appeal of this subject to popular passions, Dryden spoke of "recommending a protestant play to a protestant patron" in dedicating it to Lord Haughton when it was published in early 1681.

Finally, there were signs from both political camps that Dryden was believed, by some at least, to have wavered for awhile in his allegiance to the court. The Tory author of a pamphlet with the ironic title *A Modest Vindication of the Earl of Shaftesbury* exploited a Polish joke going the rounds of the court circle by pretending that Shaftesbury had been offered the crown of Poland, had eagerly accepted it when it was sent to him in a cloak bag, and had now drawn up a list of appointments to his royal household; among them, *"Jean Drydenurtzitz,* Our Poet Laureat for writing Panegyricks upon *Oliver Cromwel,* and Libels against his present Master King *Charles* II of *England,"* apparently alluding not only to the *Heroique Stanzas* Dryden had written to the memory of Cromwell but to the common belief that he was the author of Mulgrave's *Essay upon Satire.*[1] On the Whig side, Robert Gould would later charge, in *The Laureat,* an attack on Dryden published in 1687, that he had written *The Spanish Fryar* when the government stopped payment on his pension, which led him to join the opposition for awhile in disgust.

Here, then, were more than enough ingredients for another Whig legend about Dryden, if his nineteenth-century biographers

had chosen to build on them as they did with the story of his purpose in writing *Absalom and Achitophel.*[2] None of them accepted
the rumors of Dryden's temporary defection from the court, however. In fact, they spent an inordinate amount of time refuting
them. Edmond Malone led off Dryden's defense in 1800, arguing
in answer to *The Laureat* that, as the poet must have realized and
come to accept, his pension was stopped only because of "the poverty of the Exchequer."[3] But it was Sir Walter Scott, eight years
later, who mounted the first full-scale defense of Dryden's political loyalties throughout the Exclusion Crisis. As evidence that
Dryden "was considered as disaffected to the court" at the time
The Spanish Fryar was produced, he cited both *The Laureat* and
A Modest Vindication of the Earl of Shaftesbury, but he insisted
the play afforded no reasonable ground for such a suspicion. In
holding up "to contempt and execration the character of the
Roman catholic priesthood," Scott wrote, Dryden was partaking
"in some degree of the general ferment which the discovery of the
Popish Plot had excited; and we may easily suppose him to have
done so without any impeachment to his monarchial tenets, since
. . . the chiefs of the loyal party joined in the cry. Indeed, that
mysterious transaction had been investigated by none more
warmly than by Danby."[4]

That might have been expected to settle the matter, but it did
not. Robert Bell in 1854 tried and acquitted Dryden again on the
charge that he had deserted the court for a time, and even W. D.
Christie, no admirer of Dryden's where politics were concerned,
felt compelled in 1870 to come to his defense, or at least to relieve
the Whigs of the imputation that he was ever a colleague of
theirs.[5] It was therefore something of an anticlimax when Louis I.
Bredvold in 1932 proved that the payment of Dryden's pension
was not stopped in 1680: he had in fact received three install-
ments that year.[6]

Freed from the nineteenth-century obsession with giving a
favorable turn to what Dryden *did* do during the early years of
the Exclusion Crisis, his modern biographers have been at leisure
to develop their own obsession with filling the void of what, to all
appearances, Dryden did *not* do. Their predecessors had been so
little concerned with Dryden's tardy entry into the political lists
that they ignored the matter. George Saintsbury's manner of
introducing his discussion of *Absalom and Achitophel* in 1881 is

typical of the time. "For the first eighteen years of Charles the Second's reign," he writes, "the nation at large felt little interest, of the active kind, in political questions. Dryden almost always reflected the sympathies of the nation at large. The Popish Plot, however, and the dangerous excitement which the misgovernment of Charles on the one hand and the machinations of Shaftesbury on the other produced" had brought a sudden end to the mood of political indifference. "*Absalom and Achitophel* was published about the middle of November, 1681."[7] Saintsbury ignores the reflection that if Dryden was responding in *Absalom and Achitophel* to the popular passions of 1678, he waited three years to do so.

This is a reflection, however, which Dryden's modern biographers are unwilling to accept. They wish to find not only consistency but coherence in Dryden's writings during the Exclusion Crisis. Unable to abide what amounts to a political vacuum in Dryden's career during three years of intense excitement on the part of lesser writers, his biographers have set to work finding something for him to do. Out of this understandable wish they have tried to create a new Dryden, the prose pamphleteer and political playwright of the years 1678 to 1681.

The prose pamphleteer was the first to emerge. In 1935 Roswell G. Ham in an influential article argued that Dryden's post as historiographer royal, which he had held since 1670, carried with it the obligation of writing political tracts on behalf of the government; that during the heated debates of 1678 to 1681 he would have felt compelled to begin carrying out his official responsibilities at last; and that one such result was an anonymous pamphlet published in the spring of 1681, *His Majesties Declaration Defended,* which Ham attributed to Dryden on the basis of various parallel ideas he found in this pamphlet and in Dryden's acknowledged political writings beginning with *Absalom and Achitophel.*[8] This suggestion had become so firmly entrenched by 1961 that Dryden's biographer found it "inconceivable" that he "should not have written for the King during the months of greatest strain," and concluded that "there seems little reason to doubt that he was drawing his pen for the royal cause under the cloak of anonymity, as was the contemporary fashion in party controversy," while conceding that "he has set his editors and biographers a task of the greatest difficulty to identify his contributions to the mass of pamphlet literature."⁹

Five years ago, in an important article published in *Modern Philology,* Edward L. Saslow confronted that task and disposed of it decisively. He showed that Dryden's post of historiographer royal did not carry any expectation that he write political pamphlets and that neither contemporary testimony nor the canon of Dryden's acknowledged works can show a single case of his doing so during the reign of Charles II. As for *His Majesties Declaration Defended,* Saslow demonstrated that the supposedly parallel ideas found in that anonymous pamphlet and in some of Dryden's later writings, when they do not prove on closer examination to be dissimilar, are simply commonplaces shared by numerous political works of the period.¹⁰ That seems to have eliminated, once and for all, Dryden's putative career as an anonymous pamphleteer.

Dryden's second new role, that of political playwright, has been created not by attributing new writings to him but by discovering political content in his acknowledged work for the theater. A synoptic account of the several versions of this story yields the following: Dryden first attacked Shaftesbury on two separate occasions as early as March 1678, portraying him as Limberham, the fumbling lecher in his comedy *The Kind Keeper,* and following this almost immediately with "an unequivocal attack" on him, though not by name, in the dedication to Danby of *All for Love.*¹¹ Later, when the excitement over the Popish Plot was at its height, Dryden returned to Shaftesbury again, this time portraying him as Creon, the evil conspirator in the version of *Oedipus* he wrote with Nathaniel Lee.¹² Stung by these insults and seeking a delayed revenge, Shaftesbury may have been responsible for the Rose Alley ambuscade in which Dryden suffered a beating in December 1679.¹³ By the following spring Dryden was engrossed in "an immediate and almost total concern with the political scene," and in the summer and autumn of 1680, "now fully committed to the succession of the Duke of York," he chose a country retreat where he devoted his time to "reading widely and thinking deeply" about political questions, "for there can be little doubt that these months marked the actual beginning of *Absalom and Achitophel,*" which would not be published for another year.¹⁴ Furthermore, from 1679 onwards Dryden had been making his sentiments on the developing political crisis clear in the prologues and epilogues he was writing to his own plays and to those of other dramatists.

The suggestion that Dryden portrayed Shaftesbury as Limberham has a long and checked history. The government itself may have believed that someone was being caricatured in *The Kind Keeper,* for the play was suppressed after the third night. This naturally encouraged speculation about Limberham's identity. Samuel Derrick suggested Lauderdale in 1760 and Malone countered by proposing Shaftesbury. The latter suggestion, although rejected by Scott as improbable, was revived in our own time to supply Shaftesbury with additional motivation for arranging the Rose Alley ambuscade. Susan Staves has recently reconsidered the matter and concluded that Dryden was not personating anyone in *The Kind Keeper,* but that the audience gratuitously applied the character of Limberham to some individual, probably Lauderdale, the King's favorite, it being unlikely that the government would have intervened to spare Shaftesbury embarrassment.[15]

The passage in which Dryden supposedly attacks Shaftesbury in his dedication to Danby of *All for Love* occurs in the midst of a general criticism of those "malecontents" who are dissatisfied with the present state of affairs under Danby and "would persuade the people that they might be happier by a change."

He who has often changed his party, and always has made his interest the rule of it, gives little evidence of his sincerity for the public good; it is manifest he changes but for himself, and takes the people for tools to work his fortune. Yet the experience of all ages might let him know, that they, who trouble the waters first, have seldom the benefit of fishing; as they who began the late rebellion, enjoyed not the fruit of their undertaking, but were crushed themselves by the usurpation of their own instrument.[16]

It was again Malone who first suggested that Shaftesbury was intended here, and in this case Scott concurred, describing this passage as "a pointed allusion to the Earl of Shaftesbury, . . . now at the head of the popular faction."[17] This identification has long been accepted without question, the one traditional detail in the modern account of Dryden's early opposition to Shaftesbury. The explanation for its popularity emerges in the words of one of Dryden's twentieth-century biographers:

Here Dryden boldly attacks the leader of the Whigs, the Earl of Shaftesbury, in a passage that contains the germ of his character of Achitophel
more than three years later. . . . These were prophetic words, not arrived
at through a special sense of prevision but through Dryden's special
sense of the workings of history. . . . Already Shaftesbury's probable
course was partly charted in Dryden's mind. . . . And already the wrath
of a righteously aroused loyal poet is enlisted to wreak a devastating revenge upon the "disturber of a nation."[18]

The parallel immediately evoked by Dryden's supposedly "prophetic words" in 1678 is with his Achitophel three years later,
who in turn becomes the medium through which the reader recognizes the historical Shaftesbury of 1681. But in March 1678
Shaftesbury was not the leader of the Whigs, for that party had
not yet come into existence, and while there was certainly a group
in Parliament trying to bring about the downfall of Danby's
administration, the issues on which its members were united—
matters such as war with France, the state of the treasury, and
toleration for the dissenters, which Dryden discusses in his dedication—were very different from those which later would rivet
the attention of the Whigs. Nor was Shaftesbury the leader of this
group, much less the "head of the popular faction" or the "disturber of a nation." He had won his freedom only a few weeks
earlier from the Tower, where he had spent a year's imprisonment for contempt since February 1677. Speaking of Shaftesbury's position at the time of his release, his biographer, K. H. D.
Haley, writes: "There is no satisfactory evidence that he had yet a
very great following either inside or outside Parliament." In any
case, Haley points out, "his imprisonment in 1677 had prevented
him from acting as an effective leader for twelve months, and
even for the session of January to July 1678 the main lines of opposition policy had been formulated before he left the Tower."[19]
There is no discernible reason why Shaftesbury, who had only
been allowed to resume his seat in the House of Lords on February 27, should have been singled out by Dryden some three weeks
later in the course of attacking Danby's enemies, chief of whom
was not in any case Shaftesbury but the duke of Buckingham,
described by Danby's biographer, Andrew Browning, as "now the
Treasurer's most inveterate foe." Imprisoned at the same time as
Shaftesbury the previous year, Buckingham had been kept in
close confinement on Danby's orders. "The humiliation inflicted

upon him at this time he never forgot," Browning writes, and
"the last expiring flashes of his brilliant intellect were to be
devoted almost entirely to accomplishing the treasurer's ruin."
Buckingham had won his release from the Tower in June 1677,
much to the resentment of Shaftesbury, who was forced to sit by
helplessly while the duke moved about freely, "working for the
ruin of Danby" (in Browning's words) "even before Parliament
met" in January 1678.[20]

To modern readers Dryden's words describing one "who has
often changed his party, and always has made his interest the rule
of it" inevitably recall the common charge against Shaftesbury
repeated in *The Medal* in 1682. But the accusation of having
often changed his party, or "allegiance," out of self-interest was
not directed solely at Shaftesbury, as Dryden could have testified
himself. No one was more vulnerable to this imputation than
Buckingham: a Cavalier at the time of the civil wars who returned
to England in the 1650s in hopes of winning a pardon from Cromwell's government and recovering his estates; a member of the
Cabal who later went into opposition to the court; a patron of
Danby's who had become his bitter enemy; an ally of Shaftesbury's, with whom he had recently quarreled.

Whether or not Buckingham is intended in this passage, he is
at any rate a far more probable target of Dryden's criticism than
Shaftesbury, not only on political but on personal grounds. There
is no evidence that Dryden bore Shaftesbury any grudge at this
time, whereas he had good reason to feel resentment toward
Buckingham, who had portrayed him as Bayes in *The Rehearsal*
as long ago as 1671. Dryden's mood for paying off old scores is
shown by the fact that the preface to *All for Love,* published at
the same time as the dedication, contains his attack on Rochester,
though again not by name.

One of the latest accretions to the myth of Dryden the political
playwright is the suggestion that in December 1678 he attacked
Shaftesbury by portraying him as Creon in the version of *Oedipus*
he wrote with Lee. We are told that "Creon's character clearly
anticipates the sinister side of Achitophel in Dryden's great verse
satire . . . and Dryden gives him the essential trait to be found
later in Achitophel: he is, in his own words, a 'daring' pilot, sinister but sublime." Once again it is the parallel with Dryden's por-
trait of Achitophel three years later that is being used to authenti-

cate the identification of Creon with Shaftesbury. In this case, however, a parallel is also drawn between Creon's behavior in the play and Shaftesbury's role in capitalizing on the Popish Plot. Creon, we are told, "is presented as a clever malcontent, driven by envy, who stirs up the crowd against the king of Thebes by a series of false rumors and accusations aimed at friends of the throne." His false charge of complicity in the slaying of Laius against two members of the Theban court is meant "to suggest the basic premise of the Popish Plot, that the life of the king was threatened by the Catholics, including his brother James and his own queen," while "the appearance of the Theban crowd in full cry upon the stage" would remind the audience that "mob violence was Shaftesbury's most intimidating threat" during the excitement over the Plot.[21]

These suggestions might be plausible if the play had indeed been written and produced at the end of 1678.[22] But it is now generally accepted that *Oedipus* was first performed during the autumn of 1678 and that Dryden and Lee must have finished writing it no later than September, when rumors of a Popish Plot were only starting to reach the public.[23] Titus Oates and Ezerel Tonge made their first appearance before the privy council on September 28, and threats of mob violence did not materialize until even later. As for Shaftesbury, the opportunity had still not arisen for him to assume the role of a popular leader. That occasion was offered him by the fortuitous conjunction of two events late in the following month: the discovery of Sir Edmund Berry Godfrey's body on October 17, and the opening of Parliament on October 21, providing him with a public forum at the ideal psychological moment.

The belief that Dryden spent the summer and autumn of 1680 thinking and reading about political questions while beginning work on *Absalom and Achitophel,* although it has by now acquired authority by repetition, also originated in a mistake about the date of first performance of one of his plays. On the assumption that *The Spanish Fryar,* the last play Dryden wrote before abandoning the theater, was produced in March 1680, it seemed reasonable to conclude that he was at leisure after this date to turn to new interests.[24] His comedy is now known to have had its first performance some eight months later, when a letter of 1 November 1680 reports a visit to the theater "to see the new play, The Spanish Frier." Dryden was presumably at work on the play over the previous summer.[25] In any case, we have no evidence of what Dryden was reading in 1680, and if he began work on *Absalom and Achitophel* at this time, it must have been a very different poem from the one he published in November 1681, which is closely tied to the events and attitudes of the latter year.

When we turn to Dryden's prologues and epilogues, we appear to be on firmer ground. It is common practice in Restoration prologues and epilogues to allude to contemporary events of interest to the audience, and those which Dryden wrote during the excitement over the Popish Plot and the Exclusion Crisis are no exception. Many, though not all of them, mention the public events taking place during these months. By considering them as a uniform group of personal statements written at this time, Dryden's biographers have argued that, no longer able to remain silent, he was expressing his sentiments on the developing political situation. But Dryden wrote some twenty-seven prologues and epilogues to his own plays and those of fellow dramatists between the supposed discovery of the Popish Plot and the end of 1682. In using them, it is essential to pay close attention to their chronology and to consider as well the audience for whom each of them was written. Approximately half of these prologues and epilogues, those written before mid-1681, are markedly different from the remainder, composed after that time. And throughout these four years Dryden was writing his contributions to the theater for two very different audiences. The majority were designed for regular performances of plays during the season at one or the other of the two London theaters. But during the summer, when the London theaters were closed, Dryden also wrote prologues and epilogues for special performances at Oxford before the members of the university.

The prologues and epilogues Dryden wrote before mid-1681 display the usual characteristics of that minor genre. Rather than either personal testaments or political propaganda, they are addresses by one of the players to the audience, attempting to win their good will. They create in advance a favorable frame of mind among the spectators about to watch the play or send them home afterward in a contented mood, prepared to recommend the play to their friends. Dryden creates a rhetorical stance in each of these prologues and epilogues which is adapted to its particular audience. For an academic audience at Oxford he adopts a humorous tone tempered by a subtle deference that is always gratifying to an assembly of scholars. At Drury Lane or Dorset Garden, he adopts a bantering tone toward his audience of Londoners, producing the kind of comic raillery that in the epilogue to his own *Troilus and Cressida* was appropriately spoken by the actor who played Thersites. This good-humored abuse is part of the recognized contact between the players and the London audience, which is amused without being offended by the expected banter and won over by rough camaraderie.

All Dryden's prologues and epilogues before some time in 1681, however different the tone in which he solicits the audience at Oxford or London, aim at the same objective: to create a bond of mutual interest between players and spectators by exploiting a shared contempt or hostility toward some alien group. Before the university audience at Oxford, that bedrock of allegiance to the religious and political establishment, Dryden's prologues in the summers of 1679 and 1680 express a mutual antagonism toward dissenters from the Established Church, dissidents from the court, and Scotch rebels, implying a firm alliance between scholars and players.

> But 'tis the Talent of our *English* Nation,
> Still to be Plotting some New Reformation:
> And few years hence, if Anarchy goes on,
> *Jack Presbyter* shall here Erect his Throne.
> . . . .
> Then all you Heathen Wits shall go to Pot,
> For disbelieving of a Popish Plot.

This is a prospect as dreadful for the players as it is for their academic audience. "Nor shou'd we scape the Sentence, to Depart, / Ev'n in our first Original, A Cart." Actors and scholars would be common sufferers in a fate where "Religion, Learning, Wit, wou'd be supprest." Therefore they are natural allies in opposing any change in church or state:

> This is our comfort, none e're cry'd us down,
> But who dislik'd both *Bishop* and a *Crown*.[26]

This mood of sturdy Toryism is as fleeting as an English summer and vanishes long before the first frost. Back in London for the winter season, Dryden caters to very different sympathies in his prologues and epilogues for the audience at Dorset Garden. Naturally, they are filled with complaints about the political turmoil of this "distracted Age," because "Noise, Madness, all unreasonable Things" have driven down the market for serious drama. "Therfore thin Nourishment of Farce ye choose" at a time when "A Meal of Tragedy wou'd make ye Sick."[27] But the shared attitudes that create a strong bond between the players and the London audience are xenophobia and anti-Catholic prejudice.

> When Murther's out, what Vice can we advance?
> Unless the new found Pois'ning Trick of *France:*
> And when their Art of *Rats-bane* we have got,
> By way of thanks, we'll send 'em o'er our Plot.[28]

Poisoning is, in fact, endemic to foreigners, especially those who live in Catholic lands:

> They have a civil way in *Italy*
> By smelling a perfume to make you dye,
> A Trick would make you lay your Snuff-box by.
> Murder's a Trade—so known and practis'd there,
> That 'tis Infallible as is the Chair—
> But mark their Feasts, you shall behold such Pranks,
> The Pope says Grace, but 'tis the Devil gives Thanks.[29]

Or again, the Londoners are cajoled by a witticism at the expense of the Catholic victims of the Popish Plot trials, who affirmed their innocence on the scaffold with a solemn oath and were said to have been promised a pardon by the pope for perjuring themselves in their last moments:

> I cou'd rayl on, but 'twere a task as vain
> As Preaching truth at *Rome,* or wit in *Spain,*
> . . . .
> If guilty, yet I'm sure oth' Churches blessing,
> By suffering for the Plot, without confessing.[30]

The poet we perceive in these early prologues and epilogues is not a man troubled by the mounting political crisis and forced to express his feelings about the situation but a professional man of the theater doing his best to insure that a play will be favorably received by the audience before whom it is performed. When we examine the prologues and epilogues Dryden began writing about the middle of 1681, however, we notice a significant change. Several playfully anti-Whig lines in the epilogue to John Banks's *The Unhappy Favourite,* produced at Drury Lane about May 1681, are noteworthy not so much for what they tell us about Dryden as for what they indicate about his estimate of a changing political climate among London audiences. Again, in a prologue he wrote for the performance of a play at Oxford in the summer of 1681, Dryden adopts a more serious tone than previously in praising the loyalty of the university, though of course he is telling the academic audience what it wants to hear.

The first unequivocal sign of a decisive change appears in Dryden's prologue for a command performance of *The Unhappy Favourite* before the King and Queen at Drury Lane, given either toward the end of the season in the spring of 1681 or, just as probably, the following autumn. This prologue ignores the play it ostensibly introduces to present a serious political argument in support of the king. It is very close, in many respects, to the famous passage on government in lines 753-810 of *Absalom and Achitophel.* It marks an unmistakable turning point in the character of Dryden's prologues and epilogues, from casual pieces subordinated to the play they accompany and the audience whose favor they solicit, to political propaganda independent of both play and particular audience. In fact, beginning with his next prologue and epilogue, for Lee's *Mithridates,* first performed in October 1681, the eight theater pieces Dryden wrote for London productions during the remainder of 1681 and throughout 1682 would all be separately published as political broadsides that could easily stand by themselves without the play that occasioned them. But while Dryden's political prologues and epilogues for other dramatists were being heard at Drury Lane from about the middle of 1681, the audience in the theater was of course unaware of their authorship, and not a single one was published under Dryden's name or publicly attributed to him before the appearance of *Absalom and Achitophel* in November. Until the publication of that poem, therefore, and the rapid spread of rumors that he was its author, Dryden's emergence at the eleventh hour as a Tory spokesman remained unknown to the public at large.

This brings us back once more to the question of Dryden's public image in 1680 and most of 1681 and, inevitably it seems, to the
problem of *The Spanish Fryar*. Scott dismissed the problem too
easily when he argued that in catering to anti-Catholic prejudice
Dryden was doing no more than the chiefs of the loyal party who
"joined in the cry" over the Popish Plot, none of them more
warmly than Danby. Those members of the court party had done
so when the Plot was first broached in the autumn of 1678, and
they soon had reason to regret their folly most bitterly. It was a
very different political atmosphere in which *The Spanish Fryar*
was produced in November 1680, the month in which the second
exclusion bill moved easily through the House of Commons and
was only stopped in the upper house. Bredvold was correct in
pointing out that the play is more anticlerical than anti-Catholic,
but it was performed with an epilogue by Dryden's friend Robert
Wolseley which is unmatched for virulence throughout the entire
period except by Oldham's *Satires upon the Jesuits*. We can easily
believe that Dryden was simply writing a play whose subject
would be certain of winning it instant popularity. But appearing
at a time when the Whigs had been using anti-Catholic prejudice
to encourage popular fears at the prospect of a popish successor,
Dryden's comedy could hardly have failed to raise suspicions that
the author was no friend to the court.

More than enough has been written, however, about the theatrical performance of *The Spanish Fryar*. I want to turn to its publication, in March 1681, about which very little has been said
beyond quoting the single phrase from its dedication, "a protestant play to a protestant patron." That patron, John Holles, Lord
Haughton, has received hardly any attention from Dryden's biographers, for a perfectly good reason: he was a youth who had only
recently celebrated his nineteenth birthday and was as yet an
insignificant figure. Dryden confesses "that what I have written,
looks more like a Preface, than a Dedication," but in his final
paragraph he turns to the proper business of a dedication and
makes the young man the occasion for praising his family. That
paragraph is worth our attention.

It is difficult to write justly on any thing, but almost impossible in
praise. I shall therefore waive so nice a subject; and only tell you, that,
in recommending a protestant play to a protestant patron, as I do

myself an honour, so I do your noble family a right, who have been always eminent in the support and favour of our religion and liberties. And if the promises of your youth, your education at home, and your experience abroad, deceive me not, the principles you have embraced are such, as will no way degenerate from your ancestors, but refresh their memory in the minds of all true Englishmen, and renew their lustre in your person; which, my lord, is not more the wish, than it is the constant expectation, of

Your lordship's
Most obedient, faithful servant,
JOHN DRYDEN[31]

Who were the members of this noble family of Holles who had been "always eminent in the support and favour of our religion and liberties?" The patriarch of the family was Denzil Holles, still remembered today as one of the famous five members whom Charles I tried to arrest on the floor of the House of Commons in January 1642, on the eve of the first civil war. Raised to the peerage after the Restoration, Denzil Holles was instrumental in helping to organize an opposition among the members of the upper chamber, and it was at his house in early 1674 that Shaftesbury and his fellow peers held the meetings at which they began to formulate a concerted policy against the administration.[32] Lord Holles died in February 1680, but as his last public action he was one of seventeen Whig peers, including Shaftesbury, who led off the great Petitioning Movement in December 1679 by calling on the king to allow Parliament to meet to redress the nation's grievances, just as, some forty years earlier, he had supported the Grand Remonstrance to the king's father.[33]

The second member of the family, Denzil's son and heir, Sir Francis Holles, was elected to his father's old seat in the House of Commons in the spring of 1679 and was promptly marked down by Shaftesbury on his famous list of "worthy" and "honest" men on whom he could depend in the approaching session.[34] His hopes were not misplaced. In May 1679 Sir Francis Holles voted for the first exclusion bill.[35]

But for dedicated service to the Whig cause carried out in the limelight, no other member of this noble family could equal Lord Haughton's father, Gilbert Holles, earl of Clare. He too had been one of the signers, along with his uncle Denzil, of the petition to the king in December 1679, and as a Whig pamphlet immediately made public, was one of a smaller number of peers who presented it in person to Charles II.[36] On 30 June 1680 Lord Clare was one of nineteen Whig leaders, including Shaftesbury, who appeared before the grand jury of Middlesex and sought to have the duke of York indicted as a popish recusant. The attempt failed, but it was well publicized in a Whig broadside giving the names of those who had taken part.[37] Lord Clare was not a man to make a secret of his political sympathies. In the great debate in the House of Lords on 15 November 1680, he not only voted for exclusion but was one of a smaller number of Whig peers, Shaftesbury among them, who signed a protest against the rejection of the bill, thus insuring that their support of the second exclusion bill would be made a matter of public record.[38] Most recently, Lord Clare had been one of sixteen Whig peers, again including Shaftesbury, who on 25 January 1681 signed a petition calling on the king to allow the approaching parliament to meet at Westminster rather than at Oxford, "where neither Lords nor Commons can be in safety, but will be daily exposed to the Swords of the Papists and their adherents, of whom to many have crept into Your Majesties Guards." The king ignored this provocation, but again a Whig broadside immediately appeared listing the names of the signers.[39]

That famous Parliament, where the Whigs were expected to make their third attempt to pass an exclusion bill, was about to meet at Oxford on the twenty-first of the month when Dryden's play and its dedication went on sale in the second week of March 1681. We can easily believe that Dryden esteemed the Holles family on personal grounds and that he may have been obliged to them for favors he wished to repay. But in deciding at this moment to single out for public praise their "support and favour of our religion and liberties" and to express the hope that the young Lord Haughton would embrace their principles, he could not have failed to raise doubts about his own political sympathies.

These doubts would have been compounded by the manner in which his new book was publicized. At the time of the Exclusion Crisis, books reflecting support for either party were normally offered for sale in a newspaper sharing the same political feelings. Jacob Tonson chose to advertise *The Spanish Fryar* not in Nathaniel Thompson's Tory newspaper revived on 9 March, *The*

Loyal Protestant and True Domestick Intelligence, in which he would appropriately publicize *Absalom and Achitophel* the following November, but in Langley Curtis's stridently Whig newpaper, *The True Protestant Mercury,* where in the following year would be advertised such angry Whig rejoinders to Dryden as *Azaria and Hushai, The Medal Revers'd,* and *Absalom Senior.* The issue of *The True Protestant Mercury* for 9-12 March 1681, carried advertisements for only two books: Dryden's Protestant play and the second edition of Henry Care's *History of the Damnable Popish Plot,* the popular Whig answer to Roger L'Estrange's Tory *History of the Plot.*

The mistaken impression that Dryden was leaning toward the Whigs would have been encouraged, therefore, much less by the performance of *The Spanish Fryar* the previous year, which has been blamed for these rumors, than by its publication, expanded by Dryden's dedication, in the spring of 1681. It was an impression that would persist until the following autumn, when *Absalom and Achitophel* appeared to dispel it. *A Modest Vindication of the Earl of Shaftesbury,* the Tory pamphlet nominating Dryden as the Whig poet laureate, was assigned by Scott to the year 1680, and Bredvold accepted this date since he believed that the pamphlet was written in reaction to the appearance of Mulgrave's *Essay Upon Satire* in November 1679 and the beating of Dryden in Rose Alley in December of that year. But *A Modest Vindication of the Earl of Shaftesbury* made its first appearance not in 1680 but on 5 September 1681, some two months before *Absalom and Achitophel* was published.[40] Nor is this the only evidence that Tory writers were suspicious of Dryden's political sympathies before the appearance of his poem finally set all doubts to rest. A Tory poetic broadside satirizing the Whig bookseller Benjamin Harris, *The Saint Turn'd Curtezan,* published on 13 April 1681, a month after *The Spanish Fryar,* includes a gratuitous sneer at Dryden's humiliation in the Rose Alley ambuscade, a favorite topic for comment among his enemies.[41]

To eager partisans in the political struggle, such as these Tory pamphleteers fiercely committed to the side of the court and busily engaged against the Whig enemy, Dryden's friendly tribute to a prominent Whig family at this time and in these circumstances may well have represented a betrayal. But not everyone was a committed partisan in March 1681, in spite of accounts of the Exclusion Crisis which would lead us to believe that the entire population was sharply divided into two warring camps. There was still a large middle sector of Englishmen, loyal subjects of their king, who remained interested spectators of the bitter conflict without considering themselves either Whig or Tory. They could stand on the sidelines without any "impeachment to their monarchial tenets," in Scott's rotund phrase, because what was in conflict was not their political principles but the opposed political parties, an innovation to which many Englishmen were slow to adjust. The evidence we have been considering of Dryden's behavior between 1678 and 1681—his disengagement from partisan activities, his preoccupation with his own work for the theater, his apparent obliviousness to the political inferences that could be drawn from some of his actions—suggests that as late as the spring of 1681 he was himself part of this numerous body of uncommitted Englishmen, faithful to his own political principles but slow to enlist as an active Tory partisan.

Dryden's long-standing support of the Restoration Settlement in church and state was grounded in a view, widely accepted at the time, of the English constitution as a mixed government in which a precarious balance must at all times be maintained between the divergent interests of the king and his subjects. In his dedication of *All for Love* in March 1678, he expressed his political faith in general terms that transcend the particular compliment intended to Danby.

Moderation is doubtless an establishment of greatness; but there is a steadiness of temper which is likewise requisite in a minister of state; so equal a mixture of both virtues, that he may stand like an isthmus betwixt the two encroaching seas of arbitrary power, and lawless anarchy. The undertaking would be difficult to any but an extraordinary genius, to stand at the line, and to divide the limits; to pay what is due to the great representative of the nation, and neither to enhance, nor to yield up, the undoubted prerogatives of the crown. These, my lord, are the proper virtues of a noble Englishman, as indeed they are properly English virtues; no people in the world being capable of using them, but we who have the happiness to be born under so equal, and so well poised a government;—a government which has all the advantages of liberty beyond a commonwealth, and all the marks of kingly sovereignty, without the danger of a tyranny. . . . The nature of our government, above all others, is exactly suited both to the situation of our country, and the temper of the natives. . . . And, therefore, neither the arbitrary power of One, in a monarchy, nor of Many, in a commonwealth, could make us greater than we are.[42]

Intestine conflict is endemic to a mixed government, for on each side different interests are at stake: liberty of the subject on the side of the great representative of the nation, and the prerogative on the side of the crown. But out of the continual opposition of those interests, with each side restraining the other while advancing its own under the same difficulties, comes that equipoise which is the peculiar character of a balanced constitution, without which either arbitrary power or lawless anarchy would prevail.

In spite of cries of "arbitrary power" from the Whigs, and of "Forty-one is come again" from the Tories, there were still many Englishmen in March 1681 who were not convinced of the reality of either specter, who believed that kingly sovereignty must be preserved, but who also believed that it was in no immediate danger of being lost if Parliament continued to meet and press its own legitimate interest in insuring that the liberty of the subject would continue beyond the lifetime of the present king. It is in that light, I suggest, that we can read Dryden's tribute to a family who, not as private persons — for "every remonstrance of private men has the seed of treason in it" — but as members of Parliament, had "been always eminent in the support and favour of our religion and liberties," exercising their proper responsibilities as part of the great representative of the nation.[43]

Less than a fortnight after he had made that tribute public, Dryden would express one more time his sanguine hopes for the present safety of the balanced constitution. At Oxford on 19 March 1681, the Saturday before Parliament's opening on Monday, the king and members of both parties met on neutral ground to witness a performance of Charles Saunders's *Tamerlane the Great* and to hear an epilogue that Dryden had written for this occasion. Coming at midpoint between his earlier prologues and epilogues and those of a very different kind which would follow later, this epilogue is an anomaly from which both the theatrical orientation of the first group and the partisan propaganda of the second are absent. Neutrality would in any case be necessary before such a mixed audience, but the particular solution Dryden adopted was to appeal to the balanced constitution in which he had all along placed his faith. He characterized members of both parties assembled as responsible Englishmen whose "daies on publick thoughts are bent / Past ills to heal, and future to prevent," each side pursuing its own legitimate interest, "The Kings

Prerogative, the Peoples right," which, if preserved in equal proportion, may yet lead to harmony and "a prosp'rous end."

> This Place the seat of Peace, the quiet Cell
> Where Arts remov'd from noisy business dwell,
> Shou'd calm your Wills, unite the jarring parts,
> And with a kind Contagion seize your hearts:
> Oh! may its Genius, like soft Musick move,
> And tune you all to Concord and to Love.
> Our Ark that has in Tempests long been tost,
> Cou'd never land on so secure a Coast.
> From hence you may look back on Civil Rage,
> And view the ruines of the former Age.
> Here a New World its glories may unfold,
> And here be sav'd the remnants of the Old. [44]

That was not the expectation of the court and its partisans,
and events would quickly prove them right. Confronted with the
prospect of a third exclusion bill, the king dissolved his new Parliament, the last he would ever summon, on 28 March. That date
marks the end of the Exclusion Crisis in a strict sense, the two-
year effort to pass or prevent an act of Parliament excluding the
heir from the throne: two years of debates, dissolutions, cam-
paigns, and elections in which the Whigs had possessed the initiative. With the coming of spring the initiative would pass to the
court. The remainder of the year would be taken up with a massive propaganda campaign led off on 8 April by the appearance
of *His Majesties Declaration to All His Loving Subjects, Touching
the Causes and Reasons That Moved Him to Dissolve the Two
Last Parliaments,* which announced the theme the Tory press
would dutifully follow in the coming months. The purpose of this
campaign was not to attempt the conversion of the Whig partisans, but to appeal to the instinctive loyalty of the great middle
sector of the nation, until now neither Whig nor Tory, by persuading them that during the last two parliaments the delicate
equilibrium between opposite interests upon which the constitution depended had been on the point of breaking down under
pressure from a House of Commons intent on destroying the
king's prerogative in the name of "Religion, Liberty, and Property," and that it was only by dissolving these factious assemblies
that the king had saved the nation from what Dryden had called
the "encroaching sea" of "lawless anarchy."

His Majesties Declaration closed by expressing the hope that a little time would "open the Eyes of all Our good Subjects" to the evil designs against the constitution of church and state which had been carried on under the cloak of legality. L'Estrange announced in the first issue of *The Observator* on 13 April that the purpose of his periodical would be "the Undeceiving of the People." Over the next few months the growing enlightenment of the public became a constant theme of the Tory newspapers, which announced with satisfaction that, in the words of one of them, "Mens eyes at last are open."

One of the earliest prizes in this new campaign to awaken the uncommitted from their complacency was Dryden, who by the middle of the year was certainly at work writing political prologues and epilogues and, almost surely, writing the poem of more than a thousand lines which he would finish in November. *Absalom and Achitophel,* like *The Hind and the Panther* five and a half years later, would demonstrate the power with which Dryden could assimilate and turn to his own use arguments by which he had first been persuaded himself. The great poem he published in November 1681 was the brightest weapon in the armory of government propaganda that had been growing steadily for eight months.

In a sense different from the one he intended, Saintsbury was right when he said that in writing *Absalom and Achitophel* Dryden "reflected the sympathies of the nation at large." He reflected not the segment that was committed to party factionalism from the outset of the struggle, but the nation at large who watched and waited and cast their lot only when the angry debates in Parliament had been silenced.[45]

NOTES

1. *A Modest Vindication of the Earl of Shaftesbury: In a Letter to a Friend concerning his being Elected King of Poland* (London, 1681), p. 4.

2. I have traced the growth of this myth in "Legends Not Histories: The Case of *Absalom and Achitophel*," in *Studies in Eighteenth-Century Culture,* ed. Harold E. Pagliaro (Madison: University of Wisconsin Press, 1975), 4: 13-29.

3. Malone, ed., *The Critical and Miscellaneous Prose Works of John Dryden* (London, 1800), 1: 119.

4. Scott, ed., *The Works of John Dryden* (London, 1808), 9: 443; 6: 368-369. See also 1: 233-237.

5. See Bell, *Poetical Works of John Dryden* (London, 1854), pp. 48-52; Christie, *The Poetical Works of John Dryden* (London, 1870), pp. xlvi-xlvii.

6. See "Political Aspects of Dryden's *Amboyna* and *The Spanish Fryar*," *University of Michigan Publications in Language and Literature* 8 (1932): 119-132.

7. Saintsbury, *Dryden* (London, 1881), pp. 72-73.

8. "Dryden as Historiographer-Royal: The Authorship of *His Majesties Declaration Defended*, 1681," *Review of English Studies* 11 (1935): 284-298.

9. Charles E. Ward, *The Life of John Dryden* (Chapel Hill: University of North Carolina Press, 1961), p. 150. See also pp. 154-155.

10. See "Dryden as Historiographer Royal, and the Authorship of *His Majesties Declaration Defended*," *Modern Philology* 75 (1978): 261-272. For the use of similar arguments to disprove Dryden's authorship of another anonymous prose pamphlet attributed to him by Ward, see Thomas C. Faulkner, "Dryden and *Great and Weighty Considerations*: An Incorrect Attribution," *Studies in English Literature* 11 (1917): 417-425.

11. See Ward, *Life of Dryden*, pp. 125-126, 133, 144, 150; George McFadden, *Dryden: The Public Writer, 1660-1685* (Princeton, N.J.: Princeton University Press, 1978), pp. 204-205.

12. See McFadden, *Dryden: Public Writer*, pp. 208-211.

13. See Ward, *Life of Dryden*, p. 144; McFadden, *Dryden: Public Writer*, pp. 206-207.

14. See Ward, *Life of Dryden*, pp. 148, 156; McFadden, *Dryden: Public Writer*, p. 208.

15. See "Why Was Dryden's *Mr. Limberham* Banned?: A Problem in Restoration Theatre History," *Restoration and 18th Century Theatre Research* 13 (1974): 1-11. For earlier speculations, see Derrick, *The Miscellaneous Works of John Dryden, Esq.* (London, 1760), 1: xxii; Malone, *Works of Dryden*, 1: 117; Scott, *Works of Dryden*, 1: 222.

16. Scott, *Works of Dryden*, 5: 302.

17. Ibid., 1: 221. See also Malone, *Works of Dryden*, 3: 9.

18. Ward, *Life of Dryden*, pp. 125-126.

19. Haley, *The First Earl of Shaftesbury* (Oxford: Clarendon Press, 1968), pp. 441, 461.

20. Browning, *Thomas Osborne, Earl of Danby and Duke of Leeds, 1632-1712* (Glasgow: Jackson, Son and Co., 1951), 1: 218, 235, 264.

21. McFadden, *Dryden: Public Writer*, pp. 209-211.

22. See Ward, *Life of Dryden*, p. 352, n. 1; McFadden, *Dryden: Public Writer*, p. 208.

23. See John Harold Wilson, "Six Restoration Play-Dates," *Notes and*

Queries 207 (1962): 222; William Van Lennep, Emmett L. Avery, and Arthur H. Scouten, eds. *The London Stage, 1660-1800, Part I: 1660-1700* (Carbondale: Southern Illinois University Press, 1965), p. 273.

24. See Ward, *Life of Dryden,* pp. 146, 156.

25. See Van Lennep, *London Stage, Part I,* p. 292.

26. "Prologue at Oxford, 1680," in *The Works of John Dryden* (Berkeley and Los Angeles: University of California Press, 1956-), 1: 160-161, 401 (hereafter cited as California edition).

27. "Prologue" to *The Loyal General,* ibid., 1: 163-164.

28. "Prologue" to *The Spanish Fryar,* in James Kinsley, ed., *The Poems of John Dryden* (Oxford: Clarendon Press, 1958), 1:206-207.

29. "Prologue" to *Caesar Borgia,* in California edition, *Works of Dryden,* 1: 161-162.

30. "Epilogue" to *Troilus and Cressida,* in Kinsley, *Poems,* 1: 173-174.

31. Scott, *Works of Dryden,* 6: 381.

32. See Haley, *Shaftesbury,* pp. 357, 360.

33. See the *True Domestick Intelligence* (Nathaniel Thompson), no. 45, 9 December 1679.

34. See J. R. Jones, "Shaftesbury's 'Worthy Men': A Whig View of the Parliament of 1679," *Bulletin of the Institute of Historical Research* 30 (1957): 232-241.

35. See Andrew Browning and Doreen J. Milne, "An Exclusion Bill Division List," *Bulletin of the Institute of Historical Research* 23 (1950): 205-225.

36. See *The Humble Address and Advice of Several of the Peers of This Realm, for the Sitting of the Parliament. Presented to His Majesty at White-Hall, the 7th of December 1679* (London, 1679).

37. See *Reasons for the Indictment of the D. of York, Presented to the Grand-Jury of Middlesex, Saturday June 26. 80. By the Persons here under-nam'd* (London, 1680). This broadside also describes the renewal of the attempt on June 30, in which Lord Clare was involved.

38. See E. S. de Beer, "The House of Lords in the Parliament of 1680," *Bulletin of the Institute of Historical Research* 20 (1943-45): 22-37; *Journals of the House of Lords* 13: 666.

39. *The Earl of Essex His Speech at the Delivery of the Petition* (London, 1681).

40. The date on Narcissus Luttrell's copy of the pamphlet.

41. The date on Luttrell's copy of the poem.

42. Scott, *Works of Dryden,* 5: 300-301.

43. For Dryden's censure of "private men," see ibid., p. 302.

44. "Epilogue Spoken to the King at Oxford," in California edition, *Works of Dryden,* 2: 180-181.

45. I wish to thank Professor Robert D. Hume for suggestions in dating several of Dryden's plays.

IV

HENRY FIELDING AND POLITICS AT
THE LITTLE HAYMARKET, 1728-1737

Robert D. Hume

> Fielding . . . was a young and uncer-
> tain writer. . . . At the heart of his
> literary uncertainty was a political
> uncertainty — an inability to choose
> between two different political
> groups and two different concep-
> tions of the nature of man. As Field-
> ing's political views changed, so did
> the plays he wrote, as well as the
> companies that performed them.
> His impressive abilities were wasted
> as he shifted mercurially between
> opposing political and literary
> camps.
> — Brian McCrea[1]

Few scholars have been much interested in Fielding's highly successful career as a dramatist. To most it has seemed a false start.
Readers tend to find the conventional plays derivative and sentimental, the topical ones scrappy and superficial. The plays are
most often discussed for what they tell us about Fielding's political allegiances, a touchy subject for those sensitive about charges
of tergiversation. Our understanding of Fielding's politics has

79

been greatly advanced during the past decade by the work of Bertrand Goldgar and Brian McCrea, but we may fairly say that even these studies rest on unsubstantiated assumptions about the London theaters (especially the Little Haymarket) and treat Fielding's movements from theater to theater as reflections of his "changing" political allegiances.

To understand Fielding's dramatic career, we need to ask a number of rather elementary questions. Who operated the Little Haymarket? What exactly was its repertory? What sort of managerial position did Fielding occupy at the Little Haymarket, and when? What do his changes of theater signify? Was the Little Haymarket more political than other theaters prior to 1737? What do we mean by a "political" play? A reconsideration of these matters will lead us toward a reevaluation best posed in yet another question: How significant are politics in Fielding's career prior to 1739? I am going to argue that Fielding scholars have not understood the practical realities of the London theater world of the 1730s very well; and that a long-standing predisposition to see Fielding in partisan political terms has continued to distort our understanding of the plays and the shape of his career.

THE LITTLE THEATER IN THE HAYMARKET

The importance of the Little Haymarket to Fielding's career has been almost universally assumed, and quite correctly so. About half of his plays were first staged there, including his greatest hits, *The Author's Farce, Tom Thumb, Pasquin,* and *The Historical Register.* J. Paul Hunter's capsule description is a fair representation of current scholarly opinion:

The Little Theatre at the Haymarket . . . was small and less elaborately equipped than the more prominent and prestigious houses at Drury Lane and Covent Garden. It specialized in topical satire, and its audiences expected an anti-Establishment theater of ideas rather than the revivals and conventional five-act plays presented at the other houses. Its actors, although usually younger and less experienced than those elsewhere, thus became practiced and adept at a certain kind of satirical performance. The Haymarket was Fielding's theatrical home for five of the next eight seasons [following 1728-29], and it asserted a significant control over both the frequency and the kind of writing he undertook.[2]

Though I myself have said similar things in print, this view of the Little Haymarket is neither complete nor entirely accurate.

Our knowledge of the Little Haymarket is annoyingly scanty.[3] It was built in 1720 by John Potter, a carpenter and scene painter for the Haymarket Opera House. Through the spring of 1728 it functioned as a roadhouse, booking visiting French troupes, concerts, jugglers, variety shows—everything short of the Harlem Globetrotters. We have not a scrap of evidence about its dimensions, audience capacity, or box-office maximum.[4] From Potter's petition against the 1735 playhouse bill we learn that he claimed to have spent "at least" £1000 building the theater, plus £200 for rights to the ground (plus, presumably, annual ground rent), and another £500 for his stock of "Scenes, Machines, Cloaths, and other Decorations."[5] These are startlingly low figures. Giffard's Goodman's Fields—a nice house, but done with an eye to economy—cost £2300 in 1732; Rich's Covent Garden cost £6000 the same year. Given the sums regularly spent by the major theaters on costumes and scenery (£100 for a single production was not unusual), £500 for the entire stock is a pittance.

We would like to know how many people could be seated in the theater. Three hundred is probably a safe guess as a minimum; 600-700 is perhaps a plausible maximum. The Haymarket Opera House is said to have been bigger: its normal capacity was about 760.[6] We know that in 1721-22, when Aaron Hill tried to get permission to open a "third" English theater company, he offered a rent of £270 per season for the Little Haymarket. Avery calls this "a rather large figure for a small theatre." But in fact we do not know how shall it was, or how many nights Hill thought he could operate. The Drury Lane managers paid at least £3 12s. per day (guaranteeing 200 nights use each season), or some £720 per annum.[7] Drury Lane probably held about a thousand at this time. If the Little Haymarket held 450, and Hill could operate 150 nights, a rent under £2 per night would have been quite manageable, even considering that the Little Haymarket generally charged about a shilling less per seat than the patent houses.

Following the astonishing and unprecedented success of *The Beggar's Opera* at Lincoln's Inn Fields in the spring of 1728, the Little Haymarket abruptly changed its modus operandi. Starting with a ballad opera called *Penelope* in May, and moving on to what was evidently a pirate production of *The Beggar's Opera* in June, the theater began to compete directly with the major houses. Performances were less frequent and casts much less fully advertised, but with the exception of 1734-35 (when a troupe of French comedians occupied the theater from November to June), the Little Haymarket was the venue for a substantial number of legitimate English plays every season until the passage of the Licensing Act.

The significance of the Little Haymarket as a competitive spur to the patent houses should certainly not be ignored or underestimated.[8] We should, however, take note of three significant facts. (1) We do not know who was manager at the Little Haymarket—if, indeed, it had a manager. (2) At no time between 1728 and 1737 was there a Little Haymarket company in the sense that there were regular acting companies under contract at Drury Lane, Lincoln's Inn Fields, and Goodman's Fields. (3) We cannot be certain that our performance records for the Little Haymarket are complete, or even close to complete. These are extremely disconcerting admissions, and they are quite important to our understanding of Fielding's relationship with the theater.

Almost all scholars seem to have assumed that there was a permanent acting company at the Haymarket, a company run by *someone*. John Loftis's statement that in 1731-32 "the management of the Little Theatre grew more cautious" is quite typical.[9] Plainly, John Potter retained ultimate control of what was performed at (or excluded from) his theater, and Loftis, for example, calls him "the theatre's manager." But though Potter was the proprietor, there is no evidence that he functioned as manager in the sense that Wilks, Cibber, and Booth did at Drury Lane, or John Rich at Lincoln's Inn Fields (and later at Covent Garden), or Henry Giffard at Goodman's Fields.

References to management (both complimentary and apoplectic) are frequent in authors' prefaces in these years, but in quartos of plays first staged at the Little Haymarket there is a singular silence about management—no thanks and no complaints. One of the few exceptions has some interesting and unexplored implications. In the preface to *The Restauration of King Charles II* (banned before performance in early 1732), Walter Aston tells a strange tale. "Mr. *Potter* (Master of the *New Theatre* in the *Hay-*

Market)...told me, Nothing must be play'd there till a Gentle-man of the *Treasury,* and another of the Exchequer, had read and approved it." Aston duly sought permission, and thought he had it. "I distributed the Parts, printed Bills and Tickets, and had it rehearsed thrice; but unexpectedly a *Message* came, to stop the Performance; for the Actors should be all taken up."[10] This passage has been noticed in connection with censorship, but the managerial implications have been ignored. Managers nor-mally accepted or refused plays and took responsibility for get-ting them to the stage, but in this case the author was left to nego-tiate with the authorities. Authors generally advised on the assign-ment of parts and attended rehearsals, but Aston clearly implies that he not only called the rehearsals himself (a managerial func-tion) but arranged for the printing of playbills and tickets— hardly a normal part of the author's duties at the other theaters.

Did the Little Haymarket have any kind of resident staff in the 1730s? A benefit was advertised for "Mr Green, Prompter" on 2 June 1731, but we have no other certain reference to the gentle-man, and hence no way of knowing whether he was part of a per-manent staff employed by Potter (ipso facto not very likely) or if he was simply a member of the ad hoc troupe that had been enjoying a success with *The Tragedy of Tragedies* and *The Fall of Mortimer* that spring. I do note what might be a reference to the same man in an ad for a single performance at the Little Hay-market, Wednesday, 26 January 1737. "As Mr Green could not possibly be sure of the House till Monday Night late, he hopes the Shortness of Time will plead his Excuse for not waiting on his Friends, and that they will favour him with their Company not-withstanding." This appears to imply that the three little pieces that made up the bill were simply jobbed into the theater on short notice when Mr. Green was able to arrange a date, presumably with Potter. A resident company with a manager would not work this way.

One could easily collect a multitude of modern scholarly refer-ences to "the young company at the Little Haymarket." This commonplace tends to obscure our lack of evidence that the the-ater was ever occupied by a regular repertory company in these years. Ads that omit casts make analysis maddeningly vague, but such facts as we have suggest two conclusions. First, different companies used the Haymarket each season.[11] Second, the principal "company" generally consisted of a handful of regulars plus others drawn from a large pool of fringe actors at liberty. Even the regulars changed with disconcerting frequency.

For the latter part of 1727-28, for example, analysis of advertised casts shows that the following distinct groups were using the Little Haymarket: (a) Mme Violante's mimes and tumblers; (b) a musical group that mounted *Penelope*; (c) a "New Company of English Comedians"; (d) a "New Company" that mounted *The Beggar's Opera*; (e) a group of actors — Giffard, Reynolds, Miss Mann, et al. — who prove to be the nucleus of the principal company using the theater in 1728-29. Or consider the season of 1732-33, more typical of these years. In September a pickup summer company occupied the theater. During the regular season most performances were by groups drawn from a mixed bag of minor professionals, though an English opera company also used the premises occasionally. On 28 May the Goodman's Fields company used the Little Haymarket for a benefit (possibly because management had refused the benefit at Goodman's Fields?). In June a company drawing personnel from both the English opera group and the regular company pool started a summer season. At least once (12 July) "a Company of Gentlemen" took over the house for a performance of *The Fair Penitent*. Late in July a few of the winter regulars staged a performance with a group of unknowns.

On the basis of a survey of the distinct groups that used the Little Haymarket between 1728 and 1737, I am convinced that it never ceased to be, de facto, a roadhouse. Potter appears to have rented it night by night (probably for longer on some occasions) to any group who wanted it.[12] We simply do not know how the extended company (if we may call it such) that used the house most often chose plays, bargained with authors, and made casting decisions. Could it use Potter's scanty set of scenes and costumes? Was use of them an optional extra? Did each performer provide his or her own clothes? We do not know. The repertory of the extended company is suggestive, a mixture of warhorses (*The Beaux Stratagem, Venice Preserv'd*) and contemporary drama, much of it brand new. I would hypothesize that the actors put on a few sure-fire pieces and also struck bargains with authors for new plays, terms doubtless varying with the author and the play. The large number of author benefits on the first or second night suggests an arrangement quite different from the third-night author benefit long traditional at the patent houses. An author who had underwritten the costs of a production might well have been able to claim any profit beyond the expenses and salaries he or she had guaranteed to cover.

The extended company deserves a further word of explanation. Most seasons a handful of regulars reappear in a lot of the productions for which we have casts. In 1729-30, for example, Wells, Mullart, Lacy, Stoppelaer, Dove, Hicks, Mrs. Mullart, Mrs. Clarke, Mrs. Nokes, and a few others seem to have been the heart of the company. They were joined by an ever-shifting succession of others, most of whom worked at the Little Haymarket only once, or very occasionally. Sometimes a performer would come over from another theater temporarily (Mrs. Killbee from Lincoln's Inn Fields), or a newcomer from Dublin would be snapped up (Paget, who arrived in June 1730). Most seasons there is a small, fairly stable core of performers and a large pool of interchangeable parts, drawn on as needed and available. The amount of recasting done within a single month is evidence that this group did not operate as a repertory company. The best modern comparison I can offer is the difference between a group like the New York Philharmonic and the pickup orchestras assembled in New York for anything from a new musical to a morning of work on television commercials. The Drury Lane and Lincoln's Inn Fields actors were almost invariably hired for the season, and this was also the case at Goodman's Fields. The Little Haymarket performers seem to have been freelancing. A hit like *The Author's Farce* or *Pasquin* gave the lucky ones hired for that show a spell of prosperity, but the norm was short-term work.[13]

Logic tells us there must have been someone among the freelancers each season who got up the productions of old plays and helped cast and stage the new ones. Giffard would be a plausible candidate for 1728-29; someone like Mullart might have taken over in 1729-30 after Giffard got a regular engagement at Goodman's Fields. Fielding's dislike of the treatment he received at the hands of the "Great Moguls" at Drury Lane and Lincoln's Inn Fields — a dislike shared by a high percentage of his fellow authors — probably explains his readiness to deal with a theater whose modus operandi seems to have been do-it-yourself.

Our sense of the Little Haymarket's offerings would be distinctly more solid if we were certain that we possessed complete performance records. Unfortunately, this is not the case. As far as I am aware, no one has asked the question heretofore, but an examination of the offerings recorded in *The London Stage* raises some qualms. Three patterns emerge clearly. Very occasionally, the theater had a smash hit like *Pasquin,* at which time it operated five or six days a week. The more normal pattern in times of relatively frequent ads is two or three performances a week. But for significant stretches every season, we find blanks of many days and sometimes weeks. Conceivably the theater was dark most of these nights. (Potter did book in nontheatrical entertainments not recorded in *The London Stage.*) But we have to allow for the possibility that handbills and a house bill were sometimes regarded as sufficient advertising. This idea is reinforced by an examination of the extant ads: an astonishing number are for benefits. There are two possible explanations. (1) The extended company of fringe professionals who used the theater tended not to advertise unless a benefit was involved or a poor turnout feared. (2) The extended company treated benefits as the principal component of each actor's income, not as a special bonus. Whatever the truth of the matter, we would be rash to assume that we can be certain what was performed at the Little Haymarket.

What we do know of the repertory does not altogether bear out the cliches about "topical satire" and "anti-Establishment theater of ideas." If, for example, we consider the season of 1735-36, during which *Pasquin* enjoyed its phenomenal run, we find the following: *Jane Shore* (1715), *Love and a Bottle* (1698); *A Bold Stroke for a Wife* (1718), *The Recruiting Officer* (1706), *The Inconstant* (1702), *The Beaux Stratagem* (1707), *The Spanish Fryar* (1680), *The Twin-Rivals* (1702), Young's *Revenge* (1721), *The Careless Husband* (1704), *Aesop* (1697), *The Provok'd Husband* (1728), and *The Beggar's Opera* (1728). Most of these plays were standard fare at the patent theaters. The difference in the Little Haymarket's offerings of old plays lies in a heavy bias toward post-1700 works. At this time more than 50 percent of the repertory plays at Drury Lane and Covent Garden were pre-1695, and more than 80 percent were pre-1708.[14] Of course the Little Haymarket also mounted a flock of new plays: Charke, *The Carnival;*

Drury, *The Rival Milliners*; Haywood (?), *Arden of Feversham*; anon., *The Contract*; anon., *The Heroick Footman*; Dorman, *The Female Rake*; Cooper, *The Nobleman*; Phillips, *The Rival Captains*; Lillo, *Fatal Curiosity*; anon., *The Comical Disappointment*; "Jack Juniper," *The Deposing and Death of Queen Gin*. Most of these works proved quite ephemeral.

We can legitimately say of the Little Haymarket that it offered far more new plays than the other theaters and that many of them were topical. Having just read my way through all Little Haymarket plays that were preserved and printed, I am prepared to say flatly that few of them qualify as theater of ideas or even as anti-Establishment. One could more accurately characterize the Little Haymarket plays as an odd combination of earnest amateur efforts and rollicking farces, most of them very lightweight indeed. The Little Haymarket did launch some genuinely experimental drama at a time when other houses tended to be unreceptive. Lillo's *Fatal Curiosity* (1736) springs to mind, though of course that must be credited to Fielding's judgment. One fact is obvious, however: the Little Haymarket repertory is far less political than has generally been assumed.

It is hard to say how much influence the Little Haymarket exerted on the kind of writing Fielding undertook. Obviously the actors could not compete with the personnel of the major houses in heavyweight repertory, but they must have been good enough to make productions of standard mainpieces presentable. Since the Little Haymarket did not have a "Great Mogul" making script decisions, Fielding did not have to tailor his pieces to anyone else's preconceptions. If we survey the new plays staged before *The Author's Farce,* we will find little in the way of inspiration. Samuel Johnson of Cheshire's *Hurlothrumbo* (1729) might have given Fielding a notion toward *Tom Thumb.* But just about all of the other new plays fall into standard categories, from Wandesford's dreary *Fatal Love* and Hatchett's *The Rival Father: or, The Death of Achilles* to ballad operas such as Coffey's *The Beggar's Wedding* and farces such as Mottley's *The Craftsman.* Such works were staged at all the theaters. To understand why Fielding turned to the Little Haymarket we will need to consider the vexed problem of his dealings with various theaters, especially Drury Lane.

FIELDING'S RELATIONSHIPS WITH THE
LONDON THEATERS

Scholars have almost unanimously assumed that Fielding's changes of theatrical venue signal political shifts on his part. Thus Goldgar tells us that "Fielding's shift to Drury Lane [in 1732]...represented a sincere bid for [Walpole's] patronage," and that "his return to the Haymarket with *Don Quixote in England* signaled a move toward the opposition."[15] Likewise, Brian McCrea's book relies heavily on this assumption. ("As Fielding's political views changed, so did the plays he wrote, as well as the companies that performed them," p. 51.) McCrea's narrative is riddled with terms indicative of this sense of vacillation: "shifts," "returned to," "rejoined," "left," "moved to," "shifting between." Unfortunately, this entire theory is unsound, and modern critics, who have taken it over from Wilbur Cross, have been seriously misled by it.

The plain, dull truth is that Fielding was a freelance writer who peddled his plays where he could get them accepted. I am not aware of a shred of evidence that Fielding ever signed a contract with a particular theater.[16] Such exclusive arrangements were common in the late seventeenth century (Dryden, Shadwell, Lee, and Crowne were all house writers at various times), but aside from people employed by a theater in another capacity (Christopher Bullock as actor at Lincoln's Inn Fields, John Thurmond as dancing master at Drury Lane), exclusive arrangements were not common after 1708. At the patent theaters an author was entitled to the profits of the third night (gross take minus a fixed house charge). If a play ran six nights or longer the house usually allowed the author profits on the sixth and every third night thereafter through the first unbroken run. That ended any obligation to the author.[17] A script was completely beyond the author's control once it had been produced. Technically, he held publication rights, but only if pirates were uninterested in the play. Other theaters could mount the piece if they cared to, altered any way they chose.[18]

Fielding's first play, *Love in Several Masques*, was accepted by Drury Lane and produced in February 1728. Given the inveterate hostility of the triumvirate managers to risking time and money on new plays, this was quite a triumph, equivalent to having one's first short story published by *The New Yorker*. How much Fielding was helped by the recommendation of Lady Mary Wortley Montagu we do not know. Fielding's next two efforts were refused by the Drury Lane managers—an early version of *Don Quixote in England* and *The Temple Beau*. Fielding seems to have agreed with the verdict on the former;[19] the latter he peddled to Goodman's Fields, which produced it in January 1730.

Why Fielding went to the Little Haymarket in the first place has gone almost unconsidered. Scholars have generally ignored the issue or accepted Cross's muddled guess. Cross assumes that Fielding would have stayed with Goodman's Fields, but neighborhood opposition to the playhouse made it a bad bet. "Anticipating this result of the controversy [a silencing "by order of the King"], Fielding had already thrown in his fortunes with the Little Theatre in the Haymarket, where, on February 12, 1730, a ballad-opera entitled 'Love and Revenge, or the Vintner Tricked' was performed for his benefit."[20] We should note, however, that Goodman's Fields performed full blast until 29 April and that the silencing lasted less than two weeks. As for Fielding's throwing in his lot with the Little Haymarket, the 12 February benefit was almost certainly for the actor Timothy Fielding, who had been performing there regularly that winter.

Henry Fielding's first documented connection with the Little Haymarket is the production of *The Author's Farce* there on 30 March. Why did he not offer the play to Goodman's Fields? Perhaps he did, but in fact Goodman's Fields was not a promising venue for an ambitious writer. The company's basic repertory policy stressed eighteenth-century classics, much the same repertory as Drury Lane and Lincoln's Inn Fields, but concentrating on post-1700 plays. At no time did Goodman's Fields plunge heavily into new plays. Fielding had already been rejected at least twice by Drury Lane and probably resented it. (The 1730 version of *The Author's Farce* is of course in part a satire on Wilks and Cibber as managers.) At Lincoln's Inn Fields John Rich was famous for his commitment to the pantomime Fielding despised and almost as celebrated for his harsh treatment of importunate authors ("It will not do").[21] We may guess, however, that Fielding did approach Rich, since he tells us that *The Wedding Day*, his "third dramatic performance," was rejected by Rich, after which he laid it aside until Garrick asked for it in 1743 (see the preface to *Miscellanies*). This must have taken place in 1729-30 or 1730-31. In short, there is a very high probability that Fielding took his work to the informal company occupying the Little Haymarket because he had no choice.

We do not know with whom Fielding bargained for performance at the Little Haymarket or on what terms *The Author's Farce* was produced. No one seems to have commented on the lack of an advertisement for an author's benefit the third night. Nor, apparently, did Fielding get a benefit when *Tom Thumb* was added to the bill on the ninth night. Indeed, the first benefit advertised is 13 May, the seventeenth night of *The Author's Farce* and the ninth of *Tom Thumb*, and that remained the only author benefit despite the astonishing forty nights achieved by *The Author's Farce* this season. The peculiarity is reinforced when we note that Fielding received third- and sixth-night benefits for his *Rape upon Rape,* premiered 23 June. What financial arrangements Fielding made for *The Author's Farce* and *Tom Thumb* we can only speculate. The probability would seem to be that he accepted some sort of profit-sharing arrangement in place of a benefit, perhaps because he was unable to invest any cash up front or was unwilling to guarantee expenses. The seventeenth-night benefit I would explain as a thank-you for an unprecedented success and the usual benefit arrangement for *Rape upon Rape* as a sign of the actors' confidence in the young author.

We do not know Fielding's intentions at the start of the season of 1730-31. *The Modern Husband* appears to have been extant in draft by September 1730.[22] We do not know whether Fielding held the play for more work or whether he submitted it unsuccessfully to one or more of the theaters. Cross seems to me quite right in saying that "its subject was such as to make any theatre . . . hesitate to take it." I differ with him, however, when he asserts that the play was not mounted at the Little Haymarket because "the company at the Haymarket could have done nothing with it."[23] Granted, the Little Haymarket actors were not in a league with Drury Lane's established stars, but if the company could present passable performances of *The Provok'd Husband* and *The Beaux Stratagem* (as they evidently did in 1730-31), there is no reason they could not have made a respectable job of *The Modern Husband.*

One sign of a flirtation with John Rich, almost unremarked by modern scholars, is a production of *Rape upon Rape* (renamed *The Coffee House Politician*) at Lincoln's Inn Fields in December. I take this as evidence of more than the usual piracy because Fielding was allowed an author's benefit on 7 December—highly unusual, even though the ads call the play "revis'd." Fielding's smashing success with *The Author's Farce* and *Tom Thumb* might well have interested John Rich in his work. But *The Modern Husband* was not the sort of play Rich cared for, and perhaps manager and playwright did not hit it off. At any rate, all of Fielding's new plays this season came out at the Little Haymarket—*The Tragedy of Tragedies, The Letter Writers,* and *The Welsh Opera.* Had *The Grub-Street Opera* been performed, the Little Haymarket would, of course, have been the venue. We may note that Fielding received regular author benefits throughout the runs of these plays.

Fielding's move to Drury Lane in the season of 1731-32 is almost always treated as a momentous matter, a kind of public announcement of a change in his political views. Thus Goldgar: "in the move to Drury Lane, the dedication to *The Modern Husband,* and the epilogue to *The Modish Couple* Fielding unmistakably and publicly aligned himself with the Walpole camp."[24] Passing over the dedication and the epilogue for the moment, we need to ask whether writing for Drury Lane amounted to a public endorsement of Walpole in 1732. The answer is clearly negative. Under the triumvirate (i.e., until September 1732) Drury Lane was certainly pro-Whig and pro-ministry. But as John Loftis rightly says, in practice this meant that the theater "did not present plays patently hostile to Walpole. Yet Drury Lane cannot be said to have actively supported Walpole or his policies."[25]

The facts of Fielding's return to Drury Lane are extremely simple. First, Drury Lane was the best and most prestigious company. Every writer hoped to have plays staged at Drury Lane. Any ambitious author given a chance to have his work produced by a wealthy, (apparently) stable, and celebrated management, instead of at a fringe theater by hedgerow actors working on a pickup basis, would be out of his mind not to accept. And second, Fielding had little choice. The Little Haymarket was suppressed by the authorities in July 1731, and when he came to town that fall (at an unknown date) there would have been no way to guess when it might reopen, if ever. Fielding's choices for 1731-32 were

(a) Lincoln's Inn Fields, where he had evidently not got on with Rich a year earlier; (b) Goodman's Fields, whose management was little disposed to mount new plays; and (c) Drury Lane. Given Fielding's successes of the previous two seasons, Wilks and Cibber were probably glad to have his work (unflattering portraits in *The Author's Farce* notwithstanding), and the chances are that Fielding was delighted with the opportunity.

An argument often repeated by modern scholars to prove the distinctness of the Drury Lane repertory versus that of the Little Haymarket is the lack of revival of Fielding's early shows when he moved to Drury Lane. The argument is used more generally to suggest the difference of the Little Haymarket from all three of the other theaters. The facts, however, contradict this tidy theory. *The Author's Farce* was not revived at Drury Lane in 1732 for the good reason that it satirized Wilks and Cibber. After their departure from management, Fielding rewrote the show and staged it at Drury Lane in January 1734 as a satire on Colley and Theophilus Cibber.[26] *Rape upon Rape* and *The Letter Writers* had basically failed (though of course Rich did pick up the former at Lincoln's Inn Fields). *The Welsh Opera* was probably under a political cloud. *Tom Thumb* (revised as *The Tragedy of Tragedies*) did get produced at Drury Lane in May 1732 and was revived a year later. It was also staged at Lincoln's Inn Fields in 1732, and Goodman's Fields had added it to the repertory there as early as March 1731. We may deduce from performance records that these plays did not transplant very successfully, but the record does not show a tidy distinction between Fielding's plays staged at Drury Lane and those produced at the Little Haymarket.

Fielding continued to stage all his new plays at Drury Lane during the season of 1732-33. *The Modern Husband* and *The Mock Doctor* had enjoyed good runs in the spring of 1732; *The Old Debauchees*, *The Covent Garden Tragedy*, and *Deborah* had not. But Fielding was a good enough bet that the managers would have been daft to refuse a script from him. Unfortunately for Fielding, the triumvirate management, in power since 1709, abruptly disintegrated at the start of the 1732-33 season. The company had a stormy year: young Theophilus Cibber, "renting" his father's share, squabbled fiercely with John Highmore, an amateur dabbler who had bought half of Booth's share, and John

Ellys, a painter who represented Wilks's widow. This bickering group had every reason to be happy with Fielding, whose *Miser* was a great success. How Fielding felt about the unappetizing Theophilus Cibber and the state of the theater we do not know, but he could scarcely have been rapturous.

Fielding's return to the Little Haymarket in the season of 1733-34 is one of the most misunderstood episodes in his theatrical career. Goldgar says that "his return to the Haymarket with *Don Quixote in England* signaled a move toward the opposition as clearly as his earlier change of theaters . . . had signaled a move toward the court party." McCrea says simply, "In 1734 he left Drury Lane and brought *Don Quixote in England* to the Haymarket theatre."[27] This is quite misleading. What happened had nothing to do with politics.

In the spring of 1733 Colley Cibber sold his share of Drury Lane to Highmore, thereby outraging his son. The sale gave Highmore control of the theater. At the start of the season of 1733-34 Theophilus led a walkout of Drury Lane actors, who objected to Highmore's interference. The rebels moved over to the Little Haymarket, where they acted daily from 26 September to 9 March.[28] Highmore was left with a handful of loyalists (notably Kitty Clive) and had to hire a group of actors without regular employment (some of whom had previously worked at the Little Haymarket) in order to put on any sort of season at all. Fielding's sympathies, and perhaps his sense of prudence, were with Highmore rather than with Theophilus Cibber and the rebels. At any rate, Fielding gave *Don Quixote in England,* not to the Drury Lane actors temporarily ensconced in the Little Haymarket, but to the scratch company assembled by Highmore at Drury Lane. The play actually went into rehearsal at Drury Lane. In February 1734, however, Highmore sold out in disgust to another amateur, Charles Fleetwood, who gave in and bought back his principal performers. On 8 March Theophilus Cibber and his cohorts regained possession of Drury Lane. This displaced most of the scratch company, who took *Don Quixote in England* with them to the vacant Little Haymarket, where it opened on 5 April, advertised as "By the Persons who rehearsed it in Drury Lane before the Union of the Companies." In short, not Fielding but the actors took *Don Quixote in England* to the Little Haymarket, and no political motive should be ascribed to Fielding.[29]

The *Don Quixote in England* tangle provides occasion to remark that we must beware of treating a theater name as indicative of a changeless *Ding an sich*. In the years at issue, Rich at Lincoln's Inn Fields/Covent Garden and Giffard at Goodman's Fields represent stable managements with settled repertory policies. The Little Haymarket had no manager, no stable acting company, and no fixed repertory policy. Drury Lane was very much a known quantity until September 1732 and again by 1735-36. In the three intervening seasons one hardly knows what is meant by "Drury Lane." In 1733-34 the Drury Lane actors performed their usual repertory at the Little Haymarket. Had Fielding given them *Don Quixote in England* one could legitimately argue that he had given it to the Drury Lane company. Would this have constituted a political statement?

What Fielding would have done in 1734-35 had the Little Haymarket been open to him we do not know. He had pilloried Theophilus Cibber in his revision of *The Author's Farce* (performed by the loyalists at Drury Lane with success in 1733-34), and he might well have preferred to take his work elsewhere. Since, however, the Little Haymarket was exclusively occupied by a troupe of French comedians from 26 October to 2 June, Fielding evidently found it expedient to take *An Old Man Taught Wisdom* and *The Universal Gallant* to Drury Lane. Neither was a success, and at some point Fielding must have developed his considerable dislike for the arrogant and incompetent Fleetwood.

Taking the political view, we might assume that Fielding was driven back to Drury Lane in 1734-35 by the fortuitous unavailability of the Little Haymarket, but that he would naturally hasten back there with *Pasquin* in 1735-36. In actuality, Fielding's first thought seems to have been to approach John Rich about having a play produced at Covent Garden. In a mocking dedication to Rich of *Tumble-Down Dick* (Little Hay, April 1736), Fielding says, "as *Pasquin* has proved of greater Advantage to me, than it could have been at any other Play-House, under their present Regulations, I am oblig'd to you for the Indifference you shew'd at my Proposal to you of bringing a Play on your Stage this Winter." In short, Fielding went back to the Little Haymarket when Drury Lane turned sour and he was rebuffed at Covent Garden.

Once again we can only guess at Fielding's financial arrangements with the Little Haymarket performers. No author's benefit is advertised at any time during *Pasquin*'s sixty-four performances this season. Almost all authorities have assumed that Fielding was serving as manager/entrepreneur, a hypothesis which seems highly likely to me. What Fielding thought he might do beyond the spring of 1736 is anyone's guess. In the event, he reassembled "The Great Mogul's Company of English Comedians" the following winter, after which the Licensing Act brought Fielding's theatrical career to an abrupt close.

Fielding's changes of theater can be fully explained without reference to politics. As Goldgar has convincingly argued, what we see between 1728 and 1737 is an ambitious young playwright aggressively seeking his own advantage wherever it lies. Fielding wanted to be a *playwright*. Exactly how much nondramatic writing he did prior to 1737 is impossible to say, but certainly he was not publishing such work under his own name. Had he merely wanted to earn a living with his pen, there were plenty of possibilities open to him; but evidence that he wished to pursue them remains scanty and inconclusive.[30] Playwrights must have venues for their plays, and successful though he was, Fielding did not always find it easy to peddle his work. With this understood, we can proceed to the vexed matter of political drama in the 1730s.

POLITICS ON THE LONDON STAGE, 1728-1737

For a general account of political drama in the early eighteenth century, the reader can turn to Loftis. My concerns here are much more specific. We need to inquire, first, what sorts of political plays are to be found on stage in the decade at issue, and second, whether the Little Haymarket's offerings are demonstrably more political than those of the other theaters prior to the season of 1736-37, which must be treated as a special case.

What counts as a "political" play? This is by no means merely a semantic or a pedantic question. If Cross and a host of others see *Tom Thumb* as a systematic debunking of Walpole, but Bertrand Goldgar finds no evidence of an audience responding to it in political terms, then we have a problem. (I have dealt with some of the theoretical questions at length elsewhere.[31]) Neither apparent intention nor audience reaction is an altogether reliable criterion. Whatever we may think Fielding was up to in *Tom*

Thumb, and however tidily we can expound "satiric hits," the play is de facto nonpolitical if we can find no evidence that anyone in the 1730s audience saw it in political terms.[32] Before about 1715 this would not be a safe assumption, but the feisty thirties newspapers were quick to crow (or sling mud) when they thought a play was making a political point. *Tom Thumb* is treated as a harmless piece of foolery by both Walpole's papers and the opposition press, potent evidence that people were not responding to it in political terms, however appropriate the political reading seems to us. Conversely, an apparently harmless play could be "explained into a satire," as Walpole's propagandists claimed was done with *The Beggar's Opera.* For the purposes of my investigation here, I will consider all the plays treated as political by Loftis, Goldgar, and Jean Kern.[33]

On the basis of a reading of these plays, of which about forty are preserved, I would suggest that we need to distinguish between *topical allusion plays* and *application plays.* Most of the former are comedies, most of the latter tragedies, though the generic distinction is not absolute. Topical allusion plays refer openly to current events (and sometimes to real people, thinly disguised), generally in a snide or hostile way. *Pasquin* is a good example. Application plays rely on the audience to draw parallels and see connections: for example, applying the lessons of Scanderbeg, the Earl of Essex, or Charles I to the times and court of George II, as in Havard's *Scanderbeg,* Ralph's *The Fall of the Earl of Essex,* and Havard's *King Charles the First.* The difference between the two types is illustrated by comparing *The Beggar's Opera,* which caused a flap but did Walpole little harm, and *Polly,* which was firmly suppressed.[34] Both censorship and journalistic uproar in the 1730s suggest that application plays were taken a great deal more seriously.

Just how political were the offerings at the Little Haymarket? Pat Rogers sums up the usual view when he says that "the management...[of the Little Haymarket] sailed closer to the wind than any other house, and so the theatre was closed by the authorities at regular intervals."[35] With the freak exception of *Don Quixote in England,* all the "political" plays mounted there fall in two periods, 1728-1731 and 1736-1737. Since such "significant control" as the Little Haymarket may have exerted over Fielding (in Hunter's phrase) must have derived from expectations generated by plays in the early period, let us consider them.

Only eleven titles are germane. The first three produced suggest to Loftis that the Little Haymarket was "sympathetic to Walpole in the season of 1728-9." Mottley's *The Craftsman* (October 1728) is a very lightweight afterpiece farce built on a love plot and incidentally ridiculing "the journal of that name, its fictional author, Caleb D'Anvers, and the bumpkin squires who read it."[36] The tone is so light and good-humored that one can hardly see the piece (which limped through six nights) as much of a satire. Odell's *The Smugglers* and *The Patron* ran a single night as a double bill in May 1729. The former is a romantic farce that capitalizes on the taste for low-life engendered by *The Beggar's Opera* and tries to expose illegal practices that hurt the public, as the author explains in his dedication to George Doddington, "One of the Lords Commissioners of His Majesty's Treasury." The noble depiction of Trusty, the honest exciseman, would certainly have pleased Walpole. I do not know quite what to make of *The Patron, or The Statesman's Opera.* As Loftis observes, the piece "seems to be rich in political innuendo, though the butt of its satire is not at all clear."[37] Lord Falcon, "a minister of State," is a lying scoundrel, bamboozled into giving the deserving Merit a government post of £400 per annum in return for the favors of a prostitute posing as Merit's wife. From someone other than Odell one might take this as a hit at the way business was done in Walpole's administration. But Odell was a Walpole loyalist who became deputy licenser of plays after 1737. If this damp squib was meant as a hit at the administration, it found no favor, and it was forgotten or forgiven. Loftis somewhat misleadingly calls these three plays evidence of a "flirtation between the Little Theatre in the Haymarket and the Minister."

On the politicality of *The Author's Farce* (March 1730). *Tom Thumb* (April), and *The Tragedy of Tragedies* (March 1731), I entirely agree with Goldgar. One can espy (or think one espies) all sorts of flippant or snippy "political" allusions, but dead silence on the subject in contemporary sources forces us to treat them as effectively nonpolitical. One hint of Fielding's noninvolvement at this point is an addition grafted onto *Tom Thumb* (30 November 1730) called *The Battle of the Poets,* evidently by Thomas Cooke, with whom Fielding was later friendly. *The Battle* is a tart, amusing satire on the contention of Cibber, Theobald, Dennis, Ridpath, and Stephen Duck for the vacant laureateship. Uncharacteristically, Fielding seems not to have been amused, and the

Daily Journal carries a notice signed "Henry Fielding" stating that he has "never seen this additional Act, nor [is] in any ways concerned therein."[38] Obviously Fielding did not control the use the Little Haymarket actors made of his play, even though he was taking his work there this season. His disavowal may be pique at unauthorized additions or may suggest a desire not to antagonize Cibber and Drury Lane.

The Welsh Opera (an afterpiece first staged with *The Tragedy of Tragedies* in April 1731) is certainly an audacious indulgence in *lèse-majesté*. That it never reached the stage in mainpiece form (as *The Grub-Street Opera*) comes as no surprise, but whether the original afterpiece was written as a party satire on Walpole is another matter. Almost all criticism has focused on *The Grub-Street Opera,* a very different work indeed.[39] Fielding gives us Sir Owen Apshinken as the henpecked George II; Lady Apshinken as Queen Caroline; Master Owen ("in love with Womankind") as the stupid and womanizing Prince of Wales; the butler Robin as Sir Robert Walpole; Sweetissa the waiting woman as Walpole's mistress, Molly Skerrit; William the coachman, Robin's rival for Sweetissa, as the opposition leader William Pulteney; John the groom as John, Lord Hervey; and Thomas the gardener as Thomas Pelham-Holles, duke of Newcastle. Fielding's unkind characterizations are hilarious but entirely indirect. The work is a low burlesque, ridiculing both royal family and parliamentary leaders by diminishing them to the level of an ill-regulated Welsh household.

McCrea calls *The Welsh Opera* an "attack on Walpole,"[40] but once again Goldgar's sober historical investigations throw cold water on a political reading. *The Fall of Mortimer,* staged 12 May 1731, is a genuine political attack on Walpole, and it caused a great hubbub. On at least five occasions *The Welsh Opera* served as afterpiece for this incendiary piece. But as Goldgar says, "Neither *The Welsh Opera* nor its promised revision was mentioned in all the furor in the press . . . nor did the pamphlet warfare which raged over *The Fall of Mortimer* take any notice of Fielding. And unlike *The Fall of Mortimer* and other anti-Walpole works, his plays are not included in the list of 'false and scandalous Representations' by 'State-Incendiaries' drawn up by the grand jury of Middlesex in July."[41] *The Welsh Opera* is unquestionably cynical about the royal family and about parliamentary bigwigs, but it is just as nasty about Pulteney as it is about Walpole. How one could legitimately consider it a party document is hard to see. Scandalous yes; partisan no.

The Fall of Mortimer is an altogether different matter. Someone (William Hatchett?) altered "Mountfort's" *King Edward III* (1691) to make it aim very clearly at Walpole. Like other "Majesty Misled" plays, this one relies on an application drawn from a safely remote subject. Some bits of the prologue will give the idea: "We change the ancient for the modern Dress. . . . The *British* Constitution . . . by *one bad Man* was almost sacrific'd . . . foul Corruption was become a Trade . . . Patriot Band . . . The Monster is cast down. . . . A *Villain-Statesman,* not the *King* to blame." The king finally orders Mortimer (= Walpole) executed for his crimes (thereby becoming "a King indeed!") and says: "Such be the Fate of all, who dare abuse / The Ministerial Function" (p. 61).

We can hardly be surprised that this flagrant smear aroused the wrath of the authorities. Even so, it managed fifteen performances. Exactly how pressure was brought we do not know, but evidently some of the actors got scared. An ad for a sixteenth performance, 30 June, states: "The Company of Comedians have determined to play notwithstanding the Opposition made by some of the Company to prevent the Performance." At this point the authorities got tough and included the play in a grand jury warrant (see the *Daily Courant,* 8 July). When the play was next announced on 21 July, constables showed up to arrest the actors, who "all made their Escapes." On 20 August the actors tried to resume business, advertising the safely nonpolitical *Hurlothrumbo,* but once again constables appeared with a warrant for their arrest, and they had to take to their heels. Thus ended the first "political" phase of the Little Haymarket.

Scholars have sometimes wondered if politics lurk even in the zany *Hurlothrumbo,*[42] but this is far-fetched. *Hurlothrumbo* had been through dozens of performances since it was premiered in March 1729. It was stopped in August 1731 because the company had made itself obnoxious to the authorities. Exactly what authorities we do not really know. We may deduce, however, that there was no effective mechanism for censorship. The actors must have been warned or threatened (hence the notice of 30 June), and their defiance was met with a prosecution for operating an unlicensed theater. (Apparently the local JPs merely issued warrants for their arrest as "Rogues and Vagabonds.")[43] Presumably, Potter complained about losing the business his actor-tenants had given him and was told (perhaps late in the fall of 1731) that they could resume operations unmolested, but only if Potter would see to it that they did not stage plays obnoxious to the government; or so I would deduce from Aston's indignant preface to *The Restauration of King Charles II.* Aston's silly play strikes me as harmless, but tales of restoring Stuart kings to their rightful thrones were not popular with Georgian governments.

In the midst of all the hullabulloo, what of Fielding's *The Grub-Street Opera*? *The Welsh Opera* had been premiered with success 22 April; by 5 June the company was advertising that because of great demand it had been made into a mainpiece and was in rehearsal. I see a major difference in the political offensiveness of the two pieces, and I would hypothesize that Fielding took alarm and backed off before he got himself into serious trouble. Orator Henley's angry cracks at Fielding in *The Hyp-Doctor* (8-15 June) may well have confirmed his inclination toward prudence. *The Fall of Mortimer* came to an abrupt halt after 14 June; *The Grub-Street Opera* was advertised for the eleventh and deferred; on the fourteenth the company announced "We are oblig'd to defer the Grub Street Opera till further Notice." Did the authorities belatedly object to *The Welsh Opera*? Did they get wind of the sharper version and object even before production? Did Fielding withdraw the play? Did the actors, already in hot water, decide not to risk further provocation? We simply do not know. On 26 June an opposition bookseller named Rayner published *The Welsh Opera* with a preface saying that "the Performance of the *Grubstreet* Opera has been prevented, by a certain Influence which has been very *prevailing* of late Years." A letter evidently by Fielding appeared in the *Daily Post* on the twenty-eighth, objecting to the unauthorized publication and flatly denying that *The Grub-Street Opera* "was stopt by Authority . . . for which there could be no manner of Reason." Since there is no record of official interference, Fielding may be telling the literal truth without being entirely ingenuous.

Scholars who have seen *The Author's Farce, Tom Thumb,* and *The Tragedy of Tragedies* as a determined series of "attacks" on Walpole have naturally regarded *The Welsh Opera* and *The*

Grub-Street Opera as a continuation and intensification of the assault. Thus, Harold Gene Moss assumes that Fielding could have been prosecuted for libel (highly questionable, given the indirectness of the satire) and finds *The Grub-Street Opera* a "venture into party politics," treating it as a key link in "the progressively bitter political satire that led eventually to the Licensing Act."[44] Scholars not committed to the contextual/progressive reading tend to find the satire lightweight and randomly directed, an expression more "of political cynicism than political commitment," as Goldgar says. Jack Richard Brown, in what remains one of the best accounts of the work, notes the "tone of light-hearted banter" and concludes "that Fielding was far more interested in writing a clever play than in carrying the flag for any political faction."[45] I agree. At a guess, Fielding wrote a clever and popular burlesque, got carried away with it and pepped it up, and then decided not to risk getting himself into really hot water by proceeding with it.

By July the actors would probably not have risked performing *The Grub-Street Opera* in any case, but as several scholars have noted, Fielding's failure to publish suggests a prudent avoidance of controversy on his part. McCrea is quite right in saying that "Fielding let his *Grub-Street Opera* die without complaint or protest . . . he did not authorize its publication and try to profit from its banishment *à la* Gay." I cannot, however, concur in the conclusion that "he was eager to curry both the literary and political favor of the Whig establishment."[46] We need not postulate complex political motivations. Fielding was an ambitious young professional playwright who would undoubtedly have preferred to have his plays produced at Drury Lane and who was sensible enough not to get himself into a scandalous and damaging controversy.[47] This is cowardice or political apostasy only if we imagine that Fielding was committed to the opposition in 1730-31, an interpretation for which I can find no evidence.

Thus far we have found much less political satire at the Little Haymarket than Cross and his followers would lead us to expect. What of the other theaters? Were they even more politically toothless?

Drury Lane was widely viewed as a Whig stronghold during the long reign of the triumvirate, a truism borne out by their plays prior to September 1732. Martyn's *Timoleon* (1730) is an alle-

gorical justification of William III and the revolution of 1688, a
still timely salvo for "Revolution Principles."[48] Lillo's *The London Merchant* (1731) is political largely in ideology, but as a
trumpeting of Whig mercantilism it does not seem out of place at
Drury Lane, though it arrived via the back door of the summer
company. Mallet's *Eurydice* (1731) was accused of Jacobitism in a
contemporary pamphlet, but I must agree with Loftis that if
there are any politics in the play, they are thoroughly swamped
by neoclassical clutter.[49]

Following the advent of new management, Drury Lane occasionally produced plays with significant opposition sympathies.
Kelly's *Timon in Love* (1733) has as much social as political
satire, but it does hammer away at the theme that gold corrupts,
apparently a comment on the Walpole administration.[50] Duncombe's *Junius Brutus* (1734) is yet another defense of the revolution and William III, but it hits hard at Walpole via Tarquin's
subversion of Roman law. Lillo's *The Christian Hero* (1735), like
other "Scanderbeg" plays, preaches resistance to tyranny, opposition code for "down with Walpole!" Dodsley's *The King and the
Miller of Mansfield* (1737) shows its opposition colors in its fervent
presentation of "country" ideology.

None of these plays is political in the sense that *The Fall of
Mortimer* is political, but, with the probable exception of *Eurydice,* all of them were pretty clearly understood as political statements. To express the principles and ideology of the opposition
was within the unwritten rules; to point a finger too directly at
Walpole (much less at the king) would almost certainly have got a
theater in real trouble, as *The Fall of Mortimer* had proved. No
one really knew what the government's powers of censorship
were, but Goodman's Fields and the Little Haymarket existed in
a precarious legal limbo, while Drury Lane and Lincoln's Inn
Fields operated on royal patents that could be suspended, if not
easily revoked. A great many theater people must have remembered that in 1709 the Lord Chamberlain had on his own authority been able to silence Christopher Rich and make it stick.[51] No
theater manager would have risked producing something like the
anonymous *Majesty Misled; Or, The Overthrow of Evil Ministers,*
published in 1734 as "intended to be Acted . . . But . . . refus'd for
Certain Reasons."

The story at the other theaters is similar. John Loftis is quite right in saying that "John Rich showed restraint in the plays he produced — he clearly wished to avoid trouble," but Lincoln's Inn Fields had consistently demonstrated a Tory/opposition bias between 1714 and 1728, and Rich continued to produce plays whose "political overtones . . . could not be misunderstood."[52] *The Beggar's Opera* is the only important instance of a topical allusion play, but in four cases Rich was prepared to mount application plays with clear-cut opposition messages. *Polly* got suppressed in 1729; Madden's *Themistocles* (1729), dedicated to the Prince of Wales, uses Greek history to make a rather general comment; and Jeffrey's *Merope* (1731) merely spouts the usual opposition stuff about patriotism and liberty. Tracy's *Periander* (1731), however, is exactly what Loftis calls it, a blatant "propaganda" play denouncing Whig "luxury" and tyranny and proposing the restoration of the "ancient" form of government in the best Bolingbrokean fashion. No one seems to have called attention to the point, but Rich never again mounted a genuinely political play. I would deduce that he observed the results of *The Fall of Mortimer* at the Little Haymarket and got the message. Bond's *The Tuscan Treaty* (1733), an account of Tarquin's overthrow with much vaguer parallels to contemporary England than Duncombe's *Junius Brutus,* is about as political a play as Rich cared to venture after the spring of 1731.

At Goodman's Fields Giffard went to considerable pains to advertise his "loyalty" to George II, and he is generally described as a political noncombatant.[53] He was nonetheless willing to produce political plays of any stripe within the limits of safety. Walker's (?) *The Fate of Villainy* (1730) is a rather general criticism of courtiers who abuse their power, but Ralph's *The Fall of the Earl of Essex* (1731) comes much closer to Walpole, especially in his relations with Queen Caroline. Havard's *Scanderbeg* is quite bland.

Three political plays produced by Giffard at Lincoln's Inn Fields in 1737 span the whole spectrum. Hewitt's *A Tutor for the Beaus* (dedicated to Molly Skerrit) makes a feeble job of ridiculing the opposition. Lynch's *The Independent Patriot* is an oddly impartial hit at the world of London politics, freely damning all parties. Havard's *King Charles the First* suggests that bad ministers can lead to the downfall of kings. Havard's play was softened a bit in performance to smudge clear parallels with George II, and small wonder. The cuts are indicated in the first quarto.

From this survey we learn several things. After *The Beggar's Opera,* only the Little Haymarket does much with topical allusion plays of the comic sort. After the demise of the triumvirate, Drury Lane was perfectly willing to stage antiministerial works of the application play variety. Rich staged some opposition propaganda until he took fright in 1731. Giffard was surprisingly ready to do political pieces, including a couple of flagrant opposition allegories. The offerings of the Little Haymarket prior to 1736 are a great deal less political than its reputation would lead one to believe. The two openly obnoxious application plays, *Polly* and *The Fall of Mortimer,* both got suppressed. After 1731 the theaters did not stage application plays unless they stuck to fairly general parallels and ideology. Walpole probably did not like some of the pieces that got produced, but the London theater of the early 1730s was hardly a hotbed of partisan political activity.

FIELDING'S LAST SEASON AT THE LITTLE HAYMARKET, 1736-37

In Emmett Avery's well-known article of 1939, he made major advances in our knowledge of Fielding's activities in this crucial season.[54] Given the facts provided by Avery and by *The London Stage, Part III,* I want to ask two interpretive questions: (1) How political were Fielding's offerings at the Little Haymarket this season? (2) What were Fielding's plans for the future?

The spectacular instance of *The Fall of Mortimer* aside, the Little Haymarket was not markedly more political than the other theaters prior to 1736-37. *Pasquin* the previous spring was certainly satiric and highly topical. But while Walpole gets his lumps, the play is hard to see as a party document, either internally or on the basis of reactions at the time. Goldgar quite rightly says:

Pasquin contained nothing overtly objectionable to the government, and its popularity was not attributed at the time to any satire on Walpole which might have been suspected. The papers sympathetic to the opposition gave it no support and made no effort to capitalize upon it, with the [Tory] *Grub-street Journal,* in fact, launching its first full-scale attack on Fielding in several years. The *Journal's* criticism . . . was directed at Fielding's cynical indictment of *all* parties as equally corrupt and at the very generality of his satire on lawyers, physicians, and divines.[55]

Pasquin made a great deal of noise, but had it been viewed as an offensively partisan document, Giffard would probably not have produced it at Lincoln's Inn Fields the following season, as he did.

We can only guess at what Fielding had in mind at the end of the 1735-36 season.[56] Clearly he had no future with Giffard, who moved into the vacant Lincoln's Inn Fields theater in late September, thereby preempting any chance Fielding might have had to rent those premises. John Rich offered little hope; Fielding had pretty well burned his bridges in that direction with *Tumble-Down Dick* (April 1736) and its nasty dedication. The possibility of a rapprochement with Fleetwood at Drury Lane was his best bet among the established companies. How seriously Fielding considered or explored the possibility we do not know, but he did at some point give Drury Lane his *Eurydice,* produced there 19 February 1737. (Allowing Fielding the first night as a benefit is probably a sign that Fleetwood was anxious to produce his work at Drury Lane.) Cross and others have assumed that, as a result of its ignominious failure in one night, Fielding "fell back upon" the Little Haymarket.[57] But as Avery has proved, this cannot be right. Whether Fielding was involved with performances at the Little Haymarket in January we do not know,[58] but he was definitely in town and pursuing theatrical matters by the beginning of February, and his plans for his own troupe at the Little Haymarket were announced in the *Daily Advertiser* on 19 February, the same day *Eurydice* flopped at Drury Lane. There can be no doubt that Fielding was reconstructing "his" acting company by 15 February at the very latest.

What we do definitely know about Fielding's plans and hopes is that he wanted to build a theater to house his own company. On 4 February the *Daily Advertiser* published a notice dated 2 February:

Whereas it is agreed on between several Gentlemen, to erect a New Theatre for the exhibiting of Plays, Farces, Pantomimes, &c. all such Persons as are willing to undertake the said Building, are desir'd to bring their Plans for the same by the 2d of May next ensuing, in order to be laid before the said Gentlemen, the Time and Place of which Meeting will be advertis'd in this Paper on the last of April.

Proportions of the Ground:

The North side 120 Feet; the West, square with the North, 130 Feet; the South 110 Feet; and the East, on a Bevil, joining the Parallels.

Note, There must be a Passage left to go round the Building, and the Stage to be 30 Feet wide at the first Scene; the Distance between Wall and Wall 80 Feet; and the Scene-Rooms, Green and Dressing Rooms, to be on the outside of the last mention'd Measure.

The Stage to be either North or South.[59]

This is elucidated by a follow-up notice the 19th:

In a late Paragraph . . . it was insinuated, that there was a Design on foot for erecting a New Theatre, which by some Wise Heads was suppos'd to come from a certain Manager, in order to revive the Playhouse Bill this Session of Parliament; I think it proper therefore, in Justice to the Gentleman levell'd at, to inform the Publick, that it is actually intended for a Company of Comedians every Day expected here, late Servants to their Majesties Kouli Kan and Theodore, who in the mean time will entertain the Town in the true Eastern manner, at the New Theatre in the Hay-Market, with a celebrated Piece call'd *A Rehearsal of Kings*. I am, Sir, yours, &c. *Agent for the Company*.

The suggestion that there might be plans afoot to revive the 1735 playhouse bill as early as February is most interesting. But even more so is this evidence that Fielding intended to set up on his own. The plan was perfectly realistic. Giffard had raised the capital to build the second Goodman's Fields without difficulty five years earlier. Why should Fielding, easily the most popular playwright in London, have any trouble?

The site (at an unknown location, but presumably in the West End) was large enough for a substantial building. We can make some deductions from the dimensions given. "Between Wall and Wall 80 Feet," I take to mean that 80 feet is the combined depth of stage and auditorium, with scene rooms, dressing rooms, and Green Room added to make the full length of the theater. This is about the length of Goodman's Fields, which measured about 82 feet (Covent Garden was about 95, Drury Lane about 99). The width of 30 feet "at the first Scene" I take to mean that there should be 30 feet of clear space at the first set of closeable shutters when they were drawn off. This would imply a proscenium opening width of about 33 feet. By contrast, Drury Lane was 31 feet, 6 inches, Covent Garden about 25 feet, Goodman's Fields 23 feet. We may deduce good proportions for an attractive, fan-shaped auditorium.[60] Audience capacity is impossible to calculate with any precision from the data available, but we may note that Goodman's Fields probably held about 750. A slightly wider building might well have held 850-900. Drury Lane held about 1000 and Covent Garden about 1400, but they were seldom full. With such a building Fielding could probably have competed very successfully with the patent houses. Assuming that he liked one of the plans submitted and got financing, he could expect to be in business within a year. For the present, he had a season to offer at the Little Haymarket.

Fielding intended to open his season with *A Rehearsal of Kings,* first puffed in the press on 19 February. Sometime before the twenty-eighth he asked Aaron Hill to write the prologue and epilogue, for on that date Hill politely begged off, explaining that he had "good reasons for declining every hazard, of being considered in a light this would very unseasonably shew me in." Hill's comments, missed by the editors of *The London Stage* and ignored by others, give a highly suggestive view of the play.

I am afraid, you are in more [danger] than you imagine . . . from the choice of your subject, and the allegorical *remoteness* of your satire. — What I mean is, that the necessity your prudence was under, to disguise your design with *caution,* has so perplexed it with *doubtfulness,* that I am fearful, in the hurry of action, some of the *most meaning* allusions, in your piece, may be mistaken for scenes, which want any meaning at all; while, on the other side, among the few, who can penetrate purpose, and unravel the *satire,* as fast as they hear it, you will find *some* persons malignantly disposed, upon a supposition, that royalty, in general, should never be the mark of contempt. . . . I am heartily sorry, I had not sooner an idea of your plan; and flatter myself, I might have had the good fortune of persuading you to change it, for some other, not only of less dangerous provocation, but more promising likelyhood, to fall in with the publick capacity. . . . Upon the whole, if it were possible, in so short a time as is left to you, to substitute any other of your pieces, in place of this *Rehearsal of Kings,* I am convinced, you would avoid a disappointment, and, perhaps, a mortification.[61]

Hill was a bit of an ass, but he was a veteran playwright, a coauthor of *The Prompter,* and a knowledgeable observer of the theatrical scene. If he thought *A Rehearsal of Kings* both politically dangerous and likely to be unsuccessful, he probably knew what he was talking about.

Fielding went ahead with the production, but since the play is lost we know little about it.[62] From the exceptionally full newspaper bill, with its references to "Macplunderkan, King of Roguomania" and others, we may certainly deduce political satire.[63] The piece was advertised for 9 March, but performance was prevented "by some Persons taking clandestinely Possession of the Hay-Market Playhouse, who were about Eight o'Clock committed to Bridewell for the same. On this Account several hundred Persons were turn'd away" (*Daily Advertiser*). The performance was canceled on the eleventh "by unforeseen Accident," but the play was performed without recorded objection or disruption the fourteenth, fifteenth, and seventeenth. After that, no more is heard of it. The illegal seizure of the house on the ninth may well have been some unofficial political opposition, but evidently Hill was right about the play's lack of popular appeal.

After one night of *Pasquin* on 19 March, Fielding brought on Lillo's *Fatal Curiosity,* with *The Historical Register for the Year 1736* as an afterpiece. *Eurydice Hiss'd* replaced Lillo's tragedy on 13 April, and the two political farces ran to the end of the month. No one should doubt that *The Historical Register* is a biting attack on Walpole. *Eurydice Hiss'd,* at first sight politically harmless, can be read as a fiendishly clever satire on Walpole's loss of the 1733 excise bill, still a sore subject. The earl of Egmont attended a performance 18 April and wrote in his diary that *Eurydice Hiss'd* was "an allegory on the loss of the Excise Bill. The whole was a satire on Sir Robert Walpole, and I observed that when any strong passages fell, the Prince [of Wales], who was there, clapped, especially when in favour of liberty."[64] These works generated the kind of partisan newspaper attack and defense so conspicuously absent in relation to *The Welsh Opera* and *Pasquin.*[65]

Why did Fielding, after seven years of relative caution, abruptly join the opposition's hue and cry after Walpole? Goldgar's explanations seem convincing. Following the disappointment of the 1734 election, the opposition forces had regrouped, and by 1736 and 1737 they were barking fiercely. Fielding's growing celebrity put him in touch with Chesterfield, and with William Pitt and George Lyttelton (the last two old schoolmates), now prominent in the opposition. Between the time of *Pasquin* and *The Historical Register,* the Prince of Wales had come into open opposition. A wit who proposed to amuse the town with topical satire could hardly ignore the political frenzy building against Walpole. How personally committed Fielding felt to the opposition cause we have no way to tell. Blasts at Walpole were selling tickets, and there can be no certainty he looked beyond that welcome fact. The political difference between *Pasquin* and *The Historical Register* seems clearly implied by an anonymous attack (often ascribed to Lord Hervey) in the *Daily Gazetteer* of 7 May, strenuously objecting to open ridicule of the government in the theater. *Pasquin,* riotously popular though it was, had drawn no such blast.

There is no sign that Fielding felt any alarm. He replied with spirit in the preface to *The Historical Register* and went right on with plans for politically audacious plays. Nothing is known of *The Sailor's Opera* or *The Lordly Husband,* both anonymous shows that quickly failed, but James Lacy's *Fame,* a lost play that survived only one night, was advertised and puffed in enough detail to let us deduce topical hits. By 17 May, Fielding had evidently decided to stick with *The Historical Register* until the end of the month, when he hoped to have something else ready. On 25 May he advertised a new double bill for the thirtieth: *Macheath turn'd Pyrate* (i.e., Gay's banned *Polly,* probably with some revisions), plus *The King and Titi* (evidently an adaptation from the French designed to ridicule the king and flatter the Prince of Wales).

This was playing hardball with a vengeance, and the ad positively dared Walpole to try to do something about it.[66] Walpole had introduced the Licensing Act on the twenty-fourth, but he did not wait for its help. Ever resourceful, Walpole and Lord Chamberlain Grafton seem to have persuaded John Potter to turn Fielding out of the Little Haymarket.[67] If we can believe some MS notes by J. Payne Collier, Potter took the precaution of piling the theater high with lumber and bricks to make sure that it could not be forcibly entered and used without authorization.[68] Fielding's response to this enforced closing was silence. He could surely have created some ruckus had he wished to, and the almost preternatural lack of fuss in the papers may well suggest that he went to some trouble to stifle comment on this episode. Fielding was almost always a realist, and if he concluded that the game was lost, he may have decided that protest could only hurt him.

Fielding's plans prior to 25 May are plainly stated in his "Dedication to the Public" of *The Historical Register,* published 12 May.

The very great Indulgence you have shewn my Performances at the little Theatre, these two last Years, have encouraged me to the Proposal of a Subscription for carrying on that Theatre, for beautifying and enlarging it, and procuring a better Company of Actors. If you think proper to subscribe to these Proposals, I assure you no Labor shall be spared, on my Side, to entertain you in a cheaper and better Manner than seems to be the Intention of any other. If Nature hath given me any Talents at ridiculing Vice and Imposture, I shall not be indolent, nor afraid of exerting them, while the Liberty of the Press and Stage subsists, that is to say, while we have any Liberty left among us.

Obviously, Fielding had dropped his plan to build a new theater of his own. Possibly the owner of his prospective site had welshed; perhaps Fielding found that investors were alarmed by recurring rumors of a restriction on the number of public theaters allowed in London;[69] conceivably, John Potter offered him sufficiently attractive terms at the Little Haymarket to make a move seem more trouble than it was worth. In any event, Fielding now proposed to enlarge and beautify the Little Haymarket and to hire "a better Company of Actors."[70] This proposal implies a new kind of agreement with John Potter. Until March 1737 performance records definitely suggest that Fielding, like others, rented the Little Haymarket on a night-by-night basis. Obviously he would not put money into improving a theater in which he was merely a tenant at will. We must presume, therefore, that Potter offered a long-term lease and that Fielding had every expectation of signing such an agreement if he had not done so already.

Many critics have been inclined to believe that Fielding was uncomfortable as a playwright, but all the evidence I can find suggests that in the spring of 1737 he was entirely committed to a career in the theater. The Licensing Act turned him toward the law and ultimately toward the novels we now prefer, but only the benefit of hindsight allows us to proclaim the shift somehow right and inevitable. Fielding had suffered his share of misfires (what professional dramatist does not?), but from *The Author's Farce* to *The Historical Register* he had enjoyed a series of solid successes and several major triumphs. No writer since Congreve and Farquhar could claim equivalent success. To describe Fielding's years in the theater under the heading "Fielding's 'Undistinguished Career as a Dramatist'" (as McCrea does, quoting Woods) is to ignore his vast popular success, his personal commitment, and his plans for the future. It also tends to distract us from the theater as a central preoccupation in Fielding's life.

THE PLACE OF POLITICS IN FIELDING'S
EARLY CAREER

Fielding has almost always been viewed as a highly political writer — in particular, as a diehard opponent of Walpole. The Cross biography of 1918, splendid though it is in many ways, contributed substantially to perpetuating this distortion throughout whole generations of Fielding scholarship. McCrea rightly complains of the effect of the "Tory interpretation" of Fielding, one which views the Fielding of *Tom Thumb* as an ally of Pope and Swift in a noble and high-principled attack on Walpole.

The last decade has seen major and welcome modifications of this view, though it has not yet been replaced by anything like a satisfactory account of the young Fielding's psyche and ideology. McCrea's excellent account of Fielding's old-Whig outlook, useful though it is, naturally stresses politics in its presentation of Fielding. Even Goldgar, who has done so much to qualify overly political readings of the plays, inevitably has a hard time getting beyond the political perspective of his book to see Fielding in any other context. Readily admitting that others have pondered Fielding longer and harder than I have, I would suggest that a theater historian has some special advantages to bring to a consideration of Fielding's early career.

McCrea very fairly admits that Fielding's "political allegiances were casual [in the 1730s], and his goal of success as a playwright probably foremost in his mind."[71] But he immediately goes on to add that "those priorities should not blind us to the important roles of political principle and interest in his early career," and he can say that "in these plays" Fielding "is very much a man in search of a party and a cause," a man trying "to create a political identity." These views are essentially conformable to a long tra-

dition of Fielding scholarship. I think, however, that the burden
of proof still rests with those committed to a political view of the
early career. Having grown up with that view of Fielding, I was
certainly predisposed toward such an interpretation. A review of
the evidence, however, quickly casts doubt on political readings.

The evidence for Fielding's political convictions in the 1730s —
for his serious opposition to Walpole — is scanty. It consists of the
following:

(1) A handful of early poems, not all of them published. All are
quite imitative, and none attracted significant attention. Fielding
was barely over twenty, and for him to indulge in conventional
praise of the head of the ministry probably means very little, especially if we heed McCrea's forceful reminder that Fielding was
raised a Whig. He was not a once-and-future Tory flirting with
the party in power, his choice of nom de plume, H. Scriblerus
Secundus, notwithstanding.

(2) Four anonymous pieces published between July 1728 and
October 1730, newly attributed to Fielding by Martin Battestin,
all of them satiric at Walpole's expense.[72] The attributions,
though resting "almost entirely on internal evidence," seem very
plausible. Battestin comments that "Fielding's known writings of
this early period are either entirely unconcerned with political
matters or indiscriminate in directing incidental shafts at either
party," and that hence, "at first glance it would seem implausible
that Fielding could be the author" of these satires. Battestin concludes, however, that Fielding was prepared to utilize his "talent
to amuse" on either side of a question if money was to be made by
doing so.

(3) The supposed attacks on Walpole of 1730 and 1731: *The
Author's Farce, Tom Thumb,* and *The Tragedy of Tragedies.*
Goldgar has proved beyond reasonable doubt that these works
were not viewed as political by the original audience.

(4) *The Welsh Opera* (1731). Personal allusion to Walpole,
George II, Queen Caroline, et al. is certain. The degree of partisan intention is another matter. The lack of public fuss is counter-
weighed by the nonperformance of *The Grub-Street Opera* and
by Fielding's evident reluctance to put either piece in print. Fielding's treatment of the royal family and parliamentary leaders is
audacious but not very political in ideological or party terms.

(5) The "change" to Drury Lane in 1732. In itself, the accep-

tance of Fielding's work at Drury Lane has no political significance, though until the dissolution of the triumvirate he could not have had anything openly hostile to the ministry staged there. I am now inclined to believe that the dedication of *The Modern Husband* to Walpole is to be taken straight, as Loftis and Goldgar urge, and that Fielding would have welcomed government patronage had any been offered.[73] His writing an epilogue for *The Modish Couple* I am less inclined to take seriously.[74] Popular writers often did provide prologues and epilogues for works with which they had no connection or sympathy. Indeed, Fielding may have been asked precisely because he did *not* have any recognized connection with court or ministry. There is no proof that he had any idea who wrote the play when he agreed to supply an epilogue.

(6) *Don Quixote in England.* As I have explained, the Little Haymarket venue was accidental and without political significance. Neither Goldgar nor McCrea finds the play itself very political. Goldgar observes: "Though there are a few scenes satirizing corrupt electioneering, the play itself is of no special interest and could certainly not have been considered anti-Walpole satire; it is the dedication to the earl of Chesterfield which reveals Fielding's new direction."[75] Taken in conjunction with performance at the Little Haymarket, Goldgar considers this "a bid for favor from the opposition." Very probably the dedication is exactly that, with its references to "the cause of liberty," "general corruption," and "true patriotism." I am quite ready to believe that Fielding would have welcomed patronage from Chesterfield, and if Battestin is correct in attributing *Craftsman* essays to Fielding (starting at just this time, March 1734), then we are probably safe in seeing the dedication to Chesterfield as a serious political statement. The play itself is something else again. Electioneering was topical, and satiric complaints about election abuses can be found even in so openly pro-ministry a work as Odell's *Smugglers.* We may hypothesize that Fielding sided with the opposition Whigs on the excise bill of 1733 and that he was feeling scant sympathy for Walpole. But *Don Quixote in England* is by no means a political document, much less a partisan one.

(7) *Pasquin.* Indubitably topical and satiric, *Pasquin* was not regarded as a party document in 1736 and is not claimed as such by Goldgar or McCrea. The thoroughness with which Fielding

mocks and derides the Tory part of the opposition (as well as
Walpole and the court) is well expounded by McCrea (pp. 73-74).

(8) *The Historical Register* and other offerings at the Little
Haymarket in 1737. Here we do find evidence of partisan political attack on Fielding's part, and for the first time he drew genuinely angry objections from the ministry. Whether Fielding was
acting opportunistically or otherwise we cannot be sure. But
there is a major difference between the essentially moral/social
basis of his earlier work and the overt political aims of his activities in 1737. The degree to which Fielding was openly attacking
and defying the ministry is clearest in his advertising a production
of *Polly* for the Little Haymarket, a point unknown to Cross and
Dudden and not mentioned by either Goldgar or McCrea. An
announcement of a revival of *The Fall of Mortimer* would probably have been less directly obnoxious to the ministry. Had Fielding finally found his political identity, or did he yield to temptation in the heat of the moment?

The desire to see Fielding as a fearless opponent of Walpole has
made many scholars (e.g., Cross, Dudden, Woods, Coley, Avery)
overestimate the partisan nature of the plays, one consequence
of which is excessive distress when Fielding turns around in 1741
and writes *The Opposition: A Vision.* A less one-sided view of
Fielding's politics in the 1730s suggests that he was always, as
McCrea has argued, a sturdy Whig;[76] that within the Whig spectrum he was willing to seek his advantage where it lay and would
cheerfully have accepted government patronage in 1732 or just
about any other time; that when advantage seemed to lie in tug-
ging Walpole's tail in 1737, Fielding did so with vigor; and that
Fielding's silent acceptance of the Licensing Act suggests a lack of
passionate partisan commitment on his part at that time.[77]

Until very recently, Fielding scholars tended to exaggerate the
significance of the gulf between Walpole and the Whig opposition and hence to regard any inclination to switch camps as the
blackest of treachery. This view seems the odder since Namierite
dogma (predominant into the 1960s) belittled ideological distinctions even between Whig and Tory. I must agree with McCrea in
attributing a great deal of distorted thinking about Fielding to a
predisposition to group him with Pope, Swift, and Gay—the Tory
opposition. Current historical thinking allows for a genuine ideological split between Whigs and Tories,[78] but Fielding never gives
any hint of an inclination to change his party. Far from selling his

principles, he is willing to sell his pen to either of the feuding fac-
tions in his own party. Fielding's oft-cited defense of this position
in *The Jacobite's Journal* (26 March 1748)[79] has been received by
political idealists with about as much enthusiasm as moralists
greet Tom Jones's acceptance of money from Lady Bellaston. But
Fielding is a realist as well as a man of principle, and he is realistic about politics as well as about sex, money, and human nature.
All the fuss over tergiversation reflects our ideals and prejudices,
not his.[80]

Fielding's plays represent our fullest view of him prior to 1739.
They are vigorous, sometimes experimental, deliberately "popular," and consistently devoted to the exposure of "vice and imposture," as Fielding defines his aim in the preface to *The Historical
Register*. The irregular plays are highly topical, and in the politically supercharged London of the 1730s, that gives them political
overtones. But with the exception of *The Historical Register* (and
probably *Eurydice Hiss'd*) Fielding did not write party satire, nor
did he write or produce application plays directed at Walpole in
the fashion of *The Fall of Mortimer* or *King Charles the First*.
Snide political allusions bit more at the ministry than at the relatively faceless (and chaotically amorphous) opposition, but that
does not make them seriously partisan. When Fielding became
genuinely partisan (or perhaps just got carried away) in 1737, he
quickly drew fire of a sort he had never previously attracted.

Fielding's plays are certainly variegated. He was ready to try all
sorts of things, and some of his experiments flopped. Indubitably,
he was young, but I do not see that the inclination to experiment
makes him an "uncertain writer," as McCrea charges. I am baf-
fled by McCrea's insistence that Fielding suffered from a debili-
tating inability "to choose between . . . two different conceptions
of the nature of man" embodied in the work of Cibber and Gay.
What McCrea sees as tortured insecurity I see as breadth, complexity, and surprising maturity. Was Dryden suffering from
dreadful insecurity because he was writing *The Conquest of Gra-
nada* and *The Assignation* at about the same time? *All for Love*
and *Mr Limberham*? This seems a simplistic view of a writer's
psyche. I see no more evidence of "mercurial" shifts "between
opposing literary camps" than I do of rapid shifts in Fielding's
political allegiances. Fielding was a professional dramatist ready
to employ successful formulas, and he was prepared to take them
where he found them.

Views of Fielding's early career have long been colored and distorted by lack of interest in the plays, by desire to find political
partisanship in them, and by ignorance of the theater world in
which Fielding was trying to make a living. Certain facts now
seem clear: the Little Haymarket did not have a manager and a
resident company; it had no settled repertory policy; and the
plays staged there were no more political than those mounted at
Drury Lane and Lincoln's Inn Fields—except during the spring
of 1737. Fielding was a freelance writer who marketed his plays
where he could. Consequently, no political significance should be
deduced from his changes of theater. All the evidence suggests
that in 1737 Fielding hoped to build his own theater (or revamp
the Little Haymarket under a long-term lease) and manage his
own company there.

This much seems to me fact; what of interpretation? In my
view, little political commitment (and not all that much politics)
is to be found in Fielding's plays prior to 1737, and none of the
political material will support charges of his changing political
camps. The plays have a strong moral bent, despite their tearing
high spirits and exuberant jokiness. Tone and genre notwithstanding, Fielding's plays seem to me much more of a piece with
his later writing than most commentators have found them. To
dismiss the plays with impatience is to treat Fielding with less
respect than he deserves. Wilbur Cross is among the few scholars
to treat Fielding's theatrical career with any real understanding
of what it meant to him. Cross's summation is well worth quoting:

He had hardly more than discovered where his talent lay before his dramatic career was ended. As he used to say, "he left off writing for the
stage when he ought to have begun." But for the Licensing Act he
would have rebuilt or enlarged his theatre and continued to delight
London audiences for another decade or more. On Fielding's stage
rather than Giffard's, Garrick would have won his spurs.... The
drama, I have tried to make clear, was to Fielding much more than a
means of support; it was his soul; it was his life. Underlying all his
plays—farce as well as comedy—was a serious intent. (1: 235-236)

What I find in Fielding's highly successful decade of playwriting
and theater management is not "uncertainty" or a "search for
political identity," but a brash young man managing to sustain
his ethical commitments while aggressively pursuing success in
the commercial theater.[81]

NOTES

1. Brian McCrea, *Henry Fielding and the Politics of Mid-Eighteenth-Century England* (Athens: University of Georgia Press, 1981), p. 51. Although much of the present essay is devoted to correcting or refining McCrea's views, I should say unequivocally that I consider his book a fine piece of work and that even when I disagree with it I am indebted to him for providing a context in which Fielding's plays and politics can fruitfully be discussed.

2. J. Paul Hunter, *Occasional Form: Henry Fielding and the Chains of Circumstance* (Baltimore: Johns Hopkins University Press, 1975), p. 51.

3. Most of what is known about the theater is collected in Emmett L. Avery, ed., *The London Stage, 1660-1800, Part II: 1700-1729,* 2 vols. (Carbondale: Southern Illinois University Press, 1960), 1: xxxv-xxxvi.

4. We do know that the site size was approximately 48 by 136 feet. See Edward A. Langhans, "The Theatres," in *The London Theatre World, 1660-1800,* ed. Robert D. Hume (Carbondale: Southern Illinois University Press, 1980), p. 63.

5. *Journal of the House of Commons* 22 (1735): 456.

6. See Judith Milhous, "The Capacity of Vanbrugh's Theatre in the Haymarket," *Theatre History Studies* 4 (1984), 38-46.

7. P.R.O. C11/1175/59. I owe this reference to the kindness of Judith Milhous.

8. For a detailed analysis of theatrical competition and the repertories of the various theaters see "The London Theatre from *The Beggar's Opera* to the Licensing Act," chapter 9 of my book *The Rakish Stage* (Carbondale: Southern Illinois University Press, 1983).

9. John Loftis, *The Politics of Drama in Augustan England* (Oxford: Clarendon Press, 1963), p. 106. Likewise, Pat Rogers says that "the managers put up the price of tickets . . . when Fielding had his benefit night" for *The Welsh Opera* (*Henry Fielding: A Biography* [New York: Scribner's, 1979], p. 51).

10. Walter Aston, *The Restauration of King Charles II* (London: R. Walker, 1732), pp. ii-iii.

11. The editors of *The London Stage* imply this when they give the composite season rosters of the Little Haymarket as "all companies," though they do not discuss the problem in the introductions and make no attempt to distinguish the different groups that used the theater each season. Such an attempt could be no more than partially successful on present evidence.

12. Consider, for example, some very odd, brief breaks in the run of *Pasquin* in 1736. On 26 April a smash hit is pulled off after its thirty-ninth night, and Joseph Dorman's *The Female Rake* is given its one and only performance, benefit the author. Three weeks later Mrs. E. Cooper's *The Nobleman; or Family Quarrel* takes over the theater for three nights. These and other such instances suggest that Potter was renting

the theater to different authors and acting groups, and such deals could evidently preempt even a success like *Pasquin*—hardly likely if a resident company were in control of the theater.

13. How did the actors communicate? At a guess, I would say at a conventional hangout, a "theatrical tavern" of the sort described by Philip H. Highfill, Jr., for the period ca. 1790, at which impressarios from town and country could strike bargains with performers at liberty. See "Performers and Performing," in Hume, *London Theatre World,* pp. 154-155. Joseph Wechsberg describes a modern musical parallel in the Quat'z' Arts Café in Paris during the 1920s and 1930s. See *Looking for a Bluebird* (London: Michael Joseph, 1946), chapter 3.

14. For detailed figures see "The London Theatre from *The Beggar's Opera* to the Licensing Act" (note 8 above).

15. Bertrand A. Goldgar, *Walpole and the Wits: The Relation of Politics to Literature, 1722-1742* (Lincoln: University of Nebraska Press, 1976), pp. 112, 114-115.

16. This is by no means merely a technicality. An "attached" writer (to borrow G. E. Bentley's phrase) was paid a substantial retainer. Fielding was certainly Drury Lane's most conspicuous and best-known writer after 1732, as his appearance as "Crambo" in Edward Phillips's *The Stage-Mutineers* (Covent Garden, July 1733) suggests. But even there Fielding is treated essentially like Bayes.

17. Financial arrangements for afterpieces (a subject not yet studied in detail) seem to have varied considerably.

18. McCrea seems unclear on the nature of these arrangements. He comments that Henry Carey "wrote for and had benefit nights at Drury Lane" and seems surprised that *The Contrivances* was also performed at Lincoln's Inn Fields and Goodman's Fields and that *Betty* was mounted at Drury Lane "barely a month" after *Treminta* was produced at Lincoln's Inn Fields (McCrea, *Fielding and Politics,* p. 54). Of course Carey had benefits at Drury Lane; everyone who had a new play accepted there did. And if Lincoln's Inn Fields and Goodman's Fields picked up a successful show, Carey had nothing to do with it. He did not benefit, but he could not prevent it. For an author to have shows appear nearly simultaneously at Drury Lane and Lincoln's Inn Fields is no more surprising than for a scholar to have articles appear the same month in *Modern Philology* and *Philological Quarterly.*

19. See his comments in the preface to the edition of 1734.

20. Wilbur L. Cross, *The History of Henry Fielding,* 3 vols. (1918; reprint ed., New York: Russell and Russell, 1963), 1: 78.

21. See F. Homes Dudden, *Henry Fielding: His Life, Works, and Times,* 2 vols. (Oxford: Clarendon Press, 1952), 1: 181 (citing *The Life of Mr. James Quin* [1766]).

22. *The Craftsman* and *The Grub-street Journal* mention the play that month, and Woods (following Cross, *History of Fielding,* 1: 119) suggests that a letter of 4 September to Lady Mary Wortley Montagu concerning the play should be dated that year. See Charles B. Woods,

"Notes on Three Fielding's Plays," *PMLA* 52 (1937): 359-373, especially pp. 362-363.

23. Cross, *History of Fielding,* 1: 119.

24. Goldgar, *Walpole,* p. 113.

25. Loftis, *Politics of Drama,* p. 108.

26. McCrea (*Fielding and Politics,* p. 67) unfortunately confuses the two versions of *The Author's Farce,* asserting that Fielding's attack on Theophilus Cibber in the play predated *The Modern Husband* (1732).

27. Goldgar, *Walpole,* pp. 114-115; McCrea, *Fielding and Politics,* p. 64.

28. McCrea is confused about this episode, stating that "Cibber's preeminence was such that the Haymarket company ceded its stage to him and his son Theophilus during their conflict with the Drury Lane patentees in 1734" (*Fielding and Politics,* p. 56). In fact, Colley Cibber had no part in the rebellion and did not perform at any theater in 1733-34; nor was there a "Haymarket company" to cede its stage. McCrea's view of Colley Cibber is eccentric. ("Cibber exerted almost universal sway.") Several of his plays were repertory mainstays, but his personal unpopularity was such that any new play tended to be greeted with riotous opposition. Even *The Provok'd Husband* drew some fire in 1728. McCrea comments that Cibber's "*Damon and Phillida* was one of the most popular afterpieces of the era," but does not point out that as a mainpiece (*Love in a Riddle*) it was run off the Drury Lane stage in two nights in 1729.

29. Fielding's account of the shift in his preface is disingenuous, ignoring the end of the actor rebellion. He asserts that he "brought it on where it now appears" because of delays caused by "the Giant Cajanus" (a Dutch freak) and the advent of the benefit season. Reference to the performance calendar shows the flimsiness of this explanation. Fielding's relations with Theophilus Cibber (now manager at Drury Lane) cannot have been cordial after the new version of *The Author's Farce;* under the circumstances he was probably glad to see the play taken to the Little Haymarket by the actors for whom he had reworked it.

30. Martin Battestin informs me that he is in the process of trying to prove from internal evidence that between March 1734 and December 1738 Fielding contributed some forty-five anonymous and pseudonymous satiric essays to *The Craftsman.* If true, this is important evidence about Fielding's outlook in the mid-thirties, but it does not alter the basic fact of Fielding's primary commitment to a career in the theater.

31. "Content and Meaning in the Drama" (chapter 1 of Hume, *Rakish Stage*). For helpful analysis of audience "application" of literary texts (including plays), see John M. Wallace, "Dryden and History: A Problem in Allegorical Reading," *ELH* 36 (1969): 265-290, and "'Examples Are Best Precepts': Readers and Meanings in Seventeenth-Century Poetry," *Critical Inquiry* 1 (1974): 273-290.

32. For a highly plausible political reading of some of Fielding's plays, see Sheridan Baker, "Political Allusion in Fielding's *Author's*

Farce, Mock Doctor, and *Tumble-Down Dick,*" *PMLA* 77 (1962): 221-231. For a powerfully convincing counterview, pointing out that there is not the slightest scrap of evidence that suggests that *The Author's Farce, Tom Thumb,* or *Rape upon Rape* "were read or viewed at the time as satirizing Walpole," see Goldgar, *Walpole,* especially p. 102.

33. Jean B. Kern, *Dramatic Satire in the Age of Walpole 1720-1750* (Ames: Iowa State University Press, 1976).

34. For an excellent explanation of the "application" of *Polly* (a far less harmless work than has generally been assumed), see Vincent J. Liesenfeld, ed., *The Stage and the Licensing Act 1729-1739* (New York: Garland, 1981), pp. x-xiii.

35. Rogers, *Fielding,* p. 34.

36. Loftis, *Politics of Drama,* p. 103.

37. Ibid.

38. Printed in *The London Stage, Part III: 1729-1747,* ed. Arthur H. Scouten, 2 vols. (Carbondale: Southern Illinois University Press, 1961), 1: 97.

39. For the best disentanglement of the complex publication history of *The Welsh Opera* (June 1731, evidently set from prompt copy without authorization), *The Genuine Grub-Street Opera* (August 1731, unauthorized), and *The Grub-Street Opera* (1740s or later; false imprint with 1731 date), see the textual introduction to *The Grub-Street Opera,* ed. L. J. Morrissey (Edinburgh: Oliver and Boyd, 1973).

40. McCrea, *Fielding and Politics,* p. 67.

41. Goldgar, *Walpole,* p. 111.

42. See Cross, *History of Fielding,* 1: 112; Loftis, *Politics of Drama,* p. 106.

43. *Daily Advertiser,* 23 August 1731.

44. Harold Gene Moss, "Satire and Travesty in Fielding's *The Grub-Street Opera,*" *Theatre Survey* 15 (1974): 38-50.

45. Goldgar, *Walpole,* p. 111. Jack Richard Brown, "Henry Fielding's *Grub-Street Opera,*" *Modern Language Quarterly* 16 (1955): 32-41.

46. McCrea, *Fielding and Politics,* p. 221.

47. Martin Battestin suggests an alternative hypothesis in a personal letter: "the government bought him off — with warnings as to the dangers he was running if he continued to supply such satires to the Haymarket players, and with the very large and attractive carrot in prospect of renewing his association with Drury Lane." I cannot disprove this theory, nor do I believe it. No one in the government held that kind of patronage at Drury Lane, and I cannot imagine the managers guaranteeing acceptance of a playwright's work to oblige the ministry. The simplest explanation seems best: Fielding took fright at the ruckus (mostly over *The Fall of Mortimer*); the Drury Lane managers accepted his work in 1732 because it would pay. We have no positive evidence connecting the two events.

48. For relevant background see J. P. Kenyon, *Revolution Principles: The Politics of Party 1689-1720* (Cambridge: Cambridge University Press, 1977).

49. Loftis, *Politics of Drama*, p. 108. For the charge of Jacobitism see the anonymous *Remarks on the Tragedy of Eurydice* (London: E. Rayner, 1731).

50. *Timon in Love* was staged by the "loyal" company, not by the regular acting company, then at the Little Haymarket.

51. For details see Judith Milhous and Robert D. Hume, "The Silencing of Drury Lane in 1709," *Theatre Journal* 32 (1980): 427-447. Rich was not allowed to reopen (at Lincoln's Inn Fields) until the accession of George I in 1714.

52. Loftis, *Politics of Drama*, p. 107. On the Tory bias of Lincoln's Inn Fields 1714-28, see chapter 4.

53. See Scouten, *London Stage, Part III*, 1: lxxxii-lxxxiii, and Loftis, *Politics of Drama*, p. 106.

54. Emmett L. Avery, "Fielding's Last Season with the Haymarket Theatre," *Modern Philology* 36 (1939): 283-292.

55. Goldgar, *Walpole*, pp. 152-153.

56. We do not even know when his involvement with the Little Haymarket ended in the summer of 1736. Both Cross (*History of Fielding*, 1: 202-203) and Dudden (*Fielding: His Life*, 1: 193) assume that Fielding was managing the theater when it produced "Jack Juniper's" *The Deposing and Death of Queen Gin* (2 August), which seems to have lasted only one night as an afterpiece. But from the scrappy performance records after 2 July (the last night of *Pasquin*), I would guess that the company reverted to its usual ad hoc arrangements at that point, and consequently Fielding is unlikely to have "lent assistance" to the author of *Queen Gin*, as Cross deduces.

57. Cross, *History of Fielding*, 1: 207.

58. The company was rehearsing *The Battle of Parnassus* in public by 6 January, and on the fourteenth ran *The Defeat of Apollo* (an attack on pantomime, possibly by Eustace Budgell) with *The Fall of Bob, Alias Gin* (anon.). For the twenty-sixth "Mr Green" advertised *The Defeat of Apollo* together with a pair of topical satires (lost) called *The Mirrour* and *The Mob in Despair*. Loftis assumes that Fielding was in charge of the theater from the beginning of January (*Politics of Drama*, p. 136); Avery more cautiously says that we cannot be sure ("Fielding's Last Season," pp. 284-285). From the miscellaneous repertory offered (*Cato, The Orphan*, etc.) before *Pasquin* was revived "by Pasquin's original Company" on 25 February, I would guess that Fielding had no part in the theater's offerings prior to that time.

59. First noted and reported by Emmett L. Avery, "Proposals for a New London Theatre in 1737," *Notes and Queries* 182 (1942): 286-287.

60. For examples from this period see Richard Leacroft, *The Development of the English Playhouse* (London: Eyre Methuen, 1973), chap-

ter 5. For convenient tables of theater dimensions, see Edward A. Langhans, "The Theatres," in Hume, *London Theatre World,* esp. pp. 61-65.

61. Published in *The Works of the Late Aaron Hill* (1753), and reprinted by Jack Richard Brown, "From Aaron Hill to Henry Fielding?" *Philological Quarterly* 18 (1939): 85-88.

62. The common assertion that it was a revision of an anonymous lost play of 1692 is, however, a canard. See Judith Milhous and Robert D. Hume, "Lost English Plays, 1660-1700," *Harvard Library Bulletin* 25 (1977): 5-33.

63. The authorship is unknown. Hill implies, or seems to believe, that it was Fielding's. The puff of 8 March says it is by "a Gentleman who never wrote for the Stage." Since the same puff identifies Fielding as the author of *The Historical Register,* I am inclined to think that he was not responsible for *A Rehearsal of Kings.*

64. Cited in Scouten, *London Stage, Part III,* 2: 660.

65. For example, the *Daily Gazetteer,* 4 June: the "Drift of the Allegory throughout, is too plain to be mistaken."

66. Neither Goldgar nor McCrea mention these works, though they definitely represent a daring escalation of Fielding's political risk, if not necessarily of his political commitment.

67. For Potter's letter of 7 January 1737/8 reminding Grafton that he was owed "a Reward" for preventing "what was Intended to be Represented in my theatre in May last," see J. Paul de Castro in *Notes and Queries* 182 (1942): 346. For discussion of the episode, see Hume, *Rakish Stage,* pp. 306-307.

68. Folger MS T.b. 3. Collier's notes include a copy of a bill dated 13 June 1737 and evidently submitted by Potter to the duke of Grafton, then lord chamberlain. The bill includes £12 12s. "To taking down the scenes & decorations so that the theatre was Renderd Incapable of haveing any Play or other performance, and mens time & Carts To fill the same with deale & timber Bricks and Lime Charge of moveing those things." Also included under "Loss by my theatre" is £212 2s. "To money to Be paid by Mrs Coopper and I suppose Mr Fielding (he haveing Begun a subscription) for twenty one weeks from the first day of January next."

69. Fielding himself denounced the idea of such a restriction in an article for the *Daily Journal* published 25 March. See Thomas Lockwood, "A New Essay by Fielding," *Modern Philology* 78 (1980): 48-58.

70. How good were the performers at the Little Haymarket? They were definitely a mixed bag, and they varied considerably from season to season and even production to production. Aaron Hill's letter of 28 February makes an interesting comment: "I see clearly, by some names among your performers, that you are not in so much danger as I apprehended, on that quarter." But we may guess that after the likes of Eliza Haywood, Charlotte Charke, and James Lacy (named as performers in

A Rehearsal of Kings) the quality of the company fell off rapidly. Charke claimed to have been paid four guineas per week (plus a benefit at which she cleared sixty guineas more) during the run of *Pasquin* — excellent pay. *A Narrative of the Life of Mrs Charlotte Charke* (London: W. Reeve et al., 1755), p. 63.

71. McCrea, *Fielding and Politics,* pp. 24-25. Following quotations from pp. 75, 76.

72. See Martin Battestin, "Four New Fielding Attributions: His Earliest Satires of Walpole," *Studies in Bibliography* 36 (1983): 69-109.

73. This dedication is susceptible of a very plausible ironic reading — yet another warning to avoid overingenuity. For the ironic reading, see Hunter, *Occasional Form,* pp. 56-57, and Hume, *Rakish Stage,* pp. 209-210. Cf. Loftis, *Politics of Drama,* pp. 130-131; Goldgar, *Walpole,* pp. 112-115.

74. On this play, sponsored by Bodens but probably the work of Lord Hervey and the Prince of Wales, see Charles B. Woods, "Captain B — — —'s Play," *Harvard Studies and Notes in Philology and Literature* 15 (1933): 243-255, and Robert Halsband, *Lord Hervey: Eighteenth-Century Courtier* (Oxford: Oxford University Press, 1974), pp. 130-132. For discussion of political significance, see Goldgar, *Walpole,* pp. 101-102.

75. Goldgar, *Walpole,* p. 150.

76. McCrea deviates from his own well-argued position at the end of chapter 3 when he says that in 1737 Fielding was "still uncertain whether he belonged with the Tories or with the Whigs" (*Fielding and Politics,* p. 77). What evidence have we of serious Tory inclinations? McCrea takes Vern D. Bailey to task for such views in "Fielding's Politics," Ph.D. diss., University of California, Berkeley, 1970.

77. Martin Battestin comments that several of the essays in *The Craftsman* which he attributes to Fielding "are bitterly ironic on the subject of the Licensing Act." This would hardly be surprising, but Fielding's remaining anonymous is surely significant. However angry he was about the Licensing Act, he did not publicly burn his bridges.

78. My understanding of the split is drawn from Quentin Skinner's "The Principles and Practice of Opposition: The Case of Bolingbroke versus Walpole," in Neil McKendrick, ed., *Historical Perspectives: Studies in English Thought and Society in honour of J. H. Plumb* (London: Europa, 1974), pp. 93-128, and from such books as Kenyon's *Revolution Principles,* H. T. Dickinson's *Liberty and Property: Political Ideology in Eighteenth-Century Britain* (New York: Holmes and Meier, 1977), and Linda Colley's *In Defiance of Oligarchy: The Tory Party 1714-60* (Cambridge: Cambridge University Press, 1982).

79. "I do not think a Writer, whose only Livelihood is his Pen, to deserve a very flagitious Character, if, when one Set of Men deny him Encouragement, he seeks it from another, at their Expence; nor will I rashly condemn such a Writer as the vilest of Men, (provided he keeps

within the Rules of Decency) if he endeavours to make the best of his own Cause, and uses a little Art in blackening his Adversary."

80. For significant views of Fielding's politics (mostly ca. 1740) see Martin C. Battestin, "Fielding's Changing Politics and *Joseph Andrews*," *Philological Quarterly* 39 (1960): 39-55; W. B. Coley, "Henry Fielding and the Two Walpoles," *Philological Quarterly* 45 (1966): 157-178; and Goldgar, *Walpole,* especially pp. 207-208.

81. I am indebted to Martin Battestin and Bertrand A. Goldgar for helpful critiques of an earlier draft of this study.

V

WHERE IS HISTORY BUT IN TEXTS? READING THE HISTORY OF MARRIAGE

Susan Staves

Marriage in the eighteenth century has left behind a rich record of pleasure and pain, particularly marriage in the literate classes. For various reasons, it is possible to know more about how literate couples lived and struggled with each other in the eighteenth century than about the domestic histories of earlier centuries. The evidence provided by sources encountered in earlier periods— sermons, records of ecclesiastical courts, letters and diaries, pamphlet controversy—was supplemented by a variety of new sources in the eighteenth century. Newspapers printed both gossip and more official notices of weddings and divorces, and other matrimonial news and litigation. New magazines like *Bon Ton* and the *Town and Country Magazine* elaborated on the gossip. The development of the tort of criminal conversation led to the publication of virtually complete trial transcripts through which an interested public could learn what evidence the plaintiff had of his wife's adultery and what arguments the defendant could marshal to mitigate his alleged depravity.[1] Not so often published as the criminal conversation trials but nevertheless sometimes available to the historian are the separate maintenance contracts

125

negotiated by discontented couples which enabled spouses to live apart and regularized their obligations to each other during their separations.[2] On a happier note, more and less practical suggestions for maintaining domestic peace and tranquility were available in an increasingly secular advice literature.[3] Images of contemporary domestic bliss could also be contemplated by audiences of sentimental fiction and sentimental drama. All of these verbal sources are available to anyone who wishes to read the history of eighteenth-century marriage. (There is, of course, also some numerical evidence — such as age at first marriage, portions allotted to younger sons and daughters, and so on — which is important but which I do not wish to consider here.)

Many of the verbal texts have been used in more or less systematic ways by historians now engaged in a spirited debate over the nature of the changes that occurred in marriage in early modern England. The debate is so spirited partly because it has as a clamorous subtext another debate about the nature of twentieth-century marriage, which is in some sense a product of these changes, and because there is a deep division of feeling over whether modern marriage is fundamentally, in the words of *1066 and All That,* a "good thing" or a "bad thing." An important place in the debate is occupied by the distinguished historian Lawrence Stone, whose *The Family, Sex and Marriage in England, 1500-1800,* published in 1977, gives an expansive description of marriage practices and attitudes among the various classes. Stone argues for the rise of what he calls "the companionate marriage" in the ranks of "the lesser nobility, the squirarchy and the gentry . . . and the professional and upper middle classes." He describes this new companionate marriage as follows:

The choice of a spouse was increasingly left in the hands of the children themselves and was based mainly on temperamental compatibility with the aim of lasting companionship. The wife concerned herself with household management, entertainment and leisure activities. She also often closely supervised, in an increasingly permissive mode, the upbringing of the young children. . . . The husband and wife were closely bonded by affective ties, and the wife was normally both faithful and obedient to her husband. The husband might well have a few extramarital sexual adventures, but they were not allowed to break up the marriage. Many of these marriages were accompanied by legal settlements which protected the wife's property, and decision-making power tended to be shared rather than monopolized by the husband.[4]

Stone gives a basically positive picture of this new companionate marriage, though he does acknowledge that it also entailed some "problems"; notably, that increased autonomy for individuals and increased privacy for the nuclear family also "had the effect of stripping away from a marriage one by one many of those external economic, social and psychological supports which normally serve as powerful reinforcing agencies to hold together the nuclear family," and that, as he puts it, "wives of the middle and upper ranks of society increasingly became idle drones."[5]

Stone's account has been challenged in a variety of ways. Randolph Trumbach in *The Rise of the Egalitarian Family* describes instead an eighteenth-century shift from earlier "patriarchy" to "domesticity": patriarchy presuming that heads of households had property in things and persons, domesticity establishing a limited degree of household equality between husband and wife, an equality from which servants were excluded. For Trumbach, the aristocracy rather than the gentry and the new middle classes were the principal agents of this change.[6]

Stone's companionate marriage depends upon strong "affective ties" between husband and wife, and Stone explains the modern ability to form such ties by a "growth of affective individualism" in his innovating classes. He contrasts this affective individualism with a lack of affect in the lower classes and with a lack of such affect in the sixteenth and early seventeenth centuries, when a "majority of individuals ... found it very difficult to establish close emotional ties to any other person."[7] This line of argument has met with strong resistance from a number of readers, including the Marxist historian E. P. Thompson, who, employing the rhetorical overkill to which British historians seem attached, has declared that Stone's view of the modern family is not supported "by any relevant evidence" and that parts of his book, such as those dealing with plebeian sexual behavior, "should be pulped." Thompson treats with sarcasm Stone's belief that the importance of romantic love in marriage was tied to literacy:

But by 1600 or 1800 the English peasantry and working people had not had any chance to learn about love, because learning requires literacy. They did not learn to love each other because they couldn't read novels, and they couldn't have a companionate marriage because, until both husband and wife could read the newspapers, they could have little in common to "talk about."

Not surprisingly, Thompson is also unconvinced by a picture of couples bonded together by affection rather than economic interest, believing instead that in the classes which Stone sees as creating the companionate marriage "economic interests are only masked or distanced" and that "genteel sensibility" is itself a "product of surplus value." Moreover, Thompson argues, "there cannot be any such historical entity as the family. For familial relations are inextricably part and parcel of every other kind of relation and occupation: that is, they are components of a whole way of life." For most people, Thompson maintains, family relations are intermeshed with the structures of work, and "feeling may be *more,* rather than less, tender, or intense *because* relations are 'economic' and critical to mutual survival."[8]

Claims that the rise of companionate marriage or the egalitarian family meant an improvement in the position of women have also been greeted with skepticism or frank denial. Some feminist historians have been more impressed with the damage to women brought about by the privatization of the domestic sphere, and by the exclusion of women from the world of work, than they have been charmed by increased autonomy in the choice of marriage partners or by development of closer affective bonds between husband and wife. Writing in *Philosophy and Public Affairs,* Susan Okin, a feminist political scientist, has recently argued that the "growing idealization of families as private sanctuaries of sentiment," far from being related to a heightened appreciation of women, instead served "as a *reinforcement* of the patriarchal relations between men and women that had been temporarily threatened by seventeenth-century individualism." In particular, it reinforced the legitimacy of male rule within the household by presenting such rule—unlike political rule in the public sphere—as "based only on love."[9]

I don't propose to settle all these disputes. I would like, however, to offer some reflections on reading the texts that are the sources for the history of eighteenth-century marriage. These reflections are in part a cautionary tale to myself as I study aspects of matrimonial law and the representation of marriage in literature. They may also help to explain how there can be such radically divergent views of the subject.

There is a remarkable range of attitudes struck and tones sounded in talk of marriage in the eighteenth century. There are,

of course, the familiar voices from the pulpit. These are sometimes tinged with a newer sentiment but always suitably serious.
"No persons," said Archbishop Secker,

should ever enter the marriage bond with such as they cannot esteem
and love: and all persons, who have entered into, should use all means,
not only to preserve esteem and love, but to increase it; affectionate condescension on the husband's part, cheerful submission on the wife's;
mildness and tenderness, prudence and attention to their common
interest, and that of their joint posterity, on both parts.[10]

The lawyers, necessarily, also spoke of marriage. Blackstone
not only offered his famous maxim "the husband and wife are one
person in law" but also ventured to comment on such matters as
apparent limitations placed on the husband's power of chastising
his wife "in the politer reign of Charles the second." He concluded his discussion of baron and feme by remarking compla-
cently: "even the disabilities, which the wife lies under, are for
the most part intended for her protection and benefit. So great a
favorite is the female sex of the laws of England."[11] There is sometimes a similar chivalry in the appellate opinions. But in opinions—no doubt because the marriages that produce litigation
have often notoriously failed to exhibit "affectionate condescension on the husband's part, cheerful submission on the wife's"—
judges are more often moved to reassert the harsher necessities of
male domination and female subordination.

In parliament, also, there was talk of marriage, perhaps most
notably in the debates over the Marriage Act of 1753. Such public and official discourse about marriage as came from the pulpit,
the bench, and the houses of parliament usually, though not
invariably, expressed a sense of marriage as a public institution
that served such public purposes as the reproduction of citizens
and the orderly transmission of property from one generation to
another. Official discourse also expressed an awareness of marriage as a social institution that could accustom people to a
domestic order that was to be both a microcosm of and a building
block for a larger public order, the state. Gratification of sexual
desire absent the ordering power of marriage constituted licen-
tiousness. As Archbishop Secker imagined, in proportion as licen-
tiousness

prevails, the regularity and good order of society is overturned, the credit and peace of families destroyed, the proper disposal of young people in marriage prevented, the due education of children and provision for them neglected, the keenest animosities perpetually excited, and the most shocking murders frequently committed, of the parties themselves, their rivals, their innocent babes: in short, every enormity follows from hence, that lawless passion can introduce.[12]

Not surprisingly, in official public discourse marriage is usually spoken of in respectful tones and represented as a fundamentally stable, satisfactory institution—even though the speaker may advert to what are characterized as transient problems or to less respectful, erroneous attitudes which prompt his own discourse.

In some less official discourse, however, eighteenth-century marriage is represented in radically different ways and spoken of in very different tones. Richard Cumberland described a fashionable eighteenth-century couple in a satiric poem:

> Dorinda and her spouse were join'd,
>   As modern men and women are,
> In matrimony not in mind
>   A fashionable pair.
>
> Fine clothes, fine diamonds, and fine lace,
>   The smartest vis-a-vis in town,
> With titles, pin money, and place,
>   Made wed-lock's pill go down.[13]

In a more lurid vein, George Granville, Lord Landsdowne, composed what was apparently intended as a cautionary poem against women marrying for rank and wealth. The most vivid lines describe what happens when Cleora, having made a splendid appearance by day in the Park, must at night retire to the bedroom to "bear...the loathsome load" of a husband who infects her with venereal disease:

> The secret Venom circling in her veins,
> Works thro' her Skin, and bursts in bloating Stains;
> Her Cheeks their Freshness lose and wonted Grace,
> And an unusual Paleness spreads her Face,
> Her Eyes grow dim, and her corrupted Breath
> Tainting her Gums, infects her Ivory Teeth,
> Of sharp nocturnal Anguish she complains,

And guiltless of the Cause, relates her Pains.
The conscious Husband, whom like Symptoms seize,
Charges on her the Guilt of their Disease.[14]

Branded by her husband with a "vile Adulteress's Name," the wife rots and dies alone. Insists Granville, "Thousands of poor *Cleora*'s may be found."

In private letters marriage was spoken of with reverence, long-ing, pain, anger, disgust, puzzlement, and amused contempt. Writing from Florence to his friend Horace Walpole in England, Horace Mann reacted to news of the latest matrimonial scandal:

I have often reflected that the affair of matrimony is upon a worse foot in England than in any other country. One never, or at least very sel-dom, learns of unhappy marriages in these parts. They set out better, and certainly understand the conduct of it better: separate apartments, and less fondness and cuddling are quite necessary. Matters are really reduced to such a pitch in England that I don't wonder people should be deterred from such undertakings.[15]

Writing from England to her friend Lady Pomfret in Paris, Lady Mary Wortley Montagu reported with amusement the return of Lady Vane, who had left her husband, with her lover Lord Berkeley:

[She] went with him in publick to Cranford, where they remain as happy as love and youth can make them. I am told that though she does not pique herself upon fidelity to any one man (which is but a narrow way of thinking), she boasts that she has always been true to her nation, and notwithstanding foreign attacks, has always reserved her charms for the use of her own countrymen.[16]

To my observation that a great range of tones and attitudes appear in eighteenth-century discourse about marriage, a com-monsensical response would be, "But of course! Isn't the same true now, when men speak reverentially of marriage to fathers of women they wish to marry, joke about it in bars, and cry about it to their analysts? Hasn't the same thing always been the case?" The truth of this response needs to be borne in mind by anyone attempting a history of marriage. Dependence on a single kind of source or even on limited kinds of sources is bound to lead to a partial history. Conduct books will give one history of eighteenth-century marriage, the gossip columns and vignettes of the *Town and Country Magazine* another. Modern scholars being generally sober-minded, no one has recently attempted a history based solely on gossip columns or lewd joke books. But too many scholarly generalities about older attitudes toward marriage are based on sources such as sermons or conduct books.

Not only were there different attitudes toward marriage in different classes or social circles—among the Methodists or the rakes—but the same people were perfectly capable of taking one attitude or tone in one social circumstance and another in another social circumstance. There were many spheres of discourse about marriage in the eighteenth century, and speakers and writers were sensitive to the different decorums of the different spheres. It is hard to say now what were the rules of speech about marriage in different spheres of discourse, but we can understand something about the rules of writing about it.

Moreover, though it is true that there were multiple spheres of discourse about marriage in the eighteenth century and that there are multiple spheres of discourse about marriage now, it cannot be true that these spheres of discourse are invariant over time, transhistorical. Eighteenth-century people, for instance, did not engage in dialogues about marriage with psychotherapists. Twentieth-century people do not go to masquerades and carry on adulterous flirtations in assumed characters, speaking in high-pitched masquerade squeaks.

So far, I have not made any particular distinction between factual and fictional discourse, a distinction that has seemed obvious and important to historians. Indeed, Stone, who depends massively upon literary sources in *The Family, Sex and Marriage,* has implausibly characterized his use of such sources as putting "frosting on the cake of hard data."[17] The distinction between factual and fictional discourse about eighteenth-century marriage, however, is not so obvious or so easy to apply as may at first appear. In an important discussion of early eighteenth-century narratives, Lennard Davis has described the textual world of which early novels were a part as one in which novels and news were not clearly differentiated, "when there was no standard veracious discourse in the realm of narrative," but only a general "news/novel discourse." He points out, for instance, that in early titles *news* and *novel* seem to have been used interchangeably; that laws attempting to regulate publication had difficulty defining a category of *news*; that both news and novels frequently appeared in serial format; and that, partly in relation to this format, both established "a mode of presenting the past, more specifically the recent past, without the powerful retrospective implications of a treatise on history."[18]

When we attempt to read the history of eighteenth-century marriage, it is useful to realize that it is often quite impossible to tell on the basis of internal evidence whether a particular narrative is fact or fiction. Consider the following letter addressed in the late eighteenth century to a husband by a wife who has eloped from him:

> By what Title, or in what Manner shall I convey to him I have so cruelly wronged, so wickedly deceived, the Sentiments of Gratitude and Grief with which my Heart is overpowered! Will you believe me? Can you suppose me not totally lost to all Feeling? Alas! what shall I say, I would now redeem the past with my Life were it possible, and to the last Hour of my lingering Existence, my Thoughts shall dwell on you, and on all your Benefits; it will add Torture to Reflections, and Stings to wounded Consciences: May you be ever happy, ever cheerful: May your Children be all that is good and dutiful, and may I hope from the Husband I have wronged, that Species of Forgiveness, which I will pray Heaven to grant me, that in another World I may see his Face again. . . .
>
> Farewell; let not my Children, while they detest my Offence, hate the Person of their Mother; would she had been ever as at the Moment,
>
> Your grateful, affectionate,
> and deeply affected
> *E. S. S.*

Obviously, this is not a sixteenth-century or a twentieth-century letter. The syntax is that debased Johnsonianism into which Fanny Burney dwindles, the diction adjectively and abstractly sentimental, and the image of the writer in "the last Hour" of a "lingering Existence" virtually Richardsonian. But I doubt whether anyone could say with confidence whether this letter was actually written by a woman just eloped from her husband or whether it was part of an epistolary novel. The careful periodic sentences might incline one to guess that the letter was more likely from a novel than from the pen of a distraught woman who had only a lady's education. I have, however, quoted the letter from the *Journal of the House of Lords*, where it is given as having been introduced as evidence in the case of *Shadwell* v. *Shadwell,* as a letter of Mrs. Shadwell.[19] Shadwell claimed he had been informed by his servants that his wife had been seen having intercourse with the man who was supposed to be giving her instruction in French, that he had then sent her from his house "so soon as Lodging could be procured for her," and that from this Lodging she had sent him the penitent letter. The peers gave Shadwell his divorce, presumably believing that Mrs. Shadwell had written it. It is not entirely beyond human belief, however, that Shadwell could have written the letter himself. Perjury and forgery have always been particularly rampant in divorce litigation, and Shadwell was a barrister well aware of the value of such a document. My point is simply that nothing intrinsic to the text of the letter allows us to say with confidence that it was written by a novelist, by Mrs. Shadwell, or by Shadwell.

Much factual discourse about eighteenth-century marriage is deeply imbued with the language, assumptions, roles, and plots of fictional discourse. For example, a stock scene of eighteenth-century fiction is a wife's discovery of her husband's infidelity and the representation of her response to this discovery. In Cibber's *Careless Husband,* Lady Easy discovers Sir Charles Easy with the maid, Edging. After a painful soliloquy over the sleeping lovers, the wronged wife shows her love and forgiveness by draping her neckerchief over her errant husband's bare head, lest he catch a chill.[20] In Richardson's *Pamela,* as Pamela hears more and more of the relationship between her husband and the countess, she confronts him in her "trial" scene, declaring that she knows "the charms of my rival are too powerful for me to contend with." She begs to be sent down to live with her parents in Kent, offering "to give his wishes all the forwardness" she honorably can should he wish to divorce her, but also insisting that she cannot consent to live with a man "who lives in what I cannot but think open sin with another."[21] Similar scenes abound in eighteenth-century fiction and drama. The wife is thoroughly virtuous, not only sexually chaste but also innocent of having driven the husband into the arms of another by bad behavior. The husband expresses amazement at her restraint in not railing at him, and at her virtue.

In Elizabeth Baroness Craven's *Memoirs,* fictional scenes like this seem to shape the narrative. According to her account she married William Craven in 1767 because he importuned her; she was able to say honestly not that she loved him but that she "felt for him that regard and gratitude which his honest and warm heart deserved."[22] After thirteen years of marriage, during which he treated her kindly enough, her chief anxiety being his carelessness about money, she begins to realize that he is lying about his whereabouts. She learns of a mistress and suddenly is informed by Lord McCartney that Lord Craven's mistress travels with him calling herself Lady Craven and conducting herself "at inns in such a manner as to reflect upon and tarnish" the character of the real Lady Craven. As she narrates the scene of her confrontation with her husband, she calmly and humbly opens by asking a "favor," namely, "that he would not permit his mistress to call herself Lady Craven":

He looked much confused, rose from where he was sitting, and walked about the room some time. He then asked how long it was, that I had known that he had a mistress? To this I replied, "Above a twelvemonth." He then took some more walks across the room; when, suddenly stopping and clasping his hands together, he threw his eyes up to heaven and exclaimed, "By G—, you are the best-tempered creature in the world; for I have never suspected that you knew this!" I then told him that he must remember the spotless young creature he had married, and who had borne him seven children; and that there was one thing I must insist on, which was, that if he continued to live with that woman, I would order a bed in the room next to his; for her conduct was such that my health might suffer.[23]

When she proceeds to tell her husband what she has learned from his mistress's husband, Lord Craven begins to show indignation and resentment, but, says Lady Craven, "I continued to entreat him to consider his children, and seriously to reflect on the fatal consequences of his conduct."[24]

As the narrative of their separation develops, certain interesting deviations from the usual fictional treatments appear. For instance, she attempts to protect her own interests and those of her children by seeking legal advice, calling in first Lord Loughborough and then Lord Thurlow. Both give estimates of how much money she can expect by way of a settlement. Nevertheless, on hearing her story Lord Loughborough is reported to fly "into the most violent passion" with Lord Craven, and Lord Thurlow is supposed to have been observed with tears welling up in his eyes.[25]

Edifying as the narrative in Lady Craven's *Memoirs* is, it seems unlikely that the confrontation scene could have taken place exactly as she describes. Her *Memoirs* omit all reference to a notorious episode in 1773 in which she herself was supposedly discovered in an embarrassing degree of intimacy with the French ambassador to London. According to the *Town and Country Magazine,* Lord Craven, grown suspicious, declined to join his wife in going to the masquerade, pretending a headache.

Her ladyship dressed at home, and went to the ball. His lordship soon after followed her with two friends, who kept a constant eye upon her and the ambassador. They perceived her ladyship and his excellency retire into a private room, and the door was instantly fastened. His lordship being made acquainted with this retreat, presently forced open the door, and found her ladyship sitting upon the ambassador's knee, in such a state, as clearly proved that a few minutes would have brought on an amorous conflict.

His lordship sent his wife directly into the country, and, it is said, challenged the ambassador, who declined accepting of it on account of his public character; but promises to give his lordship the satisfaction of a gentleman, when he shall have received his letters of recall. This discovery, it is assured, has wrought so powerfully upon her ladyship's mind, as to turn her brain. It is certain that her relations have severely upbraided her upon the occasion, and the more as she had no plea of ill treatment from her noble husband; he having married her with a very small fortune, though he possesses a very ample one, and has always behaved to her with the most conjugal affection.[26]

As with the account in the *Memoirs,* we may suspect that this account, too, is not strictly accurate. Lady Craven, rather than perishing in a madhouse, continued to live with her husband for some years afterward, moving in society in the ordinary way and eventually making another marriage after his death. We have, in effect, "his" and "hers" narratives: hers giving a rather mordant view of his intellectual limitations and character and an idealized view of her own; his representing him as a generous and kindly husband and her as an ungrateful woman of too easy virtue, shocked into madness by the enormity of her offense.

The different forms the same marriage could assume in different sources is also nicely evident in the various records of the marriage of Sophia Snow and Robert Baddeley. In 1763 Sophia, daughter of a court and theatrical musician, at eighteen eloped with Robert, an actor. Both had successful careers in the theater.

By 1770 Sophia was living with a lover. When David Garrick, as the manager and moralist of Drury Lane, required that she stop living with the lover, she complied on the condition that Garrick pay her salary directly to her rather than to Robert. This occasioned a duel between Robert and George Garrick, who had complained of Robert's treatment of Sophia. The *Town and Country Magazine* described the duel in the style of mock romance:

they repaired to Hyde-park, and the seconds having marked out the ground, Mr. B———y had already fired at his antagonist, when his wife, who had received intimation of the affair, flew upon the wings of love (that is in a hackney-coach) to the field of battle, and arriving at this critical time, threw herself upon her knees, and, while she looked very languishing, (*but whether at her lover or husband is not certain*) cried out, *"Oh! spare, spare him!"* which intreaty, it is imagined, induced Mr. G——— to fire his pistol in the air, and a reconciliation took place.[27]

Such publicity perhaps seemed a distortion to Sophia, however. On an occasion in 1774 when some letters between herself and a "noble Lord" were published in the paper, she wrote—more soberly—to protest, asking, "what family in the kingdom could be safe or happy when an editor of a paper would expose their most confidential concerns brought by a malevolent enemy or a treacherous servant."[28] In 1776 Sophia was sued by John Hatchett, a coachmaker, for labor and materials. Sophia's counsel pleaded that she did not owe the money on the ground that she was a married woman whose husband was still living.[29] All argument proceeded on the premise that there was no formal separate maintenance agreement—a premise that according to other evidence, including the Garrick letters, was almost certainly incorrect. *Hatchett* v. *Baddeley* contributed to the development of a rule that eloped wives living in adultery without separate maintenance are not to have credit in their own right, nor are their husbands to be responsible for their debts. Blackstone, who was among the judges who decided *Hatchett,* took the opportunity to defend the evolving rule as desirable public policy:

And I see no hardship in a man's losing his money, that avows upon the record, that he furnished a coach to the wife of a player, whom he knew to have run away from her husband. If this were generally known to be law, it would be difficult to such women to gain credit, and this would consequently reduce the number of such wanderers.

Blackstone's vision of Mrs. Baddeley, aside from its blindness to the separate maintenance contract, sees her as "the wife of a player." He was blind also to the fact that she earned money to support herself and had in the past partially supported her husband. His sanguine hope that the new legal rule would make it so difficult for discontented wives to gain credit that they would remain with their husbands certainly had no effect on Sophia, who continued to act and also continued to receive valuable presents from lovers, including Lord Melbourne. At the time of her death Sophia received some support from an actor's fund; Robert left the property he had accumulated to one of the mistresses with whom he had lived.

To approach the idea of spheres of discourse from a different perspective, there seems to be a finite set of possible narratives about marriage in the eighteenth century. Whatever the "facts" of a particular marital relationship from a twentieth-century perspective, some facts are unnamable in some eighteenth-century spheres of discourse. For example, the more official pulpit discourse and the advice literature were willing enough to recognize that some marital situations inevitably produced pain, but such discourse freely selected and invented examples, cases, capable of being integrated into a final view of contemporary marriage as satisfactory. Naturally, Stone's ideal companionate marriage, dependent on greater equality and sharing, was not usually found in the law courts, where there were frequent occasions when disputes prompted reassertions of the need for masculine dominance and female subordination. (The wife's opportunity to choose a husband for love was sometimes invoked to make her obligations to obey him the stronger.) In *Oliver* v. *Oliver,* for instance, a wife pleaded her husband's cruelty in bar to his suit for the restitution of conjugal rights.[30] She alleged one incident of violence in which her husband, a watchmaker and dissenting minister, required her to give him the keys to the wine and ale cellars. She refused — why we do not know — and in an ensuing struggle she was bruised "in her arm and breast against the garden-steps."[31] In rejecting the wife's contention, the judge opined: "surely this was conduct enough to exasperate a husband, to the extent at least of an endeavour to obtain possession of [the keys]. . . . There is no reason to impute any malignant intention, or any other intention than that of obtaining what he had a right to possess, and which was illegally withheld."[32] Though the advice literature was willing enough to insist on a wife's duty to obey her husband, and though writers of such literature probably would have had little sympathy for Mrs. Oliver, I think it fair to say that they would not mention fact situations so sordid or where a wife's duty to obey her husband justified his infliction of such bruises.

In *Holmes* v. *Holmes,* another case in which a wife alleged cruelty in bar to a suit for the restitution of conjugal rights, the wife complained that her ironmonger husband had sent two of his men friends to her, then appeared himself:

and swore he would lie with her in the presence of the said men; and they said he was her husband, and had a right to do so, and they would hold her for him to lie with her; whereupon she got out of the window, over a palisade, and over to the next house, whither he and the said two men followed her, and he there pulled off her cap, and dragged her by the hair of her head, and attempted to drag her home, but was prevented; and that afterwards he declared that if he could get her in his power he would send her abroad, where nobody should see her, unless she would give him her money; that, therefore, she could not live safely with him, and prayed to be separated.[33]

The judge in this case ruled that the wife "had charged nothing but words, except the single fact of his dragging her by the hair, which happened after she had separated herself from him, and that was not a cruelty sufficient. . . ." Conduct books were willing enough to tell women that they must not expect the "transports and wild raptures" of a romantic courtship to continue during marriage,[34] but they were not prepared to reveal that there may be no legal recourse against a husband who proposes to exercise his conjugal rights in the presence of his friends or who tries to frighten his wife into signing away her entitlement to separate property.

Not only are some facts unnamable in a given sphere of discourse, some facts are virtually unnamable in any of the available spheres of discourse — in any of the available narratives in a finite, not an infinite, set. This is perhaps clearest in the legal records. The art of pleading developed in the Middle Ages with the counte (*narratio* in Latin), a tale or a story. The plaintiff tells his story, which at a certain point is recorded in Latin and from that point on is binding and unalterable. Though there are many possible

stories a plaintiff may tell, in order for a story to prevail it must
contain certain elements necessary to sustain the action. Not all
stories will work. In eighteenth-century criminal conversation litigation, many trials come down to the plaintiff's pathetic narrative versus the defendant's comic one.[35]

If he wishes to prevail, the plaintiff cannot say—even if it is
true—that he married his wife initially for her money, likes her so
little that he is rather glad than sorry that she has committed
adultery, and looks forward cheerfully to collecting yet more
money in the form of damages. Nor, with the possible exception
of a very private communication to a very intimate and uncen-
sorious friend, is there any sphere of discourse in which a husband
could tell such a story. Nor is there one in which a wife could
express a feeling that her adultery was entirely justified by her
husband's failings and that she was a good and decent person
nevertheless. Very rarely do we read comments so acidulous as
Anne Masterman's in the postscript to her novel *The Old Maid:*
"as for the men, I have endeavored to make some of them toler-
ably decent in my book, for the sake of variety, as it is the form
generally used in writing novels; but I must confess, they are
entirely the children of my own brain, as I could not find one
original to copy by."[36]

At the end of Mary Wollstonecraft's novel *Maria, or the
Wrongs of Woman,* Maria's lover Darnford is sued by her terrible
husband, Mr. Venables, for criminal conversation damages.
Darnford is called away on pressing business, and Maria, with
ludicrous implausibility in the light of historical knowledge, takes
"the task of conducting Darnford's defence upon herself,"
instructing his counsel and writing a statement to be read in
court. Her statement protests the "false morality" which makes
the virtue of women consist in chastity and submission, asserts her
right to freedom from Venables, the wrongfulness of representing
Darnford as having seduced a twenty-six-year-old woman, and
her determination to regard Darnford as her husband and her
fortune as her own. Her efforts merely provoke the fictional judge
to comment on "the fallacy of letting women plead their feelings. . . ."[37]

If we are to write the history of eighteenth-century marriage,
we have no alternative but to depend on the kinds of texts I have
been describing. We must be aware of the particular constraints

that limit each of them and try to correct the limitations of one kind of source by juxtaposing it with other sources. Although the more idealistic and abstract representations must be confronted with more cynical or pragmatic private ones, we cannot simply toss out the idealistic representations—because they had power. All the texts taken together made up the world in which couples lived. Yet perhaps the most serious problem that confronts us in writing a history of eighteenth-century marriage is that so much female feeling, so much female bitterness, was not only unexpressed but almost inexpressible.

NOTES

1. Susan Staves, "Money for Honor: Damages for Criminal Conversation," *Studies in Eighteenth-Century Culture* 11 (1982): 279-297; see also Peter Wagner, "Trial Reports as a Genre of Eighteenth-Century Erotica," *British Journal for Eighteenth-Century Studies* 5 (1982): 117-122.

2. Susan Staves, "Separate Maintenance Contracts," paper delivered at the Cambridge Early Modern History Seminar, March 1982.

3. Lawrence Stone, *The Family, Sex and Marriage in England, 1500-1800* (New York: Harper & Row, 1977), pp. 759-763, offers a bibliography of "Moral and Medical Tracts," which are important sources for his history. Some of Stone's conclusions from this material have been challenged; for example, by Laura A. Curtis, "A Cast Study of Defoe's Domestic Conduct Manuals Suggested by *The Family, Sex and Marriage in England, 1500-1800*," *Studies in Eighteenth-Century Culture* 10 (1981): 409-428. Also, on the current issue of whether the "Puritan" advice books in the sixteenth and seventeenth centuries advocated a new ideal of marriage or not, and for an awareness of the difficulty of extrapolating from such literature to social fact, see Kathleen M. Davies, "Continuity and Change in Literary Advice on Marriage," in R. B. Outhwaite, ed., *Marriage and Society: Studies in the Social History of Marriage* (London: Europea Publications, 1981), 58-80. Other useful studies of the advice literature include Joyce Hemlow, "Fanny Burney and the Courtesy Books," *PMLA*, 65 (1950): 732-761, and Ann Zimmerman Russel, "You Have More Power by Your Tears Than We Have by Our Arguments," chapter 1 in "The Image of Women in Eighteenth-Century English Novels," Ph.D. diss., Brandeis University, 1974.

4. Stone, *The Family*, p. 392.

5. Stone, *The Family*, p. 396.

6. Randolph Trumbach, *The Rise of the Egalitarian Family: Aristocratic Kinship and Domestic Relations in Eighteenth-Century England* (New York: Academic Press, 1978).

7. Stone, *The Family,* p. 99.

8. E. P. Thompson, "Happy Families," *Radical History Review,* no. 20 (1979): 42-50; a review originally published in *New Society,* 1977.

9. Susan Moller Okin, "Women and the Making of the Sentimental Family," *Philosophy and Public Affairs* 11 (1982): 74.

10. Thomas Secker, "Lectures on the Catechism of the Church of England; With a Discourse on Confirmation. Lecture XXV. The Seventh Commandment," in *The Works of Thomas Secker, LL.D., Late Lord Archbishop of Canterbury,* 6 vols. (London, 1811), 6:255.

11. William Blackstone, *Commentaries on the Laws of England,* 4 vols., facsimile of the 1st ed. (Chicago: University of Chicago Press, 1979), 1: 433.

12. Secker, *Works,* 6: 256.

13. Richard Cumberland, *The Observer: Being a Collection of Moral, Literary and Familiar Essays,* 3 vols. (London, 1786), 2: 159; reprinted as "The Fashionable Pair," *Scots Magazine* 47 (1786): 348.

14. George Granville, Lord Landsdowne, "Cleora," in *Poems Upon Several Occasions,* 2d ed. (London, 1716), p. 79.

15. "From Mann" (2 April 1743 NS), in *Horace Walpole's Correspondence with Sir Horace Mann,* ed. W. S. Lewis, Warren Hunting Smith, and George L. Lam (New Haven, Conn.: Yale University Press, 1954), 2: 199. Walpole had shortly before regaled his friend with an account of an examination of the duke of Beaufort for impotency, explaining that the duchess had made an accusation in retaliation for the duke's having acquired proof of her adultery with Lord Talbot.

16. "To Lady Pomfret" (January 1739), in *The Complete Letters of Lady Mary Wortley Montagu,* ed. Robert Halsband, 3 vols. (Oxford: Clarendon Press, 1965-67), 2: 133-134.

17. Lawrence Stone, "Old Views of Youth," review of *The Adolescent Idea,* by Patricia Meyer Spacks, *New York Times Book Review,* 20 September 1981, p. 12.

18. Lennard J. Davis, "A Social History of Fact and Fiction: Authorial Disavowal in the Early English Novel," in *Literature and Society: Selected Papers from the English Institute, 1978,* ed. Edward W. Said (Baltimore: Johns Hopkins University Press, 1980), pp. 120-148.

19. *Journals of the House of Lords,* 40: 609.

20. Colley Cibber, *The Careless Husband* (1705), V, v, in *British Dramatists from Dryden to Sheridan,* ed. George H. Nettleton, Arthur E. Case, and George Winchester Stone, Jr. (Carbondale, Ill.: Southern Illinois University Press, 1969), pp. 427-428.

21. Samuel Richardson, *Pamela,* 2 vols. (London: Everyman, 1914), 2: 311-312.

22. *The Beautiful Lady Craven. The Original Memoirs of Elizabeth Baroness Craven . . . ,* ed. A. M. Broadley and Lewis Melville, 2 vols. (London: John Lane, Bodley Head, 1914), 1: 28.

23. Broadley, *Beautiful Lady Craven,* 1: 43-44.

24. Ibid., p. 44.

25. Ibid., pp. 49-50.

26. *Town and Country Magazine* 5 (1772): 246-247.

27. Ibid. 2 (1770): 158.

28. Philip H. Highfill, Jr., Kalman A. Burnim, and Edward A. Langhans, *A Biographical Dictionary of Actors, Actresses, Musicians, Dancers, Managers and Other Stage Personnel in London, 1660-1800* (Carbondale, Ill.: Southern Illinois University Press, 1973-), s. v. "Baddeley, Mrs. Robert, Sophia, nee Snow" (paraphrasing her letter to the *Morning Post,* August 1774).

29. *Hatchett* v. *Baddeley* (1776), 2 Black. W. 1079; further discussion of this case is in Staves, "Separate Maintenance Contracts."

30. *Oliver* v. *Oliver* (1801), 1 Hag. Con. 359. Both this case and the one following were brought to my attention by an unpublished Harvard Law School senior essay by Laura A. Santirocco (1982), who uses them to stress the persistence of economic motives for marriage in the later eighteenth century. Her essay uses Court of Arches cases as the basis for a critique of Lawrence Stone's picture of what she calls "the triumph of the sentimental view of marriage."

31. Ibid., 371.

32. Ibid., 371-372.

33. *Holmes* v. *Holmes* (1775), 2 Lee 117-118.

34. [Eliza Heywood], *The Wife. By Mira* (London, 1756), pp. 204-205, in a chapter entitled, "The imprudence of indulging too flattering expectations in Marriage."

35. Staves, "Money for Honor," pp. 282-283.

36. Ann Masterman Skinn, *The Old Maid; or, The History of Miss Ravensworth,* 3 vols. (London, 1771), vol. 3, "Address to the Reader"; for a discussion of this unusual woman, see "Matrimonial Discord in Fiction and in Court: The Case of Ann Masterman," in *Fetter'd or Free?: Collected Essays on Eighteenth-Century Women Novelists in England, 1670-1815,* forthcoming, Ohio University Press.

37. Mary Wollstonecraft, *Maria, or the Wrongs of Women* (New York: W. W. Norton & Co., 1975), pp. 145-150.

VI

WORDSWORTH'S REFLECTIONS ON
THE REVOLUTION IN FRANCE

James K. Chandler

My title both refers and alludes. The reference is to books nine through eleven of *The Prelude* (1805), the so-called France books, in which Wordsworth brings his personal epic to its climax by recounting his response to the French Revolution. The allusion, of course, is to Edmund Burke's response to the Revolution in the book he published at the very outset of the 1790s, the same tumultuous decade that issued in *The Prelude*. The relation between these two responses is my topic. Although this relation is one of influence, it is an influence of a most complex and interesting kind. And although one might call it an influence fraught with anxiety, my concern is with ideological rather than psychological categories and I will use no Freudian terms to account for that anxiety.

Part of what makes this case so complex is the nature and extent of Burke's influence on Wordsworth's entire generation. This is the generation that came to intellectual maturity in the England of the 1790s, and the *Reflections on the Revolution in France* was arguably the decade's most powerfully influential book. Summarizing the history of that period in his 1828 *Life of Napoleon,* Hazlitt described Burke as single-handedly harpooning the great Leviathan of the Revolution in its career toward the

English ship of state.[1] Even this large claim does not do full justice
to Burke's role, however, for initially his polemic served as a prod
to the Revolution's greatest advances on England. The *Reflections* engendered a hostile radical campaign that produced scores
of pamphlets in the early years of the 1790s. J. T. Boulton has
counted more than seventy different published responses to Burke
in the early 1790s, almost all of them critical.[2] Wordsworth's own
republican pamphlet of 1793 is better understood as an attack on
Burke than on the bishop of Llandaff, to whom it is ostensibly
addressed. Wordsworth attacks the bishop for having turned his
coat, just as Burke is supposed to have done, and for having been
induced to do so specifically by partaking of the "intoxicating
bowl" of Burke's rhetoric.[3]

That the young radicals of Wordsworth's generation helped to
forge their own politics by attacking Burke's might be demonstrated in a careful analysis of pamphlets like Wordsworth's *Letter to the Bishop of Llandaff,* but the point is explicitly acknowledged by the Friends of Liberty themselves. On 14 July 1791, the
Revolution Society and the Society for Constitutional Information, the two organizations that Burke singled out for attack in
the *Reflections,* held a joint dinner meeting in London to com-
memorate the taking of the Bastille. When the dinner ended, a
series of toasts were proposed:

To the liberty of the press. — To trial by jury, and that the rights of
juries to protect the innocent are never attacked. — To the men of letters
who have made themselves advocates of the rights of man, and that
genius always defend the cause of liberty! — *To Mr. Burke, to thank him
for having provoked the great discussion that occupies all thinking
beings* (here follows universal applause, which lasts for a full half-
hour). — To the patriots of France. — To the precious memory of the
citizens who, in France, sacrificed their lives for the freedom of their
country. — To friends of the Revolution inside of Parliament and outside.[4] [Italics added]

The thirty-minute ovation after the toast to Burke may reveal a
certain irony in the Friends' salute, but it enables one to state a
truth that is itself ironic: Burke did provoke the "great debate"
that led to the very occasion at which these toasts were proposed.

The reason Hazlitt could say that Burke arrested the Revolution is that soon after this time its events, as Wordsworth later put

it, seemed to bring less and less encouragement to radical hopes and more and more warrant for Burke's fears. Eventually, many of the radicals came to recant their earlier views, though not all of them gave credit to Burke for predicting the events that led them to do so. Wordsworth himself only managed to give Burke credit a quarter of a century after the letter to Llandaff. In his 1818 address to the freeholders of Westmoreland, the man whom in 1793 he had called "an infatuated moralist" became "the most sagacious Politician of his age": "Time has verified his predictions; the books remain in which his principles of foreknowledge were laid down" (*PrW*, 3: 158). He spelled out those "principles of foreknowledge" in a passage he later composed for and added to the long since completed *Prelude*. This is a passage in which Wordsworth apologizes for having been too slow to acknowledge what other men learned from Burke. If the oddity of this maneuver betrays Wordsworth's anxiety about the matter, its summary of Burke's principles shows the accuracy of his sense of what Burke stood for:

> Genius of Burke! forgive the pen seduced
> By specious wonders, and too slow to tell
> Of what the ingenuous, what bewildered men,
> Beginning to mistrust their boastful guides,
> And wise men, willing to grow wiser, caught,
> Rapt auditors! from thy most eloquent tongue —
> Now mute, for ever mute in the cold grave.
> I see him, — old but vigorous in age, —
> Stand like an oak whose stag-horn branches start
> Out of its leafy brow, the more to awe
> The younger brethren of the grove. But some —
> While he forewarns, denounces, launches forth,
> Against all systems built on abstract rights,
> Keen ridicule; the majesty proclaims
> Of Institutes and Laws, hallowed by time;
> Declares the vital power of social ties
> Endeared by Custom; and with high disdain,
> Exploding upstart Theory, insists
> Upon the allegiance to which men are born —
> Some — say at once a froward multitude —
> Murmur (for truth is hated, where not loved)
> As the winds fret within the AEolian cave,
> Galled by the monarch's chain.[5]
>
> (BR 7; ll. 512-534)

Elsewhere I have argued that principles rather like these, though not acknowledged at the time, inform Wordsworth's poetry from as early as 1798; that is, from the beginning of the major period and from the inception of his so-called program for poetry.[6] Here I will argue that such principles inform more specifically *The Prelude*'s narrative commentary on the Revolution.

The latter argument is at once easier and more difficult than the former. It is easier because there is some prima facie evidence in its favor: Wordsworth's insertion of the Burke passage into his narrative implies that he considered those principles of foreknowledge ideologically compatible with the completed *Prelude*. The argument is more difficult because, unlike the poems of 1798, where political topics tend to be treated at a remove, *The Prelude* attempts specifically to come to terms with the alleged failure of the Revolution, and it seeks to explain this failure with Burke's principles of foreknowledge but at the same time to withhold acknowledgment of their use. Wordsworth's only recorded remark about Burke in this period (1804) is highly critical, a summary dismissal couched in the words of Goldsmith: "born for the universe he narrowed his mind / And to party gave up what was meant for mankind."[7] This kind of evidence, together with Wordsworth's tendency to camouflage Burke's ideas when he uses them, has led many commentators to find Wordsworth's strong commitment to Burkism only after the great decade of his poetry; that is, after 1808, in the period when his imagination stultified and he no longer wrote sublime poetry.[8] The case is quite otherwise. The sublime imagination that in the drama of *The Prelude* saves Wordsworth by feeding his poetry itself fed deeply on the thought of Burke.

I

One of the usual forms of evidence brought to bear in a case for intellectual influence is the verbal echo: a term, phrase, or idiom that sounds as if it comes from some earlier writing. Not surprisingly, such evidence is often adduced by critics who have argued for Burke's influence on certain of Wordsworth's relatively late works, that is, those written after his great decade. In making his case for the influence of Burke on *The Convention of Cintra*, for example, Alfred Cobban observed that Wordsworth's conclusions tend to be drawn "in phrases that wonderfully, and surely not accidentally, echo Burke."[9] Cobban's claim is certainly true, but he cites only a few examples. And though other scholars have cited others, one senses that the surface of the matter has barely been scratched.[10]

How much work remains to be done on the topic of Burke's influence on *Cintra* can be suggested by the example of an extended echo which has not, as far as I know, been mentioned in any commentary, not even in Gordon Thomas's book-length study.[11] The context for this passage is Wordsworth's suggestion that, since "Spain has nothing to dread from Jacobinism," the Spanish might profit by a reform of their Catholic institutions, such as was attempted in France in 1789, without fearing the consequences that attended the effort in France:

Nor has the pestilential philosophism of France made any progress in Spain. No flight of infidel harpies has alighted upon their ground. A Spanish understanding is a hold too strong to give way to the meagre tactics of the "Systeme de la Nature;" or to the pellets of logic which Condillac has cast in the foundry of national vanity, and tosses about at hap-hazard — self-persuaded that he is proceeding according to art. The Spaniards are a people with imagination: and the paradoxical reveries of Rousseau, and the flippancies of Voltaire, are plants which will not naturalise in the country of Calderon and Cervantes. Though bigotry among the Spaniards leaves much to be lamented; I have proved that the religious habits of the nation must, in a contest of this kind, be of inestimable service. (*PrW*, 1: 333)

In Wordsworth's view, Spain is a kind of hybrid of England and France. It has some of the former's virtue and some of the latter's vice. Wordsworth's hope for the Spaniards is that they will rely on their (English) virtue to rid themselves of their (French) vice. Here is the counterpart passage from the *Reflections*:

We are not the converts of Rousseau; we are not the disciples of Voltaire; Helvetius has made no progress amongst us. Atheists [a few paragraphs later Burke calls them "Atheists and infidels," p. 349] are not our preachers; madmen are not our law-givers... In England we have not yet been completely embowelled of our natural entrails: we still feel within us, and we cherish and cultivate, those inbred sentiments which are the faithful guardians, the active monitors of our duty, the true supporters of all liberal and manly morals.[12]

When Henry Crabb Robinson showed a copy of the *Cintra* pamphlet to his friend Thomas Quayle, the latter complained that Wordsworth's long sentences contained "a cluster of Metaphors." "I don't know who may be the Author's Model: — His Style resembles the worst of Burke's, — But I do not expect that he himself will be a Model to any body else."[13] To compare Wordsworth's two attacks on Rousseau and Voltaire is to appreciate Quayle's hunch about Wordsworth's stylistic "Model," but it is also to understand that the debt extends beyond style. Wordsworth has fully adopted Burke's view of how French "philosophism" must be combated.

In *The Prelude* one also finds passages that, to use Cobban's phrase, "wonderfully, and surely not accidentally, echo Burke." These echoes bespeak an influence that has been almost entirely neglected, for the simple reason that so few readers have thought to listen for them.[14] Cobban's discussion of Wordsworth and Burke is typical of this neglect. In fact, at least one of the passages Cobban hears echoed in *Cintra* is also echoed in *The Prelude*. In discussing the tract, Cobban singles out Wordsworth's assertion that "There is a spiritual community binding together the living and the dead; the good, the brave, and the wise, of all ages" (*PrW*, 1: 339).[15] What Cobban recalls here is the famous passage in the *Reflections* in which Burke writes that "Society is, indeed, a contract":

It is a partnership in all science, a partnership in all art, a partnership in every virtue and in all perfection. As the ends of such a partnership cannot be obtained in many generations, it becomes a partnership not only between those who are living, but between those who are living, those who are dead, and those who are to be born. (*BW*, 3: 359)

Apart from stating so central a Burkean belief, this passage is especially germane to the subject of Wordsworth's ideological development since it is the same one he ridiculed in the letter to Llandaff, citing its doctrine as an example of Burke's "unnatural cruelty." The passage in *Cintra*, however, merely elaborates a sentiment recorded in book ten of *The Prelude*: "There is / One great society alone on earth: / The noble living and the noble dead" (*Prel*, 10: 967-969).[16] Furthermore, it elaborates with material also to be found in the poem.[17]

In other telling echoes of Burke in the France books, Wordsworth, in Burkean fashion, turns Jacobin language against the Jacobin position. Book nine, for example, describes those curious moments when Wordsworth "slipped in thought" from his "earnest dialogues" with Michel Beaupuy to muse upon the legendary chateaux of the Loire Valley. Wordsworth says that at such times the imagination, though indignant at certain wrongs associated with these places, "Did often mitigate the force / Of civic prejudice, the bigotry, / So call it, of a youthful patriot's mind" (499-501). The use of "prejudice" and "bigotry" to describe the mind of the enlightened rationalist is a page taken straight from Burke, who could so readily embrace his own prejudices partly because he believed that France's "atheistical fathers have a bigotry of their own" and that "they have learned to talk about monks with the spirit of a monk" (*BW*, 3: 379). And as if to prove that his account of the slip of the mind in book nine was no slip of the tongue, Wordsworth comes back to this Burkean topos in book ten, where he describes himself in his most rigorously syllogistic phase. He was then, he says, "A bigot to new idolatry," and "like a monk who had forsworn the world" did he "Zealously labour to cut off [his] heart / From all the sources of her former strength" (74-78).

The passages I have cited from *The Prelude,* echoing as they do Burke's central statements about a society that binds generations one to another, and about the allegedly fatal self-exempting fallacy of Jacobin argument, have implications that run deeper than mere verbal mimicry. By themselves they offer evidence enough to warrant looking more carefully at *The Prelude*'s affinity with Burke's thought and its debt to his writings. One must always consider evidence other than verbal echo as such, however, and this is especially true of the present case.

First of all, there is good reason for suspecting that Wordsworth would not at this time have been able to echo Burke in any way that might count as an allusion to Burke's writings. Though his polemical attack on Burke in the letter to Llandaff had not been published, we must keep in mind the letter's fervent and unyielding insistence on the ignominy of changing one's political mind. For the young Wordsworth, no political crime was more heinous, not even that of the tyrant himself.

Secondly, at the time of his work on the France books, Wordsworth's historical, personal, and rhetorical relation to the experience of the Revolution was very different from Burke's. The *Reflections* are written against what Burke takes to be the French ideology at a time when that ideology posed, in his view, an imminent threat to English security. Wordsworth's reflections on the French Revolution are likewise inimical to French ideology, but he writes as a man who was once, in a time he calls his "youth" and under special circumstances, drawn to accept that ideology. Although Wordsworth may be said to write for much the same audience as Burke did, that audience, is, like Wordsworth himself, a decade older. Their hopes for the Revolution, insofar as they had hopes for it, are now past. There is not the same urgency in denouncing (or, as in some cases, renouncing) what the Jacobins thought. In the early 1800s, Napoleon's French army poses a more immediate threat to England than Rousseau's French ideology. In such circumstances, the ideology itself can be examined more dispassionately, less xenophobically.

A third consideration is related to the first two. Because narrative point of view in *The Prelude* is constantly shifting, especially in the France books, it is very difficult to find anything like straightforward political commentary such as one finds in Burke's *Reflections* or in Wordsworth's letter to Llandaff or his tract on Cintra. To establish the authorial viewpoint on political and social issues, as on any other issues, one must sort through some difficult changes in perspective. First, there is the authorial point of view, that of the poet who reviews his revolutionary experience from a position that purports to make political as well as psychological and poetic sense of it. Second, there is the changing perspective of the young Wordsworth who moves through the celebrated times and places described in the poem.

These two perspectives play off one another in the poem in complex ways reminiscent of certain kinds of first-person fiction or, perhaps, on a smaller scale, of first-person Romantic lyrics. Another helpful analogue here is Hegel's *Phenomenology of Spirit,* a work composed at about the same time by a man just Wordsworth's age (b. 1770) with a strikingly similar history of political sympathies. M. H. Abrams's comments on the parallels between these two texts as *Bildungsromans* need not be repeated here.[18] What is relevant is that in Hegel's autobiography of Spirit, as in Wordsworth's autobiography of Imagination, the narrative argument tends to modulate in and out of the earlier, unformed consciousness. The reader may find himself at a loss to determine the meaning of a passage in either text for precisely the same reason: a subtle shift in standpoint has occurred.

One consequence of this subtle modulation for *The Prelude* is that, despite the obvious differences between the early and the later positions, they come to be united by a bond of affinity. That is to say, once the positions are set in this relation to each other, they can be posed against a third political point of view in the poem, that of the French revolutionists themselves, just as England (both past and present) is made to stand against France. Besides the relation of the mature Wordsworth to his earlier self, two other relations are therefore possible: that of the young Wordsworth to "France," and that of the older Wordsworth to "France." Wordsworth writes the France books from a doctrinal position toward France very like the one that, both in 1793 and 1818, he recognized as Burke's. Yet he needs at the same time to make plausible his own earlier relationship with French political thought by showing its continuity with his present view.

These suggestions can be tested by looking at the first lines of the famous passage that is the heart of *The Prelude*'s discussion of the Revolution, the only part of the France books to appear in print during Wordsworth's lifetime.

> O pleasant exercise of hope and joy,
> For great were the auxiliars which then stood
> Upon our side, we who were strong in love.
> Bliss was it in that dawn to be alive,
> But to be young was very heaven! O times,
> In which the meagre, stale, forbidding ways
> Of custom, law, and statute took at once
> The attraction of a country in romance—
> When Reason seemed the most to assert her rights
> When most intent on making of herself
> A prime enchanter to assist the work
> Which then was going forward in her name.
>   (10: 689-700)

The importance of phenomenological dialectic in this passage is suggested by the title Wordsworth gave it when he published it in Coleridge's *The Friend* in 1810, "The French Revolution: As it Appeared to Enthusiasts at its Commencement." Clearly, Wordsworth is dealing with the Revolution not only as it appeared to enthusiasts but also as that appearance appears to Wordsworth as the author of *The Prelude*.

Consider, for example, the handling of that important Burkean slogan about usage, "the ways / Of custom, law, and statute." Although the author of *The Prelude* writes that these were "meagre, stale, and forbidding" in the eyes of the enthusiasts, his claim cannot be accepted as it stands. The enthusiasts would never have attributed such qualities to, or used such adjectives for, the ways of custom, law, and statute. They would have said — did say — that the ways of custom had been unjustifiable, unjust, favoritist, outmoded, irrational, unnatural, and so on — never that they were "meagre, stale, and forbidding." Just as clearly, the young Wordsworth would not have accepted the description of the new appearance of custom's ways as taking on the attraction of a country in romance. That appearance was for them that of the present world — in a future state, to be sure, but for them just as real as ever. For most of them, the future society was if anything more real, because more rational, than the delusory world of the status quo, of slavery and falsehood.

Reason is the topic of the very next lines, which perhaps make the point even more plainly: "Reason seemed the most to assert her rights / When most intent on making of herself / A prime enchanter to assist the work / Which then was going forward in her name." This formulation implies a contradiction. The Reason of the enthusiasts wields the greatest authority in her (or their) most irrational moments. This contradiction is clearly perceived, and expressed, by the author of *The Prelude*. Yet just as clearly it is not apparent to the young rationalists for whom Reason is supposed to "seem" as she does. To reach an accurate sense of the implied point of view of the poem we must therefore ask ourselves: From what perspective might the French Revolution be said to appear to its enthusiasts in this contradictory way? So far, the signs point to a perspective very like Burke's.

R. D. Havens long ago observed of these lines that "it is not generally realized that they refer less to the Revolution as a whole than to the enthusiasm aroused by the Revolution in theories of government."[19] The remark is accurate enough, but I believe it misses the point of the ironic portrayal of the Revolution's dislocation of practice into theory, the portrayal of the Revolution advanced by Burke.

One last sign worth mentioning is the language of fantasy Wordsworth uses to discuss the rationalist mind, for Burke also uses such metaphors. Burke's insinuation that the political theorists of the Revolution live in a romantic fairyland is latent in his descriptions of the human rights they advocate as "pretended" and "imaginary." It is more explicit in his criticisms of their "hocus-pocus of abstraction" and of the Jacobins' "sleight of hand" (4: 17). Most explicit of all is Burke's first use of this metaphor in his early "Vindication of Natural Society" (1756), where he speaks of the "abuse of reason" in the "fairy land of philosophy" (1: 5). This is just the sort of metaphor Wordsworth employs to describe the effect of abstract philosophy on his sense of belonging to a transgenerational human community:

> as by the simple waving of a wand,
> The wizard instantaneously dissolves
> Palace or grove, even so did I unsoul
> As readily by syllogistic words
> . . .
> Those mysteries of passion which have made
> . . .
> One brotherhood of all the human race,
> Through all the habitation of past years. . .
> (11: 79-89)

None of this is meant to suggest that Burke could himself have written a passage resembling Wordsworth's. The emphatic identification with the young English Jacobins would have been impossible for Burke both psychologically (he was not one of them) and politically (the allure of this sort of identification was part of the very power he sought to dispel). Adequately interpreted, however, Wordsworth's lines take a stand that resembles Burke's very closely. The speculative self-indulgence Wordsworth describes, though apparently born of love and joy and undertaken in behalf of the rights of men, is the exercise of a faculty that has lost its temper. In the remaining pages of Wordsworth's reflections on the Revolution, we see this self-indulgence turning into self-destruction for English sympathizers. For the French revolutionists it leads to the destruction of fellow citizens as well. The action of books ten and eleven unfolds to show an ill-tempered Reason put to uses that play havoc with the English poet's mind and the French national welfare.

This leads to a final reason why one must not rely too exclusively on verbal echoes to establish the extent of Burke's influence on Wordsworth's political reflections. In the France books Burkean assumptions tend to sink down, not to float near the surface. The central catastrophe of the France books—also that of the poem as a whole—is recounted in both its social and mental aspects from Burke's point of view. Burkean conceptions seem to underlie the very emplotment of both social and mental events. Beginning, middle, and end, the story of this young Englishman's experience with France has all been told before. Though verbal echoes can help to show that Wordsworth's story is such a retelling of Burke's, the real debt runs deeper.[20]

II

To single out a starting point for the action of the France books, we might choose Wordsworth's conversations with Michel Beaupuy, since it is from Beaupuy that Wordsworth first learns to think and argue abstractly about political matters. Beaupuy gives him his first lessons in the pleasant exercise of political theory. In the account of these "earnest dialogues" with Beaupuy the reader of the 1805 *Prelude* (that is, the text without the "Genius of Burke" lines from book seven) first encounters the Burkean code words:

> Oft in solitude
> With him did I discourse about the end
> Of civil government, and its wisest forms,
> Of ancient prejudice and chartered rights,
> Allegiance, faith, and laws by time matured,
> Custom and habit, novelty and change,
> Of self-respect, and virtue in the few
> For patrimonial honour set apart,
> And ignorance in the labouring multitude.
>   (9: 328-336)

Although these topics resemble those listed by Burke in parts of the *Reflections,* Wordsworth seems to invite us to regard them as constituting a predictable litany for the early 1790s. We are also invited to take note of their balanced arrangement, which suggests that both sides of these complex questions are being weighed by the young philosophers. The ensuing lines come as an explanation for this intellectual judiciousness. Well-balanced thoughts come from steady minds:

> For he, an upright man and tolerant,
> Balanced these contemplations in his mind,
> And I, who at that time was scarcely dipped
> Into the turmoil, had a sounder judgment
> Than afterwards, carried about me yet
> With less alloy to its integrity
> The experience of past ages, as through help
> Of books and common life it finds its way
> To youthful minds . . .
>
> (9: 337-345)

"Afterwards" is the foreshadowing word that looks ahead to the unbridled speculation recorded in books ten and eleven. The difference between now and afterwards for Wordsworth, what makes his judgment sound in the first instance but not in the second, is explicitly identified by the Burkean phrase "the experience of past ages."

Though the conversations with Beaupuy may have sent Wordsworth marching down the road of excess, these are not the first French conversations Wordsworth records in book nine. There is the prior encounter with the royalist soldiers in Orleans, who, as he says, did not "disdain / The wish to bring [him] over to their cause" (199-200). Despite the fact that Wordsworth opposes these ignoble aristocrats in the name of liberty and equality, this passage actually provides the necessary background for understanding what is meant one hundred fifty lines later by "the experience of past ages." For, just as clearly as in the Beaupuy episodes, Wordsworth also represents himself here as a young man guided by an ancient source of "experience."

Part of what it means for Wordsworth to be so guided is that he is supposed to have no specific instruction in political philosophy. He states explicitly that he was at this time "untaught by thinking or by books / To reason well of polity or law, / And nice distinctions — then on every tongue — / Of natural rights and civil" (201-204). He is further supposed to have been "almost indifferent" then "to acts / Of Nations and their passing interests" (204-205). One might suspect Wordsworth of exaggeration here, but our concern is simply with his representation of himself at this time. In view of such massive ignorance, we are meant to suppose, Wordsworth should have been the easy mark the royalists took him for. Despite the odds, however, he remains unconvinced by the royalist arguments. Indeed, "in their weakness strong," as he says, he "triumphed" (266-267).

Recounting an event that calls out for an explanation, Wordsworth does his best to provide one. He says he owes his success over the Orleans aristocrats to the personal history he has recorded in books one through eight; that is, to his good egalitarian English rearing and his good egalitarian English education at Cambridge. Newly arrived in France, the young Wordsworth still carried this experience with him "unalloyed." The only surprise would have been his defeat at the royalists' hands:

> It could not be
> But that one tutored thus, who had been formed
> To thought and moral feeling in the way
> This story hath described, should look with awe
> Upon the faculties of man, receive
> Gladly the highest promises, and hail
> As best the government of equal rights
> And individual worth.
>
> (9: 242-249)

In what sense were Wordsworth's moral sentiments formed by the experience of past ages? The answer is that "England" is the product of ages-old experience and that in tutoring Wordsworth it confers on him the benefit of this long experience. This is indicated at the start of Wordsworth's explanation. He says that not only was he born in England (191-192) but he was born in a district "which yet / Retaineth more of ancient homeliness, / Manners erect, and frank simplicity, / Than any other nook of English land" (218-221).

We must not be put off the track by Wordsworth's claim to egalitarian sentiment. Burke believed, or argued anyway, that no one exceeded him in championing the cause of equality. His cause, however, was the ancient English tradition of equality, handed down from father to son, not the egalitarianism generated out of cosmopolitan discussion of the abstract rights of men. The stronger the chain through which the manners and attitudes of this way of life are passed on, the better the chance they will be retained. The English sense of equality is both an inherent and an inherited characteristic of "ancient homeliness." In one of his famous speeches on the American colonies, Burke defended his plan of reform for colonial affairs from the objection that it was rashly innovative. His proposal, he said,

is the genuine produce of the ancient, rustic, manly, homebred sense of this country. I did not dare to rub off a particle of the venerable rust that rather adorns and preserves, then [sic] destroys, the metal. It would be profanation to touch with a tool the stones which construct the sacred altar of peace. I would not violate with modern polish the ingenuous and noble roughness of these truly constitutional materials. Above all things, I was resolved not to be guilty of tampering, the odious vice of restless and unstable minds. I put my foot in the tracks of our fore-fathers, where I can neither wander nor stumble.[21]

Burke is best known for defending his English sense of tradition from working-class attacks. These defenses have created a mis-leading sense of where he stood on these matters, even in the works of the 1790s. The language of the family, so dominant in works like the *Reflections,* is ultimately rooted in the rustic domesticity Burke discusses here.[22]

I make no claim that Wordsworth knew Burke's celebrated speeches on America, though they are some of the books in which Burke's "principles of foreknowledge" were laid down. What I do claim is that the above passage is an accurate version of Burke's vision of tradition, what in the *Reflections* he calls the "collected reason of the ages" (*BW,* 3: 357), that "long experience" which he says is necessary to political and moral virtue.

One of the most fundamental principles of Wordsworth's re-flections, as of Burke's, is that tradition diminishes as a guiding political force in direct proportion to the practice of abstract political theory; that is, in proportion as one begins "To think with fervour upon management / Of nations—what it is and ought to be" (10: 685-686). It is a principle developed by Burke not primarily to remedy the situation of the French radicals themselves, but to warn about what happens to the young Englishmen who enlist in their ranks. In the *Appeal from the New to the Old Whigs,* Burke put the matter concisely. Accord-ing to the theory of the French politicians, he explained, "doctrines admit of no limit, no qualification whatsoever." Thus, "No man can say how far he will go, who joins with those who are avowedly going to the utmost extremities. What security is there for stopping short at all in these wild conceits?" (*BW*, 4: 205).

This principle is pointedly illustrated in book ten of the 1805 *Prelude,* the "middle" of the France narrative. Indeed, with this and other such Burkean passages in mind, book ten seems an extended gloss on Burke. Here is Wordsworth's account of the period following the establishment of the Directory.

> This was the time when, all things tending fast
> To depravation, the philosophy
> That promised to abstract the hopes of man
> Out of his feelings, to be fixed thenceforth
> For ever in a purer element,
> Found ready welcome. Tempting region that
> For zeal to enter and refresh herself,
> Where passions had the privilege to work
> And never hear the sound of their own names —
> But, speaking more in charity, the dream
> Was flattering to the young ingenuous mind
> Pleased with extremes, and not the least with that
> Which makes the human reason's naked self
> The object of its fervour. What delight! —
> How glorious! — in self-knowledge and self-rule
> To look through all the frailties of the world,
> And, with a resolute mastery shaking off
> The accidents of nature, time, and place,
> That make up the weak being of the past,
> Build social freedom on its only basis:
> The freedom of the individual mind,
> Which, to the blind restraint of general laws
> Superior, magisterially adopts
> One guide — the light of circumstances, flashed
> Upon an independent intellect.
>   (10: 805-829)

In contrast to the earlier passage about political theory ("O pleasant exercise of hope and joy . . ."), Wordsworth seems less concerned here to establish the plausibility of his youthful views and more concerned to show their error. In these lines we therefore find more densely and explicitly the terms and slogans of the position Wordsworth attributed to Burke first in 1793, then again in 1818, and later.

In these lines one does not have to listen hard to hear Burke's attacks on the misleadingly pure realm of political metaphysics, on the self-defeating effort to separate principles entirely from feeling and passion, and on the delusive weakness of naked, un-habituated reason. Besides hearing such echoes, however, one must recognize a whole constellation of derivative ideas at work. Wordsworth's account of this radical philosophy is that it seeks to chart out a human future based on "the hopes of man," without respect to what Burke repeatedly calls the medium of human life and what Wordsworth calls here "the accidents of nature, time and place." It sees the "infirmities" of this medium as belonging to a past human condition with which coming times will be dis-continuous, just as the pure realm of abstract philosophy is (as they falsely assume) discontinuous with the quotidian world of human feeling. The usual Burkean puns operate in this constella-tion, either explicitly or implicitly. Pure abstraction is the product of human reason in extremity. Reason in extremity stands in opposition to reason in the medium; that is, reason through habits and the accidents of nature, time, and place. It is also reason in the extremes of Platonic absolutes, such as the 'Ideas' of light and darkness. One wonders if reason in extremity is not also reason in the altogether, what Burke called the human reason's naked self.

Burke's remarks about the degeneration of a mind beset with theory hold still deeper implications for the story of Wordsworth in France. They suggest an answer to the ominous question posed in the *Appeal from the New to the Old Whigs* ("What security is there for stopping short at all in these wild conceits?"):

Why, neither more nor less than this, — that the moral sentiments of some few amongst them do put some check on their savage theories. But let us take care. The moral sentiments, so nearly connected with early prejudice as to be nearly one and the same thing, will assuredly not live long under a discipline which has for its basis the destruction of all prej-udices, and the making the mind proof against all dread of sequences flowing from the pretended truths that are taught by their philosophy.
(*BW*, 4: 205)

The "moral sentiments" can check the power of this philosophy, but only up to a point. To place them too long under its savage discipline is to risk one's moral life.

III

Burke's writings on the Revolution offer a schema that explains the course not only of Wordsworth's decline in *The Prelude* but also of his crisis and recovery. France is the land of abstract speculation. Young Wordsworth is introduced to such speculation early, but his moral sentiments, formed on the strength of ancient, homebred English experience, preserved him from moral harm through even repeated exposure to danger. Although "from the first, wild theories were afloat," he says that for a long time he "had but lent a careless ear" to their "subtleties" (10: 774-776). In this school, however, the moral sentiments must grow weaker every day, and eventually Wordsworth falls vulnerable to near despair. As "events brought less encouragement," he was impelled, as he later puts it, to find a new "proof of principles": "evidence / Safer, of universal application, such / As could not be impeached, was sought elsewhere" (10: 788-790). "Elsewhere," of course, turns out to be that "purer element" of abstraction and naked reason.

The Prelude shows the young Wordsworth pursuing almost to completion the course of moral self-annihilation Burke described in 1790. The poet describes himself at war with himself, laboring to cut off his heart from "all the sources of her former strength" (11: 78) and nearly succeeding. So vigorous a campaign did he wage that, in what he would later call "the crisis of that strong disease, / The soul's last and lowest ebb," he is finally supposed to have lost all feelings of conviction and to have given up on moral questions. In this moment in *The Prelude* Wordsworth deliberately heightens the parallels between the social and the psychological aspects of the Revolution:

> Thus I fared,
> Dragging all passions, notions, shapes of faith,
> Like culprits to the bar, suspiciously
> Calling the mind to establish in plain day
> Her titles and her honours, now believing,
> Now disbelieving, endlessly perplexed
> With impulse, motive, right and wrong, the ground
> Of moral obligation — what the rule,
> And what the sanction — till, demanding proof,

And seeking it in every thing, I lost
All feeling of conviction, and, in fine,
Sick, wearied out with contrarieties,
Yielded up moral questions in despair.

(10: 888-900)

The moral sentiments, according to Burke "so nearly connected with early prejudice as to be nearly one and the same
thing, will assuredly not live long under a discipline which has for
its basis the destruction of all prejudices." That the sentiments
under attack in Wordsworth's crisis, the sources of his former
strength, are all supposed to be intimately connected with his
prejudices is clear from the metaphor of the tribunal. (That they
are connected with his early prejudices is clear from the whole
structure of *The Prelude*.) The crisis passage presents that debili-
tating process in which emotions that ought to be taken as
"already judged," and therefore as the basis for other judgments,
are themselves subjected to the most rigorous inquisition. "False"
bottoms continue to fall away under the weight of analysis, and
Wordsworth is left with no moral ground on which to stand.

This figure of the court of reason also heightens the social-
psychological parallels in the overall narrative. Wordsworth's
metaphor analogizes the epistemological challenge to the mind's
prejudices (its "passions, notions, shapes of faith") with the legal
challenge to prescriptive rights. "Titles" (892) is glossed quite
properly in the recent Norton edition of the poem as "deeds to
prove legal entitlement." The rationalist challenge to titles and
honors is thus the Revolution's challenge to those time-honored
rights that stem not from deductive proof but simply from long
usage. In fact, Wordsworth's metaphor clarifies the analogue
between Burke's crucial concepts in a way that even Burke himself never did. Prescriptive rights are like prejudices in that they
too should be already judged, and Wordsworth's readers would
have been well aware that courts like those set up to challenge
privileges and prescriptive titles in France later sat in judgment
on the very lives of the French men and women in question. In
other words, what Wordsworth has ultimately offered is an analogy between his psychological crisis and the Reign of Terror itself,
a dual Terror adumbrated by Burke years earlier.

IV

Reading Wordsworth's France narrative in the light of Burke's writings, especially those of 1790 and 1791, one is tempted to conclude that Burke accurately predicted the fate of young English radicals like Wordsworth in considerable detail, just as he predicted so much about the Reign of Terror. But such a conclusion takes *The Prelude*'s account of that crisis at face value. If my claims about Burke's influence are in any way true, we face a far more complicated matter than straightforward prediction.

We can safely presume that *something* eventually befell Wordsworth—some form of disappointment, let us say, with the course of the Revolution—which led him to reconsider what he came to call Burke's "principles of foreknowledge." But to the extent that he already accepts these principles at the time the France books were composed, they inevitably influence the retrospective account of the experience. To put it another way, Burke's comments may seem to anticipate Wordsworth's crisis so completely simply because Wordsworth used Burke's terms to reconstruct it. While it would be impossible to determine to just what extent we have Burke's prediction, on the one hand, and Wordsworth's Burkean reconstruction, on the other, two facts are pertinent. First, many scholars have expressed great difficulty in locating in Wordsworth's mid-twenties a crisis of precisely the same description as the one we find in *The Prelude*. Second, the letter to Llandaff, as my earlier discussion suggests, does not finally sound like the work of the mind represented in books ten and eleven.

If Burke's anticipation of the debility and crisis depicted in *The Prelude* is striking, what is more striking and perhaps more important is his anticipation of the recovery. In that same passage of the *Appeal,* Burke said that only a person's moral sentiments, if they could somehow survive theory's inquisition, can save the mind from the false dominion of naked reason. Late in book ten Wordsworth offers a proleptic account of the regenerative process he more amply describes in the famous "spots of time" passage in book eleven:

> Nature's self, by human love
> Assisted, through the weary labyrinth
> Conducted me again to open day,

Revived the feelings of my earlier life,
Gave me that strength and knowledge full of peace,
Enlarged, and never more to be disturbed,
Which through all the steps of our degeneracy,
All degradation of this age, hath still
Upheld me, and upholds me at this day
In the catastrophe (for so they dream
And nothing less), when, finally to close
And rivet up the gains of France, a Pope
Is summoned in to crown an Emperor . . .

                                        (10: 921-933)

The "feelings of my earlier life," whose revival saves Wordsworth from a tragic fate, resemble both in kind and function
those redemptive sentiments that Burke claimed were so intimately connected with early prejudice. When the careful reader
of *The Prelude* reaches this passage, he or she should already be
aware of the Englishness of these revived feelings because prior
passages, such as the royalists episode in book nine, have already
described their origin and what they were like when they were still
strong. That knowledge is confirmed in the reference to Napoleon and to the present state of France. The French suffer the
degrading spectacle of a papal coronation, never fulfilling their
apparent national promise, because of their age-old infatuation
with papist splendor and arbitrary power.

Such evidence suggests how firmly the France books align
themselves not only with Burke but with the entire Whig tradition
Burke claimed to uphold. This is the political tradition, dating
from the first Whigs of the 1670s, that views France as the seat of
royalist papism and as a threat to the rights provided for by the
English constitution.[23] Even in his severest strictures against the
overthrow of the French government in 1789, Burke never depicted that government as the equal of England's. In a speech on
French affairs delivered (on 9 February 1790) before the publication of the *Reflections,* Burke gave a fuller account of his view of
the French monarchy than the rhetorical aims of the *Reflections*
would allow. In a discussion of why "France, by the mere circumstance of its vicinity, had been, and in a degree always must be,
an object of our vigilance, either with regard to her actual power
or to her influence and example," he describes the "perfect despotism" of Louis XIV:

Though that despotism was proudly arrayed in manners, gallantry, splendor, magnificence, and even covered with the imposing robes of science, literature, and arts, it was, in government, nothing better than a painted and gilded tyranny, — in religion, a hard, stern intolerance, the fit companion and auxiliary to the despotic tyranny which prevailed in its government. The same character of despotism insinuated itself into every court of Europe, — the same spirit of disproportioned magnificence, — the same love of standing armies, above the ability of the people. In particular, our sovereigns, King Charles and King James, fell in love with the government of their neighbor, so flattering to the pride of kings. A similarity of sentiments brought on connections equally dangerous to the interests and liberties of their country. It were well that the infection had gone no farther than the throne.

... The good patriots of that day, however, struggled against it. They sought nothing more anxiously than to break off all communication with France, and to beget a total alienation from its country and its example. (*BW*, 3: 216-217)

Burke did not consider Louis XVI the despot his grandfather was, but he thought no French monarch or royalist beyond the influence of France's inveterate penchant for splendor and magnificence, paint and gilding. Such courtly excesses may have been preferable to the barbarism of the Revolution, but they could never compare favorably with the "ancient, rustic, manly, home-bred sense" of the English. Burke claims that the solid habits of the English patriots prevented the French infection from spreading beyond the throne of Charles and James in the seventeenth century. *The Prelude* shows these same native habits saving Wordsworth from the rhetoric of the royalists in book nine and ultimately from the double reign of terror described in book eleven.[24]

In addressing the Westmoreland freeholders, Wordsworth laments the recent decay of "that tree of Whiggism, which flourished proudly under the cultivation of our Ancestors" (*PrW*, 3: 162). Like Burke in the *Appeal from the New Whigs to the Old*, Wordsworth explains that the new Whigs go wrong precisely by failing to live up to those distinguishing marks of their political ancestors: skepticism toward France and a corresponding confidence in native British character and practice. The new Whigs, according to the forty-eight-year-old poet, have in effect destroyed the balance of power between the two parties, by holding, from the beginning of the French Revolution, such a course as introduced in Parliament, discord among themselves; deprived them, in that House and elsewhere of the respect which from their Adversaries they had been accustomed to command; turned indifferent persons into enemies; and alienated, throughout the Island, the affections of thousands who had been proud to unite with them. This weakness and degradation, deplored by all true Friends of the Commonweal, was sufficiently accounted for, without even adverting to the fact that—when the disasters of the war had induced the Country to forgive, and in some degree, to forget, the alarming attachment of that Party to French theories: and power, heightened by the popularity of hope and expectation, was thrown into their hands—they disgusted even bigotted adherents, by the rapacious use they made of that power;—stooping to so many offensive compromises, and committing so many faults in every department, that, a Government of Talents, if such be the fruits of talent, was proved to be the most mischievous sort of government which England had ever been troubled with....

How could all this happen? For the fundamental reason, that neither the religion, the laws, the morals, the manners, nor the literature of the country, especially as contrasted with those of France, were prized by the Leaders of the Party as they deserved.... Is the distracted remnant of the Party, now surviving, improved in that respect?...we look in vain for signs that the opinions, habits, and feelings, of the Party, are tending towards a restoration of that genuine English character, by which alone the confidence of the sound part of the People can be recovered. (Pp. 162-163)

This is an approximate summary of the views that inform the France books. Wordsworth's use of the political labels does, however, alert us to what we might otherwise have missed: his conservatism, like Burke's, wants to be understood as the preservation of true Whiggism.[25]

What Wordsworth says about Napoleon's 1804 coronation should be compared with Southey's later reflections on Napoleon's bad-faith negotiations for peace in 1802. The Peace of Amiens, recalled Southey, "restored in me the English feelings which had long been deadened, and placed me in sympathy with my country." One crucial difference between these cases is that Wordsworth's debilitated English feelings were revived long before the coronation of 1804, or even the treaty of 1802. This much is clear from Wordsworth's tenses: "hath still / Upheld me, and upholds me at this day."[26] Here again, the most persuasive evidence is to be found in The Prelude's famous "spots of time."

Wordsworth represents these lyric passages as the initiating moments of his self-redeeming poem, and the central role they play in the earliest drafts of the poem (1798-99) bears out this claim. To read these passages in their poetic and historical context is to discover that their redemptive power is homologous with that of Burke's moral sentiments: both are strongly allied with early prejudice, insensibly formed in particular circumstances, and profoundly indebted to the English past.

NOTES

1. William Hazlitt, *Collected Works,* ed. P. P. Howe, 21 vols. (London and Toronto: J. M. Dent and Sons, 1931), 13: 52.

2. J. T. Boulton, *The Language of Politics in the Age of Wilkes and Burke* (London: Routledge & Kegan Paul, 1963), pp. 265-271.

3. William Wordsworth, *Prose Works,* ed. W. J. B. Owen and Jane Worthington Smyser, 3 vols. (Oxford: Clarendon Press, 1974), 1: 49 (subsequent references to this edition are noted here and in the text by *PrW*).

4. I have translated the text of this speech as it appeared in French in the *Gazette Nationale ou Le Moniteur Universel,* no. 202 (21 July 1791); reprinted in *Reimpression de L'Ancien Moniteur* (Paris: Henri Plon, 1863), 9: 174.

5. Citations of *The Prelude* are by book and line number to the 1805 text edited by Jonathan Wordsworth, M. H. Abrams, and Stephen Gill (New York: Norton, 1979).

6. See my "Wordsworth and Burke," *ELH* 47 (Winter 1980): 741-771.

7. William and Dorothy Wordsworth, *Letters: The Early Years: 1787-1805,* ed. Ernest de Selincourt, rev. Chester L. Shaver (Oxford: Clarendon Press, 1967), p. 491.

8. See, for example, Leslie Chard, II, *Dissenting Republican* (The Hague: Mouton, 1972), p. 150.

9. Alfred Cobban, *Edmund Burke and the Revolt Against the Eighteenth Century* (New York: Barnes and Noble, 1929), p. 147.

10. One indication of the neglect of the matter is that Burke is nowhere mentioned in Owen and Smyser's extensive commentary on *Cintra (PrW,* 1: 374-415).

11. Gordon Kent Thomas, *Wordsworth's Dirge and Promise* (Lincoln: University of Nebraska Press, 1971).

12. Edmund Burke, *Works,* rev. ed., 12 vols. (Boston: Little Brown, and Co., 1865-67), 3: 345 (subsequent references are noted in the text by *BW*).

13. Edith J. Morley, ed., *The Correspondence of Henry Crabb Rob-*

inson with the Wordsworth Circle, 2 vols. (Oxford: Clarendon Press, 1927), 1: 59.

14. For example, neither the exhaustive commentary of R. D. Havens (*The Mind of a Poet* [Baltimore: Johns Hopkins Press, 1941]) nor that of Ernest de Selincourt (Wordsworth, *The Prelude,* 2d ed., rev., ed. Helen Darbishire [Oxford: Clarendon Press, 1959]) records any connection between Burke's political writing and the 1805 *Prelude.* Besides Carl Woodring (*Politics In English Romantic Poetry* [Cambridge, Mass.: Harvard University Press, 1970], p. 105), another important exception to this trend is Herbert Lindenberger, who notes that the language of book eight is "conservative," and suggests that its diction (*roots, ancient, birthright,* and *custom*) is "less directly related to any older conservatism than to the type we associate with Burke" (*On Wordsworth's Prelude* [Princeton, N.J.: Princeton University Press, 1963], p. 250). Lindenberger goes on to make the valuable but tentative suggestion that the roots of this conservatism reach back to 1800 (p. 251).

15. Cobban, *Edmund Burke,* p. 147.

16. Willard L. Sperry, much of whose scholarship on Wordsworth is still valuable after a half-century, is the only critic I know who has connected the lines from *The Prelude* to the passage from *Cintra,* to the passage from Burke's *Reflections,* and to Wordsworth's commentary on the latter in the letter to Llandaff (*Wordsworth's Anti-climax* [1935; reprint ed., New York: Russell and Russell, 1966], pp. 66-68).

17. The second part of the sentence from *Cintra*—"the good, the brave, and the wise, of all ages"—has strong affinities with, for example, the lines from book eleven of *The Prelude,* where Wordsworth speaks of "the elevation which had made [him] one / With the great family that here and there / Is scattered through the abyss of past, / Sage, patriot, lover, hero" (61-64).

18. Abrams, *Natural Supernaturalism* (New York: Norton, 1970), pp. 236-237.

19. Havens, *Mind of a Poet* (Baltimore: Johns Hopkins Press, 1941), p. 535.

20. The following discussion of *The Prelude's* emplotment along Burkean lines by no means denies the role of other influences on Wordsworth's shaping of the action. *Paradise Lost* is an obvious case in point. We need only think of how books nine and ten of *The Prelude* follow books nine and ten of Milton's epic in showing man's fall into Satanic or Promethean forbidden knowledge.

21. Perhaps the fullest elaboration of Burke's notion of the homebred rusticity of English thought, a passage that shows his kinship with Wordsworth in an especially revealing way, occurs in a document that Wordsworth could not have seen, "Several Scattered Hints Concerning Philosophy and Learning," in *A Note-book of Edmund Burke,* ed. H. V. F. Somerset (Cambridge: Cambridge University Press), p. 90: "A man who considers his nature rightly will be diffident of any reasonings that carry him out of the ordinary roads of Life; Custom is to be re-

garded with great deference especially if it is to be an universal Custom; even popular notions are not always to be laughed at. There is some general principle operating to produce Customs, that is a more sure guide than our Theories. They are followed indeed often on odd motives, but that does not make them less reasonable or useful. A man is never in greater danger of being wholly wrong than when he advances far in the road of refinement."

In this same essay, Burke also articulates the paradox that seems to lie at the heart of Wordsworth's experiments in *Lyrical Ballads* and to have occasioned the later criticisms of Coleridge: "The more a man's mind is elevated above the vulgar the nearer he comes to them in the simplicity of his appearance, speech, and even not a few of his Notions" (p. 90).

22. On Burke's use of images and metaphors of "family," see Boulton, *Language of Politics,* pp. 112-114.

23. See J. R. Jones, *The First Whigs* (London: Oxford University Press, 1966, pp. 45; for a fuller discussion of anti-French sentiment in the 1670s, see John Miller, *Popery and Politics in England 1660-1688* (Cambridge: Cambridge University Press, 1973), pp. 108-153, especially pp. 148-152, where Miller discusses Marvell's *Account of the Growth of Popery and Arbitrary Government* (1678), an anti-French attack on the earl of Danby. This is, of course, the period to which Burke alludes in the passage quoted immediately below.

24. For a discussion of this address ("Speech on the Army Estimates") in its political context, see F. O'Gorman, *The Whig Party and the French Revolution* (London: Macmillan, 1967), pp. 45-48.

25. Wordsworth's Burkean claim to be upholding the Whig tradition sheds light, I think, on the kind of distinction Michael Friedman wishes to make when he says that Wordsworth became a "Tory Humanist" but never a "mean-spirited Tory." Friedman's suggestion that this change may have occurred as early as 1800 moves in the right direction, but, since Wordsworth's program for poetry was conceived in 1798, does not go far enough. See *The Making of a Tory Humanist* (New York: Columbia University Press, 1979), p. 234.

26. Quoted in Cobban, *Edmund Burke,* pp. 142-143.

NOTE: Parts of the present essay have appeared in Chandler, *Wordsworth's Second Nature: A Study of the Poetry and Politics* (Chicago: University of Chicago Press, 1984) and are reprinted with permission.

VII

ARTHUR MILLER'S *THE CRUCIBLE* AND THE SALEM WITCH TRIALS: A HISTORIAN'S VIEW

Edmund S. Morgan

The historian who plays the critic runs the risk of being irrelevant as well as incompetent. A work of art must stand or fall by itself, and the author of *The Crucible* has warned off historians with the statement that his play is "not history in the sense in which the word is used by the academic historian." But when a play evokes a widely known historical event, art leans on history. No one who reads *The Crucible* can see it wholly fresh. The world into which it carries us is constructed from building blocks that are labeled Puritanism, Salem Village, witch-hunt, clergyman. Part of the verisimilitude of the play and part of its dramatic tension depend on our knowledge that men and women were hanged at Salem Village in 1692 for crimes they could not have committed.

Under these circumstances it may be permissible for a historian to examine the play's depiction of history and to ask how the author's assumptions about history have affected his understanding of his characters.

I do not expect an artist who deals with history to conform to every fact known to historians about the events he is concerned with. It does not bother me, for example, that Arthur Miller has simplified the legal transactions involved in the trials and as-signed to some individuals judicial powers they did not have. Nor does it bother me that he has transformed Abigail Williams from a child into a woman and given her a love affair with his principal character, John Proctor, a love affair that is nowhere suggested by the records. Miller's Abigail is not so much a transformation as a creation. So, for that matter, is his John Proctor. It might have been better not to have given either of them the name of an actual person who figures in the historical record. But the artist's relation to the historical record has to be different from the his-torian's.

If the artist binds himself too closely to known factual details, the result may be an aesthetic disaster. The artist must bring to his work a creative imagination that transcends historical detail in order to recreate living people and situations. He must per-suade his audience that they have been transported back to the time and place in question, or at least persuade them to suspend their disbelief that they have taken such a voyage. And the his-torical record is almost never sufficiently full to equip the artist with the details he needs for persuading them, details of things said and seen and heard, without which his enterprise is doomed. Even where the record is especially full, aesthetic considerations may require violating or ignoring the details it furnishes and sub-stituting imaginary ones in order to achieve, within the limits of the particular work, the development of characters and situations through which the artist makes his statement.

In order to make use of the building blocks that the audience will recognize, the artist must have his characters say things and do things that conform in a general way to known fact. But his characters inevitably assume a life of their own. They may say and do things that actual historical people are known to have said and done, but they do a lot of other things on their own, as it were, things dictated by the author's vision of them and what they were up to. That vision may be the product of careful study of the historical record or it may not, but it can never be as closely tied to the historical record as the historian's vision must always be. In other words, the artist's reconstruction of people and events must take place on a level that is denied to historians and that most his-torians would not have the imaginative power to reach anyhow.

Nevertheless, historians do engage, in their own less imaginative way, in the same sort of activity as novelists and playwrights and perhaps poets, namely, in the provision of vicarious experience. Granted, there are many pieces of historical writing that only faintly answer this description, the analytical and didactic and often unreadable monographs that historians direct at one another and which sometimes seem calculated to mystify outsiders. But it is surely at least one function, in my opinion the highest function, of the historian to recreate the past, however analytically and didactically, in order to release us from the temporal provincialism imposed on us by the time in which we happen to have been born, giving us experience of other times to expand our understanding of what it is to be a human being.

This function the historian shares with the novelist and playwright. The novelist and playwright, of course, are not confined to recreating experience out of the distant past. Indeed, they generally deal with experience available in their own time. And when they resort to history, they turn it into the present in a way that the historian does not pretend to do. But the artist and the historian do share some problems and responsibilities.

The artist by definition is governed by aesthetic considerations; the historian is less constrained by them but by no means exempt. He is not simply a compiler of annals or a transcriber of documents. He cannot attempt to tell everything that happened. He has to pick and choose. He has to leave things out. And though his choice of what to put in may depend on many considerations other than aesthetic, he has to construct something out of the details the record does furnish, something with a shape, a structure, a book or article that will have a theme and a beginning, middle, and end. Otherwise no one will read him, not even other historians.

In building a work around any theme, the historian and the artist who deals in history confront a problem that is particularly acute in *The Crucible,* as well as in the various historical treatments of the New England Puritans, the people whom Arthur Miller tries to bring to life for us. It is the problem of separating the universal from the unique, the timeless from the temporary. History does not repeat itself. No two persons are alike. Every event is in some way unique. And yet the only reason we are capable of vicarious experience is because history does in some sense repeat itself, because all persons are alike. In seeking to broaden our experience through art or through history we have to identify with people who think differently, talk differently, act differently; and we want to know precisely what was different about them. At the same time, we have to be able to recognize their humanity, we have to be able to put ourselves in their situation, identify with them, see in them some of the same weaknesses and strengths we find in ourselves. Otherwise they become too different to be believable and so can tell us nothing about ourselves.

It is easy to err in either direction, to exaggerate similarities to the past or to exaggerate differences. And it is all too tempting to do so in such a way as to flatter ourselves and avoid some of the hard lessons the past may have to teach us. If, on the one hand, we exaggerate differences, we may fall into the trap of viewing the past with condescension, bestowing a patronizing admiration on those quaint old folk who struggled along without benefit of the sophistication and superior knowledge we have arrived at. The past will then become a kind of Disneyland, an escape from the present, a never-never land of spinning wheels and thatched roofs and people dressed in funny old costumes. Or it may become simply a horror from which we can congratulate ourselves on having escaped, a land filled with superstition, poverty, and endless toil, a world of darkness from which we have emerged into the light.

If, on the other hand, we exaggerate the similarities of the past to the present, we may indulge in a comparable complacency, finding justification for everything we do or want to do in the fact that it has been done before: the founding fathers did it; what was good enough for them ought to be good enough for us, and so on. Or we may manufacture spurious arguments for some present policy or proposal on the grounds that it worked in the past, thus equating the past with the present, a very dangerous equation, as we know from those earnest military men who are always fighting the war preceding the one they are engaged in.

Historians and novelists and playwrights who take history seriously have to recognize both similarities to the past and differences. To overemphasize one or the other is not only to distort history but to diminish the impact of the experience it offers, indeed to escape that experience and nourish a temporal provincialism.

With regard to the Salem witchcraft of the 1690s, the temptation has always been to exaggerate the differences between that time and ours. The temptation was much more in evidence fifty or a hundred years ago than it is today. In the nineteenth century, when mankind, and especially Anglo-Saxon mankind, was progressing rapidly toward perfection, taking up the white man's burden, glorying in the survival of the fittest, and fulfilling manifest destiny, the Salem witch trials were obviously something long since left behind. Although it was a little embarrassing that the witch trials were not even farther behind, the embarrassment was compensated for by thinking how rapidly we had all progressed from that dreadful era of superstition and old night.

In the twentieth century, as perfection has eluded us and we have manufactured our own horrors to dwarf those at Salem, we have grown a little less smug. We even find something uncomfortably familiar in the Salem trials, with their phony confessions, inquisitorial procedures, and admission of inadmissible evidence. And yet there remains a temptation to flatter ourselves.

The temptation showed itself recently in the extraordinary publicity given to an article about the possibility of ergot poisoning as a cause of the symptoms displayed by the allegedly bewitched girls at Salem. Ergot poisoning comes from eating bread or flour made from diseased rye grain and produces seizures and sensations comparable to those that the Salem girls experienced or said they experienced. Although the evidence for ergot poisoning at Salem is extremely tenuous, and although if true it would in no way diminish the horror of what happened there, the article in a professional scientific journal was seized upon by the press as though modern science had now explained the whole episode. I can account for the attention given this article only by the flattering implication it seemed to carry (though probably not intended by the author) of the superiority of our own enlightened understanding of what happened in those benighted days. Yet what would be explained by ergot poisoning was only the odd behavior of a few teenage girls, not the hysteria of their elders, in which lay the shame of what happened at Salem.

Evidently the Salem trials are still something we feel uncomfortable about. We want to think that we would not behave the way people behaved then, we would behave better, we would not be fooled by a batch of bad bread. And that brings me back to *The Crucible*. Arthur Miller has probably done more than anyone else to remind us we are not so much better. The *Crucible,* as we all know, was written in the midst of the McCarthy era, and it was intended, I think, to suggest that we were behaving, or allowing our authorized representatives to behave, as badly as the authorities at Salem. There are no overt comparisons. The play is about Salem. But its success depends in part on the shock of recognition.

Let us look, then, at the design of *The Crucible*. How has the author dealt with the problem of similarity and difference? In spite of the apparent parallel with our own times, has he not flattered us a little, allowed us an escape from the hard lessons of Salem and thus denied us the full range of experience he might have given us?

The protagonist of *The Crucible* is John Proctor, a simple man in the best sense of the word, a strong man who does not suffer fools gladly. He has little of formal piety and even less of superstition. His wife is more devout but less attractive. She lacks his human warmth, or at any rate she has wrapped it in a shroud of piety and righteousness. Her husband has consequently found it the more difficult to resist the charms of an unscrupulously available serving girl, Abigail Williams. We cannot blame John Proctor. He is, after all, human, like you and me. But his wife does blame him, and he blames himself.

The antagonist of the play wears a mask, not literally but figuratively. And the mask is never fully stripped away because the author himself has never quite gotten behind it. The mask is Puritanism, and it is worn by many characters, to each of whom it imparts an inhuman and ugly zeal. Elizabeth Proctor wears it when she reproaches her husband for his weakness. Thomas and Ann Putnam wear it when they grasp at witchcraft as the source of their misfortunes. But mostly it is worn by the ministers, Samuel Parris and John Hale, and by the judges, Danforth and Hathorne. They are never explicitly labeled as Puritan; the author sees them so well as men that he has furnished them with adequate human motives for everything they do. Arthur Miller is too serious an artist to give us only a mask with no flesh and blood behind it. His object, indeed, is to show us human weakness. Nevertheless, the mask is there.

The men who kill John Proctor are easily recognized as Puritans. Miller has provided them with all the unlovely traits most of us associate with that name: they are bigoted, egotistical, bent on suppressing every joy that makes life agreeable. The worst of the lot, the most loathsome man in the play, is a Puritan clergyman. Samuel Parris, we are told, never conceived that "children were anything but thankful for being permitted to walk straight, eyes slightly lowered, arms at the sides, and mouths shut until bidden to speak." We are also told that in this horrid conception Parris was not unusual. He was "like the rest of Salem."

Puritanism sometimes seems more than a mask. Sometimes it becomes the evil force against which man must pit himself. Puritanism, repressing the natural, healthy impulses of children, breeds in the girls of Salem village an unnatural hysteria that proves the undoing of good men like John Proctor. Proctor seems the most un-Puritan man in the play, and Proctor triumphs in death, triumphs as a human being true to himself, triumphs over the hypocrisy and meanness that Puritanism has evoked.

The Crucible is a powerful play. Arthur Miller says he tried to convey in it "the essential nature of one of the strangest and most awful chapters in human history." He has succeeded — almost. The Salem episode was both strange and awful. If the author had known more abut the history of New England, however, it is possible that he might have found what happened at Salem less strange and more awful. To explain why, let me draw a picture of seventeenth-century Puritanism somewhat different from the one to be found in *The Crucible*. I speak not exactly as the devil's advocate but as what in this context may amount to the same thing, the Puritans' advocate.

Puritanism has been more often the object of invective than of investigation, and it is easier to say what it was not than what it was. It was not prudishness. The Puritans were much franker in discussing sex than most of us are outside the pages of the modern novel. The sober historical works of Governor Bradford and Governor Winthrop were expurgated when published in the present century. Puritanism was not prohibitionism. The Puritans did not condone excessive drinking, any more than we do, but they seldom drank water if they could avoid it. Puritanism was not drabness in clothing or furniture or houses. The Puritans painted things red and blue and wore brightly colored clothes, trimmed with lace when they could afford it. They forbade a number of things not forbidden today, such as the theater and card playing. They looked askance at mixed dancing and punished breaches of the sabbath. Otherwise their moral code was about the same as ours.

What distinguished the Puritans from us and, to a lesser degree, from their contemporaries was a profound vision of divine transcendence on the one hand and of human corruption on the other. The Puritan could never allow himself to forget God. Although he enjoyed the good things of life, he had always to do so with an awareness of the infinite perfection of the Being who created them. He had always to be comparing earthly pleasures with eternal ones in order to keep the earthly ones in proper perspective. This meant that he could never let himself go in sweet abandon; or rather, it meant that he must always blame himself afterwards when he did. To immerse oneself wholly, even for a short time, in the joys of the flesh was to put things above the Creator of things.

Other people have been overwhelmed with divinity in this way, but other people have found a refuge in asceticism: they have withdrawn from the world, turned their backs on the temptations that constantly invite man's attention away from God. For the Puritan, asceticism was no way out. God, he believed, had placed him in the world and created its good things for his use. He was meant to enjoy them. To turn his back on them was to insult their Maker. He had, therefore, to be in the world but not of it, to love God's creatures but not love them very much.

As he made his way through this too delightful world, the Puritan was inevitably a troubled person. His conduct might look exemplary to you and me, but not to him, because the errors he mourned lay more often in attitude than in act. A person might behave perfectly as far as the outward eye could detect—it was right to eat, to drink, and to be merry at it; it was right to love your wife or husband, play with your children, and work hard at your job. But it was wrong to forget God while you did so. And people were always forgetting, always enjoying food and wine and sex too much, and always condemning themselves for it. Sometimes the lapses were great and gross, sometimes trivial, but great or small they reminded Puritans constantly of their sinful nature. Every day of his life the Puritan reenacted the fall of Adam and felt the awful weight of God's condemnation for it.

The Puritan was as hard on his neighbors as he was on himself. When they visibly violated God's commands, he did not hesitate to condemn them. But his awareness of his own guilt and his conviction that all men are guilty made him somewhat less uncharitable than he may seem to us. He was a disenchanted judge who expected the worst of his fellow men and could not blame them more than he blamed himself. One of the first bands of Puritans to depart from England for the Massachusetts Bay Colony expressed the Puritan attitude well. In an address issued before their departure they implored their countrymen to consider them still as brethren, "standing in very great need of . . . helpe, . . . for wee are not," they said, "of those that dreame of perfection in this world."

The Puritan knew that God demanded perfection but knew also that no one could attain it. And because God could forgive the sinner who repented, the Puritan felt that he too must do so. Anyone who reads the records of New England churches and New England law courts will see how ready the Puritans were to forgive. A convicted drunkard who showed repentance after sobering up would generally receive the lightest of fines from the civil judge or perhaps no fine at all, but merely an admonition. The churches were even more charitable. According to Puritan practice only a small part of a congregation was admitted to church membership, only those who could demonstrate that they were probable saints headed for eternal glory. When a saint was found in open sin, say breaking the sabbath or drinking too much or becoming too friendly with another man's spouse, the church might by a formal vote admonish him or even excommunicate him. But if he repented and expressed sorrow for his conduct, they would almost invariably restore him to membership even if his repentance came years later. The churches exercised an almost foolish patience toward repeating offenders. A person might get drunk pretty regularly. Each time he would be admonished or excommunicated and each time, when he repented, restored.

This combination of severity and forgiveness affected the Puritans' upbringing of their children. The Puritans never supposed that children enjoyed more innocence than their elders. Men did not learn evil as they grew; it was in them from the beginning. A parent's job was to repress it in his children; just as a ruler's job was to repress it in his subjects. But the methods of repression need not be cruel or unbending. A wise parent was supposed to know his children as individuals and fit his discipline to the child's capacities and temperament. As Anne Bradstreet put it:

Diverse children have their different natures; some are like flesh which nothing but salt will keep from putrefaction; some again like tender fruits that are best preserved with sugar: those parents are wise that can fit their nurture according to their Nature.

Although Puritan parents following this precept might still find the rod the most useful instrument in correcting some children, there is no evidence that they used it any more regularly than parents do today. Samuel Sewall, one of the judges who tried the witches, records in his diary an instance when he was driven to it. His son Joseph, future minister of the Old South Church, had thrown "a knop of Brass and hit his sister Betty on the forhead so as to make it bleed and swell; upon which," says Sewall, "and for his playing at Prayer-time, and eating when Return Thanks [saying grace], I whipd him pretty smartly." In practice Puritan children seem to have been as spoiled as children in other times and ages. Parents expected them to err and corrected them without expecting perfection.

The role of the Puritan clergyman in suppressing evil was a minor one. His function was educational rather than authoritative. It was proper for the authorities in the state to ask his advice when they were having difficulties in interpreting the will of God. But it was wrong for him to proffer advice unasked, and there was no obligation on the part of the authorities to accept it after they got it. Even within his own church he had no authority. Every action of the church in admonishing or excommunicating members was the result of a vote, and in most churches unanimity was required. The minister's job was to instruct his flock, to justify the ways of God to man, to help men detect the evil in their hearts, and also to help them detect the first stirrings of divine grace. He could only hope that through his preaching God might summon some of his listeners to eternal glory.

During the eighteenth century New England preaching became increasingly hortatory and relied more and more on moving appeals to the emotions. Particularly after the Great Awakening of 1741 had set the example, preachers found it advantageous to depict the torments of hellfire vividly to their listeners, in order to frighten them into awareness of their sins. But during the seventeenth century hellfire was conspicuously missing. Seventeenth-century sermons were more didactic than admonitory; the preacher devoted most of his time to the exposition of theological doctrine and applied the doctrine to his listeners only briefly at the end of his sermon.

By the same token the seventeenth-century preacher found little occasion for discussing the devil or his demons. The evil that Puritans feared and fought lay in their own hearts, not in the machinations of the devil. This is not to say that they denied the existence of supernatural evil. They would have been an extraordinary people indeed had they done so, because scarcely anyone in the seventeenth century did. But Puritan ideas on the subject were conventional, the same ideas that seventeenth-century Europeans and Englishmen held. And Puritans were rather less interested in supernatural evil than their contemporaries. Puritans were too preoccupied with natural evil to pay much attention to supernatural.

Why, then, the hysteria at Salem in 1692? If Puritans gave less attention than their contemporaries did to the devil, why did the devil give more attention to them? Why were there not much greater epidemics of witchcraft and witch-hunting in England and Europe than in Massachusetts? The answer is that there were. During the sixteenth and seventeenth centuries some thousands of witches were executed in the British Isles, an estimated 75,000 in France, 100,000 in Germany, and corresponding numbers in other European countries.

The European trials have mostly been forgotten and the Salem ones remembered because the European ones were too widespread and too common to attract special attention. The human imagination boggles at evil in the large. It can encompass the death of Anne Frank but not of several million anonymous Jews. It can comprehend twenty men and women of Salem Village more readily than 75,000 in France. The Salem episode is the more horrible simply because we can take it in.

But even though we take it in, we can never quite understand it. In the effort to do so, we have tried to fasten the blame where it will not hurt any of us. Historians who should have known better once blamed it on the clergy. New ideas, we were told, had penetrated New England, ideas that were dissolving the enslavement of the people to Puritanism, ideas that threatened the dominant position of the clergy. In order to save their overweening influence, they blamed the devil and worked up the witch scare. All nonsense.

The witch scare was no heresy hunt; prosecutors and defendants alike were Puritans, and both believed in witchcraft. The role of the clergy was a deterring one. They recognized at an early stage that the trials were being conducted without regard to proper procedures. The court, on which of course no clergyman sat, was convicting on the basis of spectral evidence alone, evidence offered by a supposed victim of witchcraft to the effect that the devil tormenting him appeared in the shape of the accused. The assumption behind such testimony was that the devil could assume the shape only of a person who had confederated with him. The clergy knew that spectral evidence was considered acceptable in witch trials but that it was not generally considered sufficient in itself to warrant a conviction. The supposition that the devil could not assume the shape of an innocent person was questioned by many authorities, and courts generally demanded supporting evidence of a more objective nature. This might consist in the possession of dolls or wax images and the other paraphernalia of witchcraft. It might consist in the existence of so-called witch marks on a person's body. These were simply red or blue marks or excrescences, such as we would call birthmarks, at which the devil was supposed to suck, as on a teat. God help anyone who had both a birthmark and an old doll retained from childhood. And yet most previous trials of witches, where this kind of evidence was required, resulted in acquittals. The Salem court waived the necessity of such evidence and accepted the spectral evidence offered by a small group of hysterical teenage girls as sufficient in itself to justify conviction.

The clergy, knowing that this was dubious procedure, protested. They did not do so as soon or as loudly as they should have. And anyone occupying a position of influence and leadership who objected soon and loudly to the methods of the late Senator McCarthy is entitled to cast the first stone at the New England clergy of 1692. Some clergymen may have been caught up in the general hysteria; nevertheless, it was the belated protest of the clergy that finally brought the trials to a halt.

If the clergy did not promote the witchcraft scare, how did it happen? No one can give a complete answer. There was no leader who engineered it, no demagogue or dictator who profited from it or hoped to profit from it. It came when the times were out of joint, when the people of Massachusetts had suffered a cruel disillusionment.

Massachusetts had been founded as a city on a hill, to be an example to the world of how a community could be organized in subjection to God's commands. In the course of half a century the people of Massachusetts had seen the world ignore their example and go off after evil ways. Within Massachusetts itself, the piety of the founding fathers had waned in the second generation, or so at least the members of that generation told themselves. In 1685 the world moved in on Massachusetts. England revoked the charter that had heretofore enabled the colony to govern itself and installed a royal governor with absolute powers in place of the one elected by the people. New Englanders hardly knew at first whether to regard the change as a just punishment by God for past sins or as a challenge to a degenerate people to recover the piety and strength of their fathers. But in 1688, when England threw off its king, the people of Massachusetts gladly rose up and threw off the governor that he had imposed on them. There was great rejoicing throughout the colony, and everyone hoped and believed that God would restore the independence that might enable Massachusetts to serve him as only the Israelites had served him before. But the hope proved false. In 1691 the people of Massachusetts heard that they must serve England before God; the new king was sending a new royal governor.

A gloom settled over the colony far deeper than the depression that greeted the coming of the first royal governor. Men who had been rescued from despair only to be plunged back again were in a mood to suspect some hidden evil that might be responsible for their woes. They blamed themselves for not finding it; and when the girls of Salem Village produced visible and audible evidence of something vile and unsuspected, it was all too easy to believe them.

Although Puritanism was connected only indirectly with the witch scare, it did affect the conduct of the trials and the behavior of the defendants. Puritans believed that the state existed to enforce the will of God among men. If evil went unrebuked, they believed, God would punish the whole community for condoning it. It was the solemn duty of the government to search out every crime and demonstrate the community's disapproval of it by punishment or admonition. Once the witch trials began, the officers of government felt an obligation to follow every hint and accusation in order to ferret out the crimes that might be responsible for bringing the wrath of God on the colony. They were, of course, egged on by the people. Witch-hunts, whether in Massachusetts or Europe, generally proceeded from the bottom up, from popular demand. Even the Spanish Inquisition was much less assiduous in pursuit of suspected witches than were the people of the villages where the suspects lived. But popular pressure is not an adequate excuse for irregular judicial procedures. In their eagerness to stamp out witchcraft, the Massachusetts authorities forgot that they had a duty to protect the innocent as well as punish the guilty.

At the same time, they were trapped by their very insistence on mercy for the repentant. By releasing defendants who confessed and repented, they placed a terrible pressure on the accused to confess to crimes they had not committed. It is possible that some of the confessions at Salem were genuine. Some of the accused may actually have practiced witchcraft as they understood it. But undoubtedly a large percentage of the confessions were made simply to obtain mercy. Men and women who lied were thus released, whereas those whose bravery and honesty forbade them to lie were hanged. These brave men and women were Puritans too, better Puritans than those who confessed; their very Puritanism strengthened them in the refusal to purchase their lives at the cost of their souls.

Puritanism also affected the attitude of Massachusetts to the trials after they were over. No Puritan could do wrong and think lightly of it afterward. God was merciful to the repentant but not to those who failed to acknowledge their errors. And within five years of the witch trials, the people of Massachusetts knew that they had done wrong. They did not cease to believe in witchcraft, nor did they suppose that the devil had lost his powers or was less dangerous than before. But they did recognize that the trials had been unfair, that men and women had been convicted on insufficient evidence, that the devil had deluded the prosecutors more than the defendants. It was possible that Massachusetts had judicially murdered innocent men and women. The people therefore set aside a day, January 15, 1697, as a day of fasting, in which the whole colony might repent. On that day, Samuel Sewall, one of the judges, stood up in church while the minister, at his request, read his confession of guilt and his desire to take "the blame and shame" of the trials on himself. The jurors who had sat in the trials published their own confession. "We ourselves," they wrote, "were not capable to understand nor able to withstand the mysterious delusion of the power of darkness and prince of the air, whereby we fear we have been instrumental with others, though ignorantly and unwillingly, to bring upon ourselves the guilt of innocent blood."

These confessions brought no one back to life, but who will deny that it was good and right to make them? In 1927 the state of Massachusetts executed two men named Sacco and Vanzetti. They may have been guilty, just as some of the Salem witches may have been guilty, but experts agree that they did not receive a fair trial. A few years ago when the governor of Massachusetts acknowledged that fact officially, the people of Massachusetts, through their elected representatives, rebuked him. But today the people of Massachusetts are no longer Puritans and feel no need for contrition.

A knowledge of Puritanism can help us to penetrate behind the mask that disguises some of the characters in *The Crucible* and obscures the forces at work in the Salem tragedy. Arthur Miller knew his characters well enough as human beings so that they are never concealed from him by his faulty image of Puritanism. But he does not know them as Puritans. Too often their humanity is revealed as something at odds with Puritanism. We need to understand that their Puritanism was not really at issue in the tragedy. Insofar as it entered, it affected protagonist and antagonist alike. It conceals the issue to make Samuel Parris wear the mask of Puritanism and John Proctor stand like some nineteenth-century Yankee populist thrust back into Cotton Mather's court. Parris and Proctor were both Puritans and both men. We should not look on Proctor's refusal to confess as a triumph of man over Puritan. It was a triumph of man over man and of Puritan over Puritan. Elizabeth Proctor was a Puritan and a woman; we should not see her as a Puritan when she is cold to her husband and a woman when she is warm.

In other words, the profounder implications of the action in the play are darkened by a partial identification of the antagonist as Puritanism. The identification is never complete. If it were, the play would be merely a piece of flattery. But Miller has offered his audience an escape they do not deserve. He has allowed them a chance to think that John Proctor asserted the dignity of man against a benighted and outworn creed. Proctor did nothing of the kind. Proctor asserted the dignity of man against man. Man is the antagonist against which human dignity must always be defended; not against Puritanism, not against Nazism or communism, or McCarthyism, not against the Germans or the Russians or the Chinese, not against the Middle Ages or the Roman Empire. As long as we identify the evil in the world with some particular creed or with some other people remote in time or place, we flatter ourselves and cheapen the dignity and greatness of those who resist evil. The Germans, we say, or the Russians are inhuman beasts who trample humanity in the mud. We would never do such a thing. Belsen is in Germany. Salem Village is in the seventeenth century. It is a comforting and specious thought. It allows us to escape from the painful knowledge that has informed the great religions, knowledge incidentally that the Puritans always kept before them, the knowledge that all of us are capable of evil. The glory of human dignity is that any man may show it. The tragedy is that we are all equally capable of denying it.

VIII

THE INTRODUCTION OF HISTORY
AS AN ACADEMIC SUBJECT
AND ITS IMPLICATIONS

Arnaldo Momigliano

I

We are so used to regarding history as an obvious part of academic teaching, and especially of University teaching, that we seldom stop to consider how comparatively recent is the introduction of history into the school curriculum at any level.[1] Even less do we reflect on the consequences of this particular change in the pattern of education. The Greeks, who invented history as we understand it in the fifth century B.C., never regarded history as a specific subject for instruction in school. There were public readings of historical books for adult audiences. Herodotus is notoriously supposed to have read his books publicly and to have inspired a young man in his audience, Thucydides, to follow his example, with the results everybody knows. The story may be untrue, but it is typical. In Greece you did not learn history at school. You read it privately or somebody read it to you in polite company. The same happened in Rome.

There was of course plenty of incidental history to be learned at school from poets, orators, and philosophers, and conversely, historical episodes could be turned into themes for poetry, oratory, and philosophy. Moreover, historians such as Thucydides could be read for their style and, more specifically, for the speeches they included in their books. Everybody recognized that history offered examples and models for both good and bad behavior; isolated episodes from the past were supposed to be known to everyone. But the past as the past was not the subject of study at school, and the rules of historical method were not something you would have to learn at school, as you learned the rules of grammar, rhetoric, or mathematics. You did not come out of school with the reputation of being good at history.

Historical writing was to the ancients something both important and indefinite. It could be produced in different circumstances either to keep alive the memory of some specific event or series of events of the past, to record contemporary experiences, or to praise or blame a man and a group. There was invariably the implication that historians helped to remember what otherwise would be forgotten forever. There was a further implication that intellectual or moral improvement would come from the perusal of history books. Historians illustrated through individual cases what was permanent in human nature. The less serious or cautious authors also intimated that amusement was provided into the bargain. What no historian would admit was an inclination to lie or invent. Truthfulness was assumed; indeed, it had to be displayed.

In both the Greek and the Roman world we encounter historians who were supported by powerful protectors and in some cases were plainly in their pay, but the majority of historians seem to have kept themselves free from patrons and to be proud of their independence. Greek historians were often exiles who wrote about politics because they could no longer intervene in politics directly. Roman historians of the late Republic deliberately broke with their national tradition of official annals and made a point of competing with the Greeks in freedom of expression. A tone of aristocratic detachment was appropriate.

It is difficult to say how much of this ethos of personal responsibility and initiative remained operative in the Middle Ages. I would only like to make two elementary observations. First, the fact that medieval chroniclers were so often members—even anonymous members—of corporations does not necessarily imply that they considered themselves mouthpieces of the corporations

to which they belonged and therefore renounced personal judgment. Second, Christian historians, being Christians, were conscious that there were two histories, sacred and profane, and that
the former gave meaning to the latter; but it does not follow that
history became subsidiary to theology. Anyone who is acquainted
with the historians of the Crusades or with the early chronicles of
Italian cities will be reluctant to generalize about the corporative
or theological orientation of medieval historiography.

In any case, history as a subject remained outside the lecture
room. It was as little a part of the curriculum of medieval schools
as it had been of ancient schools. Schoolboys learned history, both
sacred and profane, incidentally. When the universities were
firmly established in the thirteenth century, nobody, as far as I
know, thought of history as an appropriate subject for instruction
in the new places. Nor did the situation change when Italian
humanism penetrated into the universities in the fifteenth
century.

One of the most conspicuous aspects of what we call Italian humanism was the conscious return to the literary genres of antiquity, with the consequence that humanistic historians had to
select their models from the surviving ancient authors and to
adapt them to contemporary conditions and needs. Nobody
could be simply a second Livy or Tacitus, even less a second Herodotus, Thucydides, or Polybius. It is interesting to see how the
process of adaptation proceeded at two different levels: in the
actual practice of historical writing and in theoretical reflections
about the historian's art. The small amount of theoretical writing
about history which had been preserved from antiquity—a few
pages of Cicero and Quintilian, a couple of pamphlets by Diony-
sius of Halicarnassus, and above all, Lucian's little treatise "How
to Write History"—was enormously authoritative in the Renaissance; but in the sixteenth century these works were used as a
starting point for new analytical discourses about what is good
history. The new theory modified ancient theory especially in its
awareness of what Christianity demanded from historians and of
what historians should do to help lawyers. In the course of time
the new practice had to take into account the new balance of
power in modern Europe, the wars of religion, and the discovery
of new continents.

History was still directed to adult minds and kept out of the
educational system. If handbooks of historical method intimated

or presupposed that history was a favorite subject of generals and aristocrats, they reflected the true situation. Traditional historiography centered in wars and politics. Even biography gave over a large proportion of its space to kings, generals, and politicians; though in the biographical genre generals had to compete with poets and kings with philosophers. The history of literature and philosophy remained little more than the biographies of poets and philosophers. Historians commended themselves to their readers for the help they could provide in understanding the intricacies of wars, diplomacy, and political feuds, or the strange customs of barbaric and remote nations. They even intimated, with Polybius in their hand, that they could help to win wars. Together with the ancient claim to truthfulness and independence went a more modern offer to provide some distraction and amusement for gentlemen of leisure. Rhetoricians, grammarians, lawyers, theologians, doctors, and mathematicians held their positions in universities for about three centuries before anyone began to think that perhaps history might become a teachable subject.

There is of course an intrinsic relationship between the fact that history was an ill-defined subject and the fact that history entered the schoolroom so late as a discipline in its own right. Simply to narrate what had transpired did not seem to require any special qualifications. What a reader was most likely to appreciate in a book of history—clarity and eloquence of exposition, good sense and moral principles in the evaluation of events—may be better acquired by studying something else. Good grammatical and rhetorical training and a command of moral, religious, and philosophical principles can be obtained without reference to history. Political and military leadership are the result of experience. True enough, history had included an element of research since its beginnings. The very word history, *historia,* had implied research since the time of Herodotus. But as long as this research was ill defined and did not seem to require any special techniques, it could be assumed that any educated person was capable of doing research for the purpose of writing history. History was so late in becoming an academic subject for two partly contradictory reasons: that it was not important enough to be taught, and that, even if it was important, it was not difficult enough to deserve being taught.

Latin composition, mathematics, law, and theology were both more important and more difficult than history. There is nothing extravagant in maintaining that it takes more time to learn to write a decent page of Latin than a decent page of history. This proposition may remind us that the requirement of speaking and writing Latin — which made the universities and many of the good humanistic schools the international institutions they were — created a hierarchy of subjects from which history was bound to suffer in more than one respect. It is perhaps not by chance that in Germany the claims of history became louder with the first reaction of German nationalism to the authority of Rome.

As long as people were satisfied that what one needed to know about history was contained in the Bible and in certain Greek and Latin authors, the question whether or not to teach history at school could hardly be very acute. By teaching enough Latin to enable people to read the Bible in Latin, the Roman historians in the original, and the Greek historians, if not in the original, at least in a Latin translation, the basic access to historical knowledge was provided. The fathers of humanistic education, such as Pier Paolo Vergerio and Vittorino da Feltre, took it for granted that schoolboys would learn classical history (or classical examples) from classical writers. Vittorino da Feltre communicated his taste for Livy to his pupil Federico da Montefeltro.

It became less easy to ignore the problem of access to historical knowledge when, for any reason, people felt the need to know the outlines of universal history, or the history of the nation to which they belonged, or the history of basic institutions such as the Catholic church or the Holy Roman Empire, which affected their lives profoundly. We begin to sense trouble when we notice that Enea Silvio Piccolomini, the future Pope Pius II, in his treatise *De Liberorum Educatione,* written for the King of Bohemia and Hungary in 1450, warns him not to waste his time over such a miserable subject as the history of Bohemia and Hungary. But here again some distinction is necessary. On a very elementary level the need for some historical information had been felt from the very beginning of university teaching, though perhaps not as much on the arts side as in theology and law. Theologians and jurists wanted lists of popes and emperors and, more generally, of world events, for orientation. We know of at least one book that was prepared for the benefit of theological and legal schools in the thirteenth century, Martinus Polonus' *Chronica summorum pontificum imperatorumque ac de septem aetatibus mundi.* Martinus Polonus was put into print (that is still considered useful) at the end of the fifteenth century. But such a subsidiary little text for reference was more suited to eliminate the need for teaching history than to elicit it. Though Ludovicus Vives was equally un-pretentious when in his *De tradendis disciplinis* of 1531 he sug-gested teaching schoolboys a very brief summary of world history from the creation to Charles V, we feel that he had to take into account something Martinus Polonus could not have known.

Let us agree, however, that appreciation of the value of history can go together with the exclusion of history from school educa-tion. This was the normal attitude until the sixteenth century and, well after the sixteenth century, went on being the attitude of individuals and groups that were second to none in their appre-ciation of history.

Take the case of John Milton, a man of universal knowledge who wrote history and wrote about history.[2] He had neat and sen-sible ideas of what history was about. He expressed them in lan-guage scattered throughout his history of Britain of 1670 and, above all, in his two admirable letters of 1657 to Lord Henry de Bras, in which he presented Sallust as a model historian and insisted that the offices of a rhetorician and a historian are as dif-ferent as the arts which they profess. But his pamphlet *Of Educa-tion,* addressed to Master Samuel Hartlib, simply excludes ordi-nary history from education and allows a minimum of church his-tory for Sundays.

As we know, Milton was not exactly a traditionalist in the mat-ter of education and thought that, with proper teaching, classical languages could be learned much more quickly than was usual. But in taking it for granted that history was of no use in schools, he made his own a traditional point of view such as can be found, for instance, in the *Didactica Magna* of his contemporary John Amos Comenius, whom he seems to have disliked. Comenius' basic indifference to history can perhaps be explained by saying that he was a utopian, and the utopian mentality does not seem to have contributed to an interest in history before Karl Marx suc-ceeded in combining a utopian turn of mind with trust in history as a discipline. But Milton is more important to us than Come-nius just because he was not an addict of utopian thinking but, rather, represents the continuity of the old, well-tried attitude to history, which was to keep it away from children and reserve it for the mature mind.

This attitude is also very explicit in Ludovicus Vives, though he opened the door to some elementary history in the school curriculum. Vives reserves serious reading of historical books for grown-up people and advises senior citizens to have historical books read to them. The same basic attitude is still to be found in Lord Bolingbroke's *Letters on the Study and Use of History,* which were posthumously published in 1752 but were written about 1735. The various ingredients of their composition need no analysis here — the contempt for the antiquarians, the middle road between skepticism and credulity in historical criticism, the strong anti-Whig or rather anti-Walpole bias, and, last but not least, the implicit dismissal of the Bible as a historical document. What is obvious is that Bolingbroke takes it for granted that history is a subject for adult minds, for "divines of all religions," for lawyers, and above all for those who want to fit themselves for the service of the public. As Bolingbroke says, "When Tully informs us, in the second book of his Tuscular disputations, that the first Scipio Africanus had always in his hands the works of Xenophon, he advances nothing but what is probable and reasonable." And Bolingbroke goes on to explain in the true spirit of Polybius: "Experience is doubly defective: we are born too late to see the beginning, and we die too soon to see the end of many things. History supplies both these defects."

When the Jesuits in their *Ratio Studiorum* of 1599 left so little space to history in their carefully thought out system of education, they were doing nothing more than continuing the classical and medieval tradition we still find echoed in Milton and Bolingbroke. What is worth noticing is that the discussions inside the society which prepared the final formulation of the *Ratio Studiorum* clearly revealed divergent opinions. Reports from German provinces of the society suggested a more important role for history in education. A report of 1586 from the Provincia Rhenana favored a course of history for the classes of humanity and rhetoric (that is, for the upper classes of the Jesuit schools), including both universal history and church history. The report from Germania Superior of the same year also asked for more time and more specific themes for history teaching; it complained that Latin historians were at present read for their style, not for their content.[3]

I am not quite certain whether the differences in this respect between the provisional version of the *Ratio Studiorum* of 1586 and its final version of 1599 are the consequences of criticisms of this kind. The final version (apart from other differences) seems to give more scope for the teaching of the institutions of Greece and Rome, but it confines such instruction to so-called vacation days and keeps history altogether out of the central part of the curriculum. History did not become a serious subject in Jesuit schools until the eighteenth century, and even then, if I am correctly informed, not everywhere at the same time. In the "province" of Austria, teaching of history was introduced in 1735. It became important in the Theresianum of Vienna, the seminary for aristocrats founded under the patronage of Maria Theresa, in 1746. In Italy ecclesiastical history was introduced into the Collegio Romano in 1741. In 1752, S. Bettinelli became the first "lector historiae" in the Collegio dei Nobili of Parma.

It would be entirely wrong, however, to deduce that the Jesuits did not appreciate history both in itself and as a subject for the self-education of mature readers. If there is a book indicative of what the Jesuits envisaged as a culture, it is the *Bibliotheca Selecta,* published by Antonio Possevino in 1593, six years before the final text of the *Ratio Studiorum,* and revised for the edition of 1603. Possevino intended to provide a model combination of knowledge and piety. He says himself that at first he conceived his work as a *Bibliotheca principum ac nobilium* and intended to guide his aristocratic readers to the acquisition of a suitable historical knowledge. But slowly the work developed into two stately volumes embracing all human knowledge. The chapters on "Historia Humana" were sufficiently large, even in the first edition of 1593, to be republished with some modifications in an independent volume, which in the Venice edition of 1597 has the telling title *Apparatus ad omnium gentium historiam.* The accent is on *omnium,* on the history of all nations. As one would expect from a Jesuit, the history of geographic discoveries has pride of place. As for method, Possevino is up to date. He knows about the problems of associating history with theology from Melchor Cano and about the use of history for law from Francois Baudouin. It is by comparing the *Ratio Studiorum* with the contemporary *Bibliotheca Selecta* by Possevino that we can understand the strength of and the reasons for the tradition that kept history out of ordinary education, even among people who fully appreciated the interest of history and, in particular, its value for the ruling classes.

II

The problem, therefore, is not to explain why history was kept out of the curriculum, but why and how it was introduced, and with what consequences. The problem is complicated enough. It will perhaps be useful to simplify it in one respect. Only a clear demand for better historical knowledge in areas beyond the limits of the classical writers could create the conditions for the introduction into education of specific lectures on history. Professors of eloquence or humanities could easily provide some instruction on Greek and Roman history (and even on what history was about) by choosing historical texts for their lectures. An early example is B. della Fonte, who lectured on Caesar's *De Bello Civili* and Lucan's *Pharsalia* in Florence in 1482.[4]

Because the evidence available about the introduction of history into the curricula of schools and universities is so unevenly distributed and incomplete, I hesitate to go beyond this point. That evidence so easily confirms my earliest "hunch" — that the German situation of the sixteenth century created the conditions for the introduction of history into education — that I am suspicious of my conjecture. The obstacle is that German scholars have worked so much more critically and in detail about education in their country or countries than have Italian, French, English, and Spanish scholars in theirs. For instance, for Italy there is nothing comparable to the *Monumenta Germaniae Paedagogica,* from which it is possible to know a great deal about the education of German princes and therefore to appreciate an important factor, the wishes and examples of rules. Nor for any other country is there a book comparable to Emil Clemens Scherer's *Geschichte und Kirchengeschichte an den deutschen Universitäten.* It appeared in 1927 and could easily have become a good model for other countries.

In Italy the emphasis on the usefulness of history for rulers is of course as great as in other countries. After all, we had Machiavelli and, before him, theoreticians of education like Pier Paolo Vergerio and Vittorino da Feltre. Any author specifically interested in giving advice about the education of a young prince had somehow to mention the ancient historians with praise. For instance, there is the curious dialogic work by Ludovico della Torre, *L'aio ovvero dell'educatione del principe giovane,* which was written about 1620-30 but remained unpublished until 1956, after having been discovered in a Hungarian library.[5] Ludovico della Torre gives advice about what books to read, but training in history is not really implied. Nor was the well-defined "mos itali-cus," the "Italian style," of legal studies conducive to a combination of legal and historical argument. The future of Alciato's historical approach to law was in the "mos gallicus," in the French and German developments.

Given the prevalence of Jesuit schools in Italy, one would not expect much history in Italian secondary schools before the end of the eighteenth century. What is surprising, however, is the apparent absence of specific chairs for history in Italian universities until the eighteenth century. Even more surprising is that when one finds a professor of history in that century one suspects the inspiration comes from Austria, that is, from German culture. This may even be the case with the chair given at Catania to the Benedictine Vito Mario Amico about 1743, and it is certainly the case with the introduction of the teaching of Italian and Lombard history in the University of Pavia by the Empress Maria Theresa in her reform of that university in the years 1771 to 1773.

The instructions about the duties of the professor of history contained in this reform are worth studying. They combine the Enlightenment idea about philosophic history with a definite depreciation of the history of the Roman Republic in comparison with the history of the Empire. From the Roman Empire the transition to what is called the "foul freedom of the Lombard cities," and later to Austrian rule, is or seems easy. What is more, this reform of 1771 justifies what had been a common association of subjects in transalpine universities, the allocation of the teaching of history to the professor of eloquence.[6] The combination that is explicit at Pavia in 1771 makes me wonder whether chairs of eloquence in other Italian universities may not have included some advanced teaching of history.

It remains true, however, that in the first half of the eighteenth century Scipione Maffei deplored the absence of any teaching of history in the universities of Turin and Padua and vainly proposed the creation of chairs for it. The same lacuna was noticed (and not immediately filled) in Bologna in 1709. The university of Turin got its first chair of modern history in 1847 and had to wait for another fifty years for the chair of ancient history. It is also certain that none of the great Italian historians and thinkers about history from the sixteenth to the eighteenth century—such as Paolo Giovio, Vico, and Muratoti—was ever a professor of history. If they taught in universities, they taught other subjects. In some Italian universities ecclesiastical history may have preceded civil history (for example, a chair of ecclesiastical history in Pisa in 1673).

Italy seems to have been later than England in providing chairs for the specific teaching of history. Oxford had its first lectureship in ancient history—the future Camden chair—in 1622; Cambridge had a generic lectureship in history in 1627; and both universities got a regius professorship of modern history in 1721. The previous attempt by the London antiquarians to create an academy for the study of antiquity and history failed in 1602 for lack of governmental support.[7] France may be nearer to the Italian pattern. At the Collège de France one has to wait until 1775 for a chair of "history and morals" and until the nineteenth century for chairs of pure history. Chairs of ancient history and of modern history were established at the University of Paris in 1808 and 1812, respectively. The great Parisian tradition of professors of history starts not earlier than Guizot and Michelet in the nineteenth century. At the University of Poitiers the first chair of history appears in 1810. In Spain I have been unable to locate a chair of political history before 1776 (Oviedo).

The information one collects about this argument is elusive, owing to three circumstances. First, we may be certain that some teaching of historical subjects went on under the name of rhetoric, humanities, and philology. Second, ecclesiastical history finds its way into the curriculum of some universities before civil and political history. Third, even when the name of history is attached to the chair, one cannot be certain that history was taught by the professor, either because he may not have taught at all or because he may have taught something else. At Trinity College, Dublin, a professorship of modern history was created in 1762, but in the early nineteenth century it was discovered that for several years the incumbent had given no lecture, nor had his assistant.[8] Aberdeen, in Scotland, had zealous professors, but the professor who taught civil and natural history, a subject created in Marischal College in 1753, increasingly tended to prefer natural to civil history. The situation had apparently not yet been clarified when the two rivals, Marischal College and King's College, were unified in 1860 to form what is now the University of Aberdeen. In *Studies in the History and Development of the University of Aberdeen* (1906), the long account of the historians of Aberdeen University is a very interesting record of works of history written by teachers and former pupils of the two colleges, but it does not say anything about the teaching of history. This is not exceptional.

Therefore, given the nature of the evidence that is available, I am prepared to be proved wrong on all my generalizations, but my impression remains that history first became important in German schools and universities, for a variety of independent reasons. The Germans had more difficulty in understanding Latin than the speakers of Romance languages. At the same time, the Germans seem to have been the first to want to go beyond the classical texts and learn more about their own history and about universal history. Patriotism combined with the religious question tended to make both ecclesiastical and legal history more important in German territories than elsewhere. The decisive factor, however, seems to have been the conviction of the German princes and nobility that history was useful for the education of future state officials. As universities multiplied in Germany in correspondence with political and religious divisions, historians were called in and asked to support the regime by rhetorical, legal, and historical arguments.

Of course it is difficult to determine in the abstract where rhetoric replaces historical or legal arguments. The first chair of history I know of in any country of Europe is the "lectura historica," conferred upon Bernhard Schöfferlin at the University of Mainz in 1504.[9] Schöfferlin died almost immediately. He had no time to impose his personality on the new discipline. He remains known as the first translator of Livy into German. The immediate successor of Schofferlin is not known, but the man who was appointed in 1513, Nicolaus Karbach, was also chiefly a translator of Livy. It seems therefore that in Mainz the first teachers of history were mainly concerned with introducing their pupils to Roman history by reading and translating texts they understood with difficulty.

Conrad Celtis had been inviting the Germans to study German history since at least his introductory lecture at Ingolstadt in 1492. At the University of Vienna he seems to have given lectures on universal history. He described them in an epigram (III, 112, Hartfelder) from which we learn that he started with the Babylonian Ninos and went on with the Medes, the Persians, and the Egyptians—that is, he followed the tradition of the Four Empires. The history of the Germans was prominent in this survey: "Hinc gentes patrias inquiram pectore docto / et quidquid gessit Teutonis ora, dabo" ("From here I shall start to inquire with learning about the events of our fatherland and I shall report what happened in German territory"). Celtis was especially interested in the interpretation of Tacitus' *Germania* and of a poem in praise of the emperor Friedrich Rotbart, or Barbarossa, *Ligurini de gestis imperatoris Friderici Augusti libri Decem,* of which he published an edition in 1507. Later in the eighteenth century Celtis was suspected of having written this poem himself, but the suspicion was proved to be without foundation.[10] The interest in Oriental history was reinforced in those years by the publication of the forgeries of Annius of Viterbo. It is significant that at the University of Rostock we find, in 1520, Johann Crusse lecturing on Babylonian history with the special warning that he was not going to follow Annius: he had a colleague at Rostock, Nicolaus Marschalk, who had been taken in by Annius.

With the spreading of the religious rebellion against Rome, history became an even more interesting subject. Following Luther, Melanchthon had a leading part in making history popular at the University of Wittenberg. For some reason he did not insist on having a specific chair of history in his reformed university, though he had asked for it in 1520. But de facto he started the teaching of universal history by lecturing on his new Latin translation of the universal chronicle that his friend Carion had written in German. He encouraged pupils in that direction. One of them, Paul Eber, though he was professor of Latin at Wittenberg, lectured on German and Jewish history and prepared elementary handbooks. After Melanchthon's death, his son-in-law Kaspar Peucer continued his teaching on universal history.

That a specific chair of history was not yet considered indispensable for the teaching of history is shown by the hesitations not only of Wittenberg but of the new Protestant University of Marburg, founded in 1529. There, the original chair of history was soon replaced by a combined chair of poetry, rhetoric, and history. The same combination we find again in Tübingen in

1530, under the inspiration of Melanchthon; later at Tübingen the chair was turned into one of rhetoric and history (in 1557). The conjunction of rhetoric and history is also characteristic of the second Protestant university, Königsberg, founded in 1544. Elsewhere the combination is history and ethics, as in Jena, the university founded in 1548. In Greifswald (1544), in reformed Heidelberg (1558), and in Rostock (ca. 1564), the chair of poetry included history. In Freiburg an independent chair of history was instituted in 1568. In Vienna, after a failed attempt to create an independent chair of history in 1552, history and poetry were put together under the title *literae politiores*. Even this chair was suppressed by the Jesuits when they took over the arts faculty of Vienna in 1623, and the University of Vienna remained without a chair of history until 1728.

This list indicates that the recognition of history was not without ambiguities. There was a problem in defining history in relation to traditional subjects such as poetry, rhetoric, and ethics. There was another problem in defining the territorial and spatial limits of history: the humanistic inclination to identify history with classical history was obviously very strong even among reformed Germans. Both German and universal history derived immediate advantage from the new situation. Ecclesiastical history, too, was introduced into teaching, especially in theological faculties.

The hundred years between 1550 and 1650 saw the expansion of history teaching. The instructions for the new University of Helmstedt in Braunschweig, founded in 1576, were inspired by Melanchthon's pupil David Chytraeus, who was himself active at Rostock. The syllabus included outlines of universal history and of Saxon history in addition to Livy and Herodotus. Indeed, if anything is evident in the curricula of history in the German universities during the first half of the seventeenth century, it is the increased importance of universal and ecclesiastical history. Theologians and lawyers were increasingly involved in the study and teaching of history. Heidelberg, where Franciscus Balduinus (Francois Baudouin) was professor for a few years, was one of the first universities to care for what he had called the "coniunctio historiae universae cum iurisprudentia." It was also in Heidelberg that Johann Jacob Grynaeus and Janus Gruterus offered early examples of the combination of ecclesiastical and political history. Strassburg, which was turned from an academy into a full university in 1621, was another place where ecclesiastical history was studied in an exemplary way.

Perhaps the most important curriculum was the teaching of Hermann Conring at Helmstedt from 1635 to 1681. Conring had an admirable command of all the sources of German history, but above all he had a clear notion of what was suitable teaching for the governing class of Germany. After him, it became obvious that historians had to be jurists and vice versa. It was a jurist, Burkhard Gotthelf Struve, who established the reputation of Jena as a center of historical studies at the beginning of the eighteenth century. He even lectured about contemporary history.

The University of Basel, which had no chair of history, had to face the situation in 1659 that students were migrating to Strassburg in order to study history. The regents therefore proposed to create a specific chair of history with the declared aim of serving the education of those who intended to devote themselves to public service. Thus, in 1659 Basel had in Cristoph Faesch the first professor of history. He taught elementary universal history for two hours a week and Tacitus' *Annals* for another two hours. A proposal to create a specific chair of Swiss history at Basel failed in 1734 and was only partially implemented in 1785, when the professor of general history was directed to devote one hour a week to Swiss history and to teach it in German, not in Latin.[11] In the second part of the eighteenth century, the new University of Göttingen played a role as a school of historical studies for the ruling aristocracy of Germany and other countries. Göttingen provided the model for nineteenth-century universities.

III

It is by now only too obvious that the spreading of the German historical method in the nineteenth century was not a sudden, almost improvised, consequence of the romantic movement. What seemed to many the novelty of Niebuhr, Savigny, and Ranke had been prepared by centuries of hard work in German universities. In the seventeenth and eighteenth centuries these universities had specifically tried to satisfy the needs of the ruling classes of small states. Such states needed all the evidence they could command to support their competing claims. They had also to face bigger things—the great monarchies of England, France and Spain, the Holy Roman Empire and the Catholic church. In the Protestant section of Germany the universities had the further task of replacing the monastic orders as repositories of tradition and history, a point that is obvious also for post-Reformation England. An element that marks Descartes as a Frenchman and Leibniz as a German is that Leibniz could never be so indifferent to history as Descartes was. If court officials were supposed to derive the greatest advantage from a training in history, theologians and lawyers were supposed to have a share in the profits. The occasional reading of historical classical texts offered to school boys by medieval and humanistic tradition was replaced by the systematic and programmatic reading of history at school and in the university, both on classical and nonclassical subjects.

The nineteenth century modified this situation in two directions, both still prevalently dominated by German professors. First, history became even more important and autonomous for the paradoxical reason that almost everything became history. History became a way of seeing how the world was formed, how man came about, what religion and morality were. The new science of economics became almost immediately a historical science. History explained nations, and nations—or the national spirit—explained history. History became a complicated substitute for revelation.

Second, if one had to swallow the new theories about the origins of man, of Christianity, of capitalism, of art and literature, one had to be reasonably sure that there was serious evidence behind the theories. The need for greater control of the evidence went together with the increasing claims of history. If the professors of history claimed to explain things that in earlier days had been the province of theology or ethics, in the nineteenth century they had to produce a technical training far more severe than it had ever been. Skilled technicians in the study of certain types of evidence had of course existed in previous centuries. Bollandists and Maurists had created new historical disciplines in the late seventeenth century. What was new in the nineteenth century was the introduction and generalization of such high standards in the examination of the evidence. The seminar method of teaching associated with the name of Ranke was only one of the devices for the dissemination of austere scientific methods in the study of evidence. Special schools—such as the Ecole des Chartes in Paris—archaeological institutes, and field research supplemented ordinary teaching.

There was a constant interdependence between the claims of history and the precautions taken in order to check these claims by analysis of the evidence. But the relationship was never simple. The controls tended to become an end to themselves. And the most daring and perhaps most interesting historical thinking never cared too much for them. Tocqueville, Karl Marx, Burckhardt, Fustel de Coulanges (at least in the *Cite Antique*) never treated evidence in a way to satisfy what Burckhardt called the "viri eruditissimi." Even Mommsen, of all people, wrote his Roman history without producing the evidence. His later *Romische Forschungen* are not a justification of what he wrote in the *Romische Geschichte*; they are rather a rectification, or a new approach.

Throughout the nineteenth century there is a tension between historical generalization and the study of historical sources. We have inherited it and made it more acute. We have also become acutely aware of the tension, and by this fact alone intensified it. The asymmetry between historical thinking and historical research, when translated into teaching terms, means that the teacher seldom manages to keep a balance between thinking and researching. The teacher of history thinks more than he knows or knows more than he thinks. What happens to the student is beyond my terms of reference.

NOTES

1. I am trying in this essay to develop an argument I first presented in my Lurcy lecture at the University of Chicago, "History in an Age of Ideologies," published in the *American Scholar* 51 (1982): 495-507. On the history of the teaching of history, see K. Bergmann and G. Schneider, eds., *Gesellschaft—Staat—Geschichtsunterricht, Beiträge zur einer Geschichte der Geschichtsdidaktik 1500-1800* (Düsseldorf: Pädagogischer Verlag Schwann, 1982). For the position of history in the Renaissance, see E. Cochrane, "The Profession of the Historian in the Italian Renaissance," *Journal of Social History* 15 (1981): 51-72. My data on German universities are mainly based on E. C. Scherr, *Geschichte und Kirchengeschichte an den deutschen Universitäten* (Freiburg, 1927),

quoted in the text; but I have tried to check them against the histories of individual universities and the original evidence. Recent work on the history of education in general is listed by G. P. Brizzi in *Università Principe, Gesuiti, La politica farnesiana dell'istruzione a Parma e Piacenza (1545-1622)*, introduction by C. Vasoli (Rome: Bulzoni, 1980), 194-196. The work being done in France, by D. Julia and others, has proved to be especially valuable. G. P. Brizzi has himself contributed much to the subject in *La formazione della classe dirigente nel Sei-Settecento* (Bologna, 1976) and *La Ratio studiorum* (Rome: Bulzoni, 1981). The periodicals *Histoire de l'education* (1978 ff.) and *History of Universities* (1981 ff.) provide information on new research. A. Borst, *Geschichte an mittelalterlichen Universitäten* (Konstanz, 1969) has proved to be of little use.

2. Milton's texts are conveniently collected by O. M. Ainsworth, *Milton on Education* (New Haven, 1928).

3. See B. Duhz, *Geschichte der Jesuiten in den Ländern deutscher Zunge im XVI Jahrh.* (Freiburg, 1907), 1: 258. For further bibliography on the Jesuits see B. Genero, *Giornale Storico letterat. Ital.* 138 (1961): 365-395.

4. C. Trinkaus, *Studies in the Renaissance* 7 (1960): 99-104.

5. L. Volpicelli, *Il pensiero pedagogico della Controriforma* (Florence, 1960), p. 250.

6. *Statuti e Ordinamenti della Università di Pavia dall'anno 1361 all'anno 1859* (Pavia, 1925), pp. 230-231.

7. K. Sharpe, "The Foundation of the Chairs of History at Oxford and Cambridge," *History of Universities* 2 (1982): 127-152.

8. W. M. Dixon, *Trinity College Dublin* (London, 1902), p. 159.

9. See L. Just, *Die Alte Universität Mainz von 1477 bis 1798* (Wiesbaden, 1957).

10. On the circle of Celtis, see G. Ritter, *Die Heidelberger Universität* (Heidclberg, 1936), 1: 474. See also J. von Aschbach, *Die Wiener Universität und ihre Humanisten* (Wien, 1877), p. 161.

11. E. Bonjour, *Die Universität Basel* (Basel, 1960), pp. 288-289, which summarizes his article in *Schweiz. Zeitschrift für Geschichte* 10 (1960).

INDEX

Designer: UC Press Staff
Compositor: Janet Sheila Brown
Printer: Thomson-Shore, Inc.
Binder: John H. Dekker and Sons
Text: 11/13 Baskerville
Display: Baskerville

.